EMPIRE TO COMMONWEALTH

EMPIRE TO COMMONWEALTH

CONSEQUENCES OF MONOTHEISM
IN LATE ANTIQUITY

Garth Fowden

Center for Greek and Roman Antiquity
National Research Foundation, Athens

PRINCETON UNIVERSITY PRESS

PRINCETON, NEW JERSEY

Library of Congress Cataloging-in-Publication Data
Fowden, Garth.
Empire to commonwealth : consequences of monotheism in
late antiquity / Garth Fowden.
p.   cm.
Includes bibliographical references and index.
ISBN 0-691-06989-1 (hard : alk. paper)
1. Byzantine Empire—Civilization.   2. Islamic Empire—Civilization.
3. Rome—Civilization—Christian influences.   4. Religion and
civilization.   5. Monotheism.   I. Title.
DF531.F69   1993
949.5'01—dc20   92-37903

For E. K.

Contents

CONTENTS

List of illustrations

PLATES

MAP

Abbreviations

ABBREVIATIONS follow the conventions of *L'année philologique*. Note also the following:

A.C.O.	E. Schwartz, ed., *Acta conciliorum oecumenicorum* (Strasbourg, 1914–)
A.M.Iran	*Archaeologische Mitteilungen aus Iran* (Berlin)
Arabie préislamique	T. Fahd, ed., *L'Arabie préislamique et son environnement historique et culturel: Actes du colloque de Strasbourg 24–27 juin 1987* (Leiden, 1989)
B.A.I.	*Bulletin of the Asia Institute* (Ames, Iowa)
B.M.C.	H. Mattingly and R.A.G. Carson, *Coins of the Roman Empire in the British Museum* (London, 1923–)
C.C.S.L.	*Corpus Christianorum, series latina* (Turnhout)
C.H.Ir.	W. B. Fisher and others, eds., *The Cambridge history of Iran* (Cambridge, 1968–91)
C.I.S.	*Corpus inscriptionum semiticarum* (Paris, 1881–)
IV cong.int.st.etiop.	*IV congresso internazionale di studi etiopici (Roma, 10–15 aprile 1972) 1: Sezione storica* (Rome, 1974)
C.S.C.O.	*Corpus scriptorum Christianorum orientalium* (Paris etc.)
C.S.E.L.	*Corpus scriptorum ecclesiasticorum latinorum* (Vienna)
E.A.C.	*Entretiens sur l'antiquité classique* (Fondation Hardt, Geneva)
Enc.Ir.	E. Yarshater, ed., *Encyclopaedia Iranica* (London, 1985–)
Enc.Is.[2]	H.A.R. Gibb, J. H. Kramers, E. Lévi-Provençal, J. Schacht, eds., *The encyclopaedia of Islam*[2] (Leiden, 1960–)
H.E.	*Historia ecclesiastica*
I.G.	*Inscriptiones graecae* (Berlin, 1873–)
I.G.U.R.	L. Moretti, *Inscriptiones graecae urbis Romae* (Rome, 1968–79)
I.L.S.	H. Dessau, *Inscriptiones latinae selectae* (Berlin, 1892–1916)
J.J.S.	*Journal of Jewish studies* (Oxford)
J.R.A.S.	*Journal of the Royal Asiatic Society* (London)
J.S.A.I.	*Jerusalem studies in Arabic and Islam* (Jerusalem)

J.S.S.	*Journal of Semitic studies* (Manchester)
P.Amherst	B. P. Grenfell and A. S. Hunt, *The Amherst papyri* (London, 1900–1901)
P.G.	J. P. Migne, ed., *Patrologia graeca* (Paris, 1857–66)
P.L.	J. P. Migne, ed., *Patrologia latina* (Paris, 1844–64)
P.O.	R. Graffin and F. Nau, eds., *Patrologia orientalis* (Paris, 1907–)
Popoli e spazio romano	*Popoli e spazio romano tra diritto e profezia: Atti del III seminario internazionale di studi storici "Da Roma alla Terza Roma"* (Naples, 1986)
Power and propaganda	M. T. Larsen, ed., *Power and propaganda: A symposium on ancient empires* (Copenhagen, 1979)
S.C.	*Sources chrétiennes* (Paris)
S.E.G.	*Supplementum epigraphicum graecum* (Leiden, 1923–)
S.P.A.W.	*Sitzungsberichte der preussischen Akademie der Wissenschaften zu Berlin, Philosophisch-historische Klasse* (Berlin)
Stud.Ir.	*Studia Iranica* (Paris)

Note on transliteration and references

SIMPLICITY and recognizability have been the criteria in the transliteration of Greek and of Oriental languages. Few diacritics have survived.

Greek sources are referred to by their conventional Latin titles. Arabic titles have simply been transliterated, since they are more familiar in that form. Titles of works in other Oriental languages are occasionally transliterated but usually given their Latin or English equivalents, according to convention.

This is essentially an essay, and the bibliography is intended only as an explanation of the abbreviated references provided in the notes. But these references, through their emphasis on more recent publications, should suffice as signposts to further reading.

Preface

THIS BOOK was conceived while I was teaching at Princeton in the spring of 1990, written during the academic year 1990–91 while I was privileged to be a member of the School of Historical Studies at Princeton's Institute for Advanced Study, and revised in the early months of 1992 during my tenure of a visiting fellowship at the Institute for the Humanities, University of Michigan, and while teaching again at Princeton. My ideas have gained much of what clarity they may have from being discussed with students and colleagues at Princeton, and with lecture audiences at College Year in Athens and the Universities of Chicago, Michigan, and Minnesota. Glen Bowersock, Peter Brown, Oleg Grabar, and Philip Rousseau have shown me by example what a community of scholars can be and do. Peter Brown in particular will find much in these pages that would never have germinated had he not sown it, twenty years ago in Oxford. He and Martin Goodman were also generous enough to read the whole book in typescript. While I learned much from their comments (and from those of the publisher's readers), nothing I have written should be held against them.

Although *Empire to commonwealth* is largely a product of my time at Princeton, I would not have had that experience but for the understanding and encouragement offered by Michael Sakellariou, Director of the Center for Greek and Roman Antiquity (K.E.R.A.) at the National Research Foundation, Athens. Since I joined it in 1985, the K.E.R.A. has afforded me the companionship of dedicated colleagues and the perfect vantage point from which to survey the late antique *oikoumene*. For their constant support and interest, I am especially grateful to Miltos Hatzopoulos, Anna Panayotou, Kelly Petropoulou, and Thanasis Rizakis.

The most difficult thing about this project was the struggle to keep it in perspective and not be distracted by beguiling side issues. Two friends helped me more than I can adequately thank them for: Philip Sherrard, who explained to me just once, at the outset and almost in passing, the real significance of my subject; and Elizabeth Key Fowden, in conversation with whom this book evolved from its conception until its penultimate draft, whose margins she filled with pungent scholia.

GARTH FOWDEN

Princeton, 21 May (SS. Constantine and Helena) 1992

Acknowledgments

FOR PERMISSION to illustrate objects or reproduce photographs in their possession I am obliged to the Bibliothèque Nationale, Paris (plates 1 and 10); the Walters Art Gallery, Baltimore, Md. (plate 2); P. K. Zachariou (plate 4, courtesy of J. J. Yiannias and S. Ćurčić); the Center for Byzantine Studies, Dumbarton Oaks, Washington, D.C., and the Whittemore Collection, Fogg Art Museum, Cambridge, Mass. (plate 6); and the American Numismatic Society, New York (plate 9b–e). The photograph reproduced as plate 8 is by Fred Anderegg, courtesy of O. Grabar. J. Blazejewski, Index of Christian Art, Princeton University, took the photographs for plate 1 (from R. Ghirshman, *Persian art: The Parthian and Sasanian dynasties 249 B.C.–A.D. 651* [Librairie Gallimard; American ed.: New York, 1962], 152); plate 3 (from H.-J. Klimkeit, *Die Seidenstrasse: Handelsweg und Kulturbrücke zwischen Morgen- und Abendland* [DuMont Buchverlag, Cologne, 1990²], 90; drawing by A. Yuyuma, Tokyo); plate 5 (from J. Mercier, *Ethiopian magic scrolls* [George Braziller, New York, 1979], pl. 6); plate 7 (from A. Musil and others, *Ḳuṣejr ʿAmra* [K. K. Hof- und Staatsdruckerei, Vienna, 1907], 2, pl. XXVI, facsimile by A. L. Mielich); and plate 10 (from R. Ettinghausen, *Arab painting* [Editions d'Art Albert Skira, Geneva, 1962], 119). The map of the Mountain Arena is based on W. C. Brice, ed., *An historical atlas of Islam* (E. J. Brill, Leiden, 1981), 19.

EMPIRE TO COMMONWEALTH

Introduction

IN THE *Life of S. Daniel the Stylite*, who lived atop a pillar by the Bosphorus in the second half of the fifth century, we read how the Byzantine emperor Leo I received a visit from Gobazes, king of Lazica. Leo took Gobazes along with him to meet the holy man.

> When he saw this strange sight, Gobazes threw himself on his face and said: "I thank Thee, heavenly King, that by means of an earthly king Thou hast deemed me worthy to behold great mysteries; for never before in this world have I seen anything of this kind." And these kings had a point in dispute touching Roman policy; and they laid the whole matter open to the servant of God and through the mediation of the holy man they agreed upon a treaty which satisfied the claims of each. After this the emperor returned to the city and dismissed Gobazes to his native land, and when the latter reached his own country he related to all his folk what he had seen. Consequently the men who later on came up from Lazica to the city invariably went up to Daniel. Gobazes himself, too, wrote to the holy man and besought his prayers and never ceased doing so to the end of his life.[1]

Implicit in this anecdote are the present essay's principal themes. The defining characteristic of late antiquity, by which I mean the period between the second-century peak of Rome's prosperity and the ninth-century onset of the Islamic Empire's decline, was its conviction that knowledge of the One God both justifies the exercise of imperial power and makes it more effective. Antecedents of this idea can be traced in the polytheist world of ancient Greece and Rome, but Constantine placed it at the center of Roman political ideology when he became a Christian. By Leo's day one could not become emperor if one was not a Christian; nor could Leo have retained power had he not convinced a sufficiently influential group of people (including such as Daniel) of the rightness, the "orthodoxy", of his knowledge of the Christians' God. Having done so, he could claim to rule over the earth as God ruled over the heavens, and kings like Gobazes were expected to recognize that claim. The Lazi lived by the eastern shores of the Black Sea, beyond Constantinople's direct control; and Gobazes himself was an intriguingly liminal figure, whose first reaction to political trouble in Lazica was to fire off embas-

---

[1] *Vita S. Danielis Stylitae* 51 (tr. Dawes and Baynes). The incident occurred in 465/6.

sies to both Constantinople and Ctesiphon, and who showed up for his visit to Leo "dressed in Persian attire" but bearing also, disarmingly for the Byzantines, "the symbols of the Christians".[2] Throughout Byzantium's history, the influence it exercised over peoples and places such as these encouraged the formation of what Sir Dimitri Obolensky, with reference to the predominantly Slavic world of Eastern Europe, has called the Byzantine Commonwealth.[3] Lazica lies near the northern edge of what I shall call the southwest Asian Mountain Arena, a region whose simultaneous liminality and centrality molded two other commonwealths that will be of central concern to us, one Christian and one Muslim.

We would do well to remember the humility of Gobazes and Leo before the holy man. But the relationship between imperial power and knowledge of God is usually quite different. In Daniel and his like, knowledge of God is embodied, vivid, and itself highly potent; but in the mouths of those who go by the canons of Church councils it can become no more than a slogan, easy for the unscrupulous ruler (or bishop) to manipulate. The Gobazes anecdote conveys the idealist's view of how power should relate to knowledge and theology interact with empire; but the present book will focus, not on the sage

> . . . in some high lonely tower,
> Where he may oft out-watch the Bear
> With thrice great Hermes,

but on the broad dynamic of late antique history and, in the first place, on Christianity's coming-of-age, its conquest of and compromise with the Roman Empire.

Our initial focus on Christianity carries the danger, though, that we will not see beyond it. Indeed, many students of late antiquity still regard Christianity, and Christian Europe in particular, as deserving a place of exclusive privilege in their reflections. This is culturally understandable but ends up imprisoning us in a Latin world that, after the collapse of the Western Roman Empire in the fifth century, was for several hundred years peripheral to the political and cultural centers—Constantinople, Damascus, Baghdad—where the consequences of Constantine's marriage of imperial Rome to Christian monotheism were worked out. By establishing his capital at Constantinople, Constantine clearly indicated his awareness of the East's importance as not only bulwark but

---

[2] Priscus fr. 25–26, 34 (Müller) = 33, 44 (Blockley).

[3] Obolensky, *Byzantine Commonwealth*, esp. the introduction and ch. 9. My indebtedness to Obolensky will be self-evident. His book appeared in 1971, just when, as a first-year undergraduate at Oxford, I was attending his remarkable lectures on Byzantine historical geography.

also now generator of Christian Rome's health and identity. It was in the East, not on the Rhine or the Danube, that Rome confronted the only enemy that had an alternative vision of empire to offer; and it was in the East that Rome eventually confronted Islam as well. When, by the fifth century, the Roman Empire appears to have become irreversibly Christian, it is tempting to suppose that a "transformation" of antiquity has been brought about. But the Christianization of the Roman Empire was not merely a "transformation" or "transition" within a limited segment of time. It was part of a wider and longer process by which the idea of empire, and in particular monarchy, was conjoined with belief in the One God—monotheism. Sasanian Iran was likewise struggling with the relationship between religion, in this case Mazdaism, and empire; and although that particular nexus of problems never came anywhere near being resolved, the religion Iran eventually adopted, Islam, was very much part of that late antique dynamic whose first phase had been Christianization.

ALREADY, these introductory remarks have used certain concepts that need explicit definition; and there are others that will soon be brought into play.

Polytheism means belief that the divine realm is populated by a plurality of gods of broadly comparable status, not fully subordinated to or comprehended within a single god of higher status. *Henotheism* denotes "affirmative belief in one god, without the sharply-defined exclusive line which makes it a belief in Him as the only God".[4] *Monotheism* means belief in one unique god to the exclusion of all others. It need hardly be added that to use language at all in regard to such matters is to betray the subtlety of human thought and intuition. Monotheism in particular is much more ambiguous as a reality than its definition might lead one to expect.[5] Space has to be allowed for angels, and for the Christian doctrine of the Trinity. But this book will proceed on the assumption that there are consequential differences among these three broad categories of belief, and especially between polytheism and monotheism. And I will argue that within monotheism, traditions such as Judaism, Christianity, and Islam behave very differently on the historical plane, whatever their common theological denominators.

Although we associate monotheism with certain dominant world religions, it does not necessarily give rise to personal proselytism or organized mission, much less to political expansionism. Always poten-

---

[4] W. E. Gladstone, quoted by the *Oxford English Dictionary*[2], s.v. "henotheism". See now, on the whole subject, Versnel, *Ter unus*.

[5] Hayman, *J.J.S.* 42 (1991).

tially and usually by tendency universalist, monotheism may also be ethnically based (Judaism). And even when clearly universalist, monotheism may be receptive to converts (early Islam) rather than actively proselytizing (Christianity). Nevertheless, this book will in practice be primarily concerned with monotheism (and to some extent henotheism) as a major factor in aspiration to and realization of *world empire*. World empire means control without serious competition of an area large enough to pass for "the world", the *orbis terrarum* or *oikoumene* whose late antique parameters will be defined in chapter 1. I will also argue in chapter 1 that Cyrus the Great created the European and southwest Asian world's first *political world empire*. Post-Achaemenid Iran and Rome each at times aspired to imitate this achievement; and when Rome adopted monotheism it became an *aspiring politico-cultural world empire*. But only Muhammad managed to make the aspiration reality; the Islamic Empire was antiquity's only *politico-cultural world empire*. Monotheism had a disadvantage, though: its more or less inflexible insistence on the austere idea that there is only one god—its doctrinal rigidity, in other words—entailed the rise of heresy. And heresy played an important part in the early Byzantine Empire's generation of and the Islamic Empire's evolution into that much looser, more pluralistic type of structure we call *commonwealth*. By using this term I intend to denote a group of politically discrete but related polities collectively distinguishable from other polities or commonwealths by a shared culture and history. Obviously commonwealth was a far cry from the universal empires that the princes of this world dreamed of; but because it was generated by empire it was never a purely cultural hypostasis. It was through this subtle, adaptable device that antiquity's achievement and influence were most comprehensively manifested and mediated to us.

Monotheism on the theological level and *universalism* on the historical level (both secular and religious) are the principal themes of this essay. Universalism is a concept frequently employed in the scholarly literature on the ancient world—especially the early principate—and the early Middle Ages,[6] but it is less often defined. Though a modern coinage, it can reasonably and conveniently be applied to the range of associations brought to the ancient mind by the expressions *orbis terrarum* and *oikoumene*. In the course of this essay, the concept of universalism will occasionally be broken down into *political universalism*, which is shorthand for "political, military, and economic universalism", and *cultural universalism*, which stands for "cultural and espe-

[6] See, e.g., Nicolet, *Inventaire du monde*; Cracco Ruggini, in *Storiografia ecclesiastica* (and note other relevant articles in this volume); Cracco Ruggini, *E.A.C.* 34 (1989): 181–201.

cially religious universalism", "religion" being understood to be a constituent part of the wider category of "culture". But more commonly it will be applied to late antiquity's distinctive and dynamic fusion of those two strands of universalism into the type of imperialism that aimed at politico-cultural world empire but, however successful, issued eventually in commonwealth. To those who would object that this is a "Christianocentric" definition, the reply is, first, that it is "Islamocentric" too, and second, that the world created by Christianity and Islam is what this book sets out to explain. If either of these religions possessed certain characteristics that gave them an advantage over, say, polytheism or Manichaeism, it is the historian's duty to explain why.

Political universalism presupposes political control; that was exercised more closely by some ancient empires than by others. None exercised it uniformly. No less slippery is the concept of cultural penetration, without which there can in effect be no cultural or religious universalism. Here the gap between claim or aspiration and reality may be even wider than in political universalism. A universalist culture or religion is one that is accessible to all human beings and tends to be accepted by them eventually, whether or not it actively proselytizes or has yet penetrated the geographical area they inhabit. This is the vertical aspect of universalism, the dimension within which human beings may relate personally to cultural or religious values, regardless of where they happen to find themselves at any particular moment. But breadth of actual geographical coverage is also, unavoidably, a factor. To be regarded as universalist by the historian (as distinct from the theologian), a culture or religion ought to be already at least as extensive as a world empire. Still, the depth and thoroughness of that coverage may vary just as much as does the political control exercised by an empire. Some areas and some social categories may be more affected than others, and a high degree of both political and cultural pluralism may persist within theoretically universalist structures. Religions, especially, may enjoy tremendous horizontal extension, as Judaism and Manichaeism did, without often or ever assimilating the landscape in the way Christianity and Islam did in their heartlands.

In a phrase, then, late antique universalism aimed at politico-cultural domination and ultimately homogenization of an area large enough to pass for "the world". I shall argue in chapter 1 that Cyrus was the first ruler in antiquity to create a genuine world empire in the political sense, but without cultural motive. This was the Achaemenid Empire that Alexander destroyed. Late antiquity lived in the shadow of these two men. Both Iran and Rome aspired, at times, to be world empires in the Achaemenid-Alexandrine mold, but in practice they simply counterbalanced each other. By tracing some of the salient features of the perennial conflict between Rome and (in particular) the Sasanians, I set the scene for the book's main argument. Chapter 2 traces some of the antecedents of Christian Roman universalism in polytheist Rome. The emphasis here is on cultural universalism, the evidence for which is much less known than that for its political counterpart. The emphasis on cultural universalism is maintained in chapter 3, though here the focus shifts from Rome's internal evolution to the eastern periphery and especially the Fertile Crescent, where more or less universalist religions approved by neither of the superpowers flourish between and beyond them. In chapter 4 we see how one of these, the missionary monotheism ascribed to Christ, is brilliantly married by Constantine to Rome's imperial impetus. The new sense of coherence and direction generated by this union lies behind the first Christian emperor's planned assault on Iran. The dream of world empire under the sign of the Cross rapidly evaporates in chapter 5 under the twin pressures of politico-military reality and the rise of heresy generated by monotheism's rigidification. In its place, mission generates the complex reality of commonwealth, the Monophysite world of southwest Asia, which I shall call the First Byzantine Commonwealth. This cultural and to some extent also political loosening of ties between Byzantine center and periphery, together with Iran's early-seventh-century military successes, points to the birth of antiquity's only realized politico-cultural world empire, that of Islam, the subject of chapter 6. The Islamic Empire owes its stupendous success and power to a combination of Cyrus's geopolitical achievement with a universalist (though not, to begin with, actively missionary) monotheism—Constantine's dream come true. But eventually the Islamic Empire dissolves under pressures similar to those that generated the First Byzantine Commonwealth, and the Islamic Commonwealth or what we call the World of Islam is born. It is ultimately through four commonwealths—the First Byzantine, the Islamic, the Second Byzantine in the Slavic world, and Western Christendom—along with Byzantium itself, quondam aspirant to world empire and anomalous survivor from antiquity, that the ancient world's legacy is transmitted to us.

As EMERGES from this brief summary, I believe that late antiquity had a "dynamic"—a direction and even to a certain extent a sense of direction. Beyond the characteristically "late antique" structural similarities among the Roman, Iranian, and Islamic empires, there was both a logical and a chronological sequence to developments. An episodic and inconclusive concern in polytheist Rome with the relationship between the structure of the divine world and that of secular political authority became, in Christian Rome, the centerpiece of public doctrine. An analogous development was provoked by Iran's transition from Arsacid to Sasanian rule in the 220s. Mazdaism never became a universalist faith, and even Constantine's marriage of political and religious universalism failed to result in a coordinated expansion of Romanitas and Christianitas. But Muhammad's fresh attempt in the same direction definitely had its moment.

Despite the emphasis in this book on Christianity and Islam and on links between universalism and monotheism, I do not wish to suggest that universalism is inconceivable without monotheism; still less, as I have said, that political expansion is a necessary consequence of the official adoption of monotheism. But universalism is, I believe, more realizable in the context of monotheism, and that is the sense in which my subtitle should be understood. Before Islam and Christianity there had, for example, been Hellenism, which lacked the focus a single god and a revealed scripture afford, but still offered gods in abundance, a language, and Homer. Thanks not least to Alexander, Hellenism spread almost unimaginably far beyond its Aegean home, and thanks to the durable *pax Romana* it sank deep roots in the lands around the eastern Mediterranean. But its most characteristic benefits were fully accessible only to the literate,[7] and "nothing like mass literacy ever came into being in antiquity".[8]

The late antique "dynamic" was not, then, inevitable, but neither was it the product of mere chance. Pre-Constantinian Christians saw God's providence in Christ's and Augustus's coincidence in time, and drew the conclusion that the Roman Empire and the Church were made for each other. It seems probable that this conclusion was part of Constantine's intellectual background. Similarly, the leaders of the early Islamic world self-consciously looked back to and learned from the empires that had gone before. By recognizing this intended dynamic in late antiquity, we can understand more clearly the relationship between the ancient and medieval worlds. We are also forced to recognize that Eurocentricity is a choice, not a viewpoint imposed by history. There are roads out of antiquity that do not lead to the Renaissance; and although none avoids eventual contact with the modern West's technological domination, the rapidly changing balance of power in our world is forcing even Western scholars to pay more attention to non-Latin perspectives on the past.

In the course of this essay I shall particularly emphasize two themes: the First Byzantine Commonwealth, since up to now only one Byzantine

[7] Isocrates, *Panegyricus* 50: "The name 'Hellenes' is given rather to those who share our culture (*paideia*) than to those who share a common blood."

[8] Harris, *Ancient literacy* 327.

Commonwealth has been recognized, namely the Chalcedonian Ortho-dox world of mainly Slavic Eastern Europe; and the roles of Iran and of Islam, both of which are still marginalized in works that treat late antiq-uity in terms of the "formation of Christendom". Islam in particular, the third of the ancient monotheisms after Judaism and Christianity, continues to be treated as an intrusion, a narrowing of Christendom's eastern and southern horizons, rather than as rooted in antiquity, even consummating it, and a decisive influence on medieval and modern Christendom's evolution.

As I wrote the final pages of this essay in late 1991 and early 1992, the collapse of one of the twentieth century's great empires, the USSR, was opening new prospects for both Orthodox Christianity and Islam. The leaders of the Chalcedonian Orthodox Churches, including those of the formerly Communist countries of Eastern Europe, were meeting in a new atmosphere of cooperation and optimism, determined to assert the role of Orthodoxy in the emergent European federation.[9] Fears were at the same time being expressed that a "new Islamic commonwealth" in the "troublesome crescent" stretching from Morocco to Kazakhstan might eventually come into conflict with a similar Christian bloc, espe-cially on the territory of the former Soviet Union.[10] In Bosnia and Azerbaijan this war was already being fought in miniature. To watch the collapse and re-formation of empires or even commonwealths cannot leave the historian unmoved. The spectrum of human interaction that is revealed ranges from the predictable to the bizarre, for empire by defini-tion intertwines everything. That history cannot be written with exclu-sive reference to elites and the events they stage or succumb to is now a truism; but it has of late become apparent that the study of majorities, of nonelite minorities, and of nonevents or long-term movements is not on its own any more satisfying. We need to find some way of meshing these approaches. And the interest of "new" historians in modes and effects of dominance and in nonmetropolitan cultures suggests that the "old" and the "new" approaches can best be linked by studying the idea and reality of empire, of political, cultural, and economic imperialism.[11]

Although the interrelationship of these forces can be—and often is—examined as it stood at particular moments, their interaction is best appreciated over time, and ideally over long periods of time. This essay does *not* propose a general theory of empire, but it does exploit the

---

[9] Makris and Myrtsidou, Καθημερινή (1 March 1992).

[10] Beedham, *Economist* (14 December 1991): 3; Akbar, *New York Times* (10 January 1992).

[11] See Kedourie's paradigmatic essay "Minorities", written in 1952: *Chatham House Version* 286–316.

privileged field offered for the historian's reflection by the Islamic Commonwealth, the Islamic Empire, and the late antique world from which they emerged. If the Latinist has late antiquity culminate in Augustine, while the Hellenist waits a century or so longer, but can hardly ignore the seventh century's political collapse,[12] the Islamist deals with a world that enjoyed an obvious advantage in terms of leisure to work the old problems through one more time. And the process is not yet finished. Without wishing to deny the late antique historian the pleasure of plotting inner transformations or even watching new perspectives open up onto the Germanic, Slavic, Arab, and Turkic worlds, the present essay suggests that, by maintaining the traditional Greco-Roman standpoint, we miss our period's main thrust.

[12] Cameron, *Christianity and the rhetoric of empire*, esp. 189, 227.

1

THE WORLD'S TWO EYES: IRAN, ROME, AND THE PURSUIT OF WORLD EMPIRE

THIS BOOK is about power and knowledge. But in the ancient world, power was not projected nor knowledge disseminated unless people were prepared to walk, ride, or hoist sail. We must begin then with the land and the seas and the peoples who lived or traveled on them. More specifically, it is in southwest Asia and the lands around the eastern Mediterranean Sea that our story mainly unfolds.

THE GEOGRAPHICAL FOCUS

Our interest in this particular part of the world is determined by the fact that three great monotheisms, Judaism, Christianity, and Islam, arose in either Palestine or Arabia. Though the empires those monotheisms generated were sometimes of enormous extent, even they had eventually to find borders. Some of these and other ancient empires claimed to control "the whole world", the *orbis terrarum* or *oikoumene*, which was ruled therefore by a *dominus orbis terrarum/mundi/orbis totius* or *kosmokrator*.[1] Those who were in the habit of traveling great distances—mainly merchants and missionaries—knew that the world in fact contained several "great empires". In late antiquity it was often considered that there were four of them. The religious teacher Mani, who grew up in third-century A.D. Mesopotamia and visited India in the course of his extensive travels, held that the "great empires" of his day were Iran, Rome, Aksum (Ethiopia), and "Silis" (China).[2] Kanishka, whose

[1] For this vocabulary and the (mis)conceptions behind it, see especially, as regards the Roman Empire, *Expositio totius mundi* 23, 28; Ammianus Marcellinus XV.1.3, XIX.2.11; also Mastino, in *Popoli e spazio romano*; Unruh, *Bild des Imperium Romanum* 15–51; Molè, in *Popoli e spazio romano*; Asche, *Roms Weltherrschaftsidee*; Rösger, in *Bonner Historia-Augusta-Colloquium 1979/1981*.

[2] *Kephalaia* 77. On "Silis": Metzler, *Klio* 71 (1989): 447–49 (an article seriously outdated from birth in many details). In this book I shall use "Iran" to denote the empire successively ruled by the Achaemenids, Arsacids, and Sasanians, even though the word acquired political as well as ethnic and geographical significance only in the Sasanian period (the one with which I shall mainly be concerned): cf. Gnoli, *Idea of Iran*, esp. 175–78.

Kushan Empire formed a bridge between China and India and whose estimated floruit has fluctuated between the later first and later third centuries A.D., but now seems to be settling in the later first or the first half of the second century, alluded in his titulature to the royal traditions of India, Iran, China, and Rome.[3] And in the *Fars-nama* we read how the Iranian Emperor Khusrau I (531–79) kept three empty thrones ready near his own: one for the emperor of China, one for the emperor of Rome, and one for the king of the Khazars, should they choose to visit him.[4] Clearly "the whole world" was a relative concept. Merchants, missionaries, and the monarchs they visited knew that the world was big enough for more than one universalism, and it is perfectly reasonable to see in the contacts, albeit largely indirect, between ancient Rome and China a forerunner of the "world system" that emerged in the thirteenth century and foreshadowed our own.[5] But like the late-eighteenth-century Chinese ruler who disdained George III's ambassador Lord Macartney and the "ingenious articles" of British manufacture he bore as gifts, the ancients saw no reason to let hard-to-come-by knowledge of other places undermine their own universal claims.[6]

The particular world we are interested in, that of southwest Asia and the lands around the eastern Mediterranean, was the strategically indispensable part of what the Greeks and Romans thought of when they talked about "the whole world". By such expressions as *orbis terrarum* and *oikoumene*, educated Greeks and Romans basically meant the *Kulturländer*, the useful parts of the world, which they defined with rather self-conscious broad-mindedness as what lay between, in the West, the Atlantic Ocean where Heracles had set the bounds of the earth; in the East, the remotest Indians who had been visited by Heracles together with Dionysus; in the North, the Scythians; and in the South, the Blemmyes and Ethiopians.[7] The earth's extremities, *ta es-*

[3] Konow, *Kharoshṭhī inscriptions* 162–65; Monneret de Villard, *Annali Lateranensi* 12 (1948): 146–49. On the Kushans, see, e.g., Frye, *Ancient Iran* 246–69; Staviskij, *Bactriane*. On Kanishka's date, see Fussman, *J.A.* 275 (1987): 338; Cribb, *Stud.Ir.* 19 (1990): 176–77.

[4] Ibn al-Balkhi, *Fars-nama* 97, esp. 13–14 (tr. Christensen, *Iran* 411–12). The immediately ensuing passage (esp. line 21) on the Iranian kings' habit of contracting diplomatic marriages adds the rulers of India to the list of those so honored. My thanks to Oleg Grabar for help with this passage. For parallels, see Grabar, *Ars orientalis* 1 (1954): 186.

[5] Abu-Lughod, *Before European hegemony*, esp. 366.

[6] Sahlins, *P.B.A.* 74 (1988): 9–28.

[7] Pliny, *Naturalis historia* VI.24.89 (Ceylon "extra orbem a natura relegata"); Pompeius Trogus, *Historiae Philippicae* I.fr.20, II.fr.35 (Seel); Justin, *Epitoma Historiarum Philippicarum* XLIV.1.1 (Seel); Philostratus, *Vita Apollonii* II.33, III.13; Eusebius, *Vita Constantini* I.8, IV.50. The late antique map called the *Tabula Peutingeriana* covers the area from Britain to the mouth of the Ganges.

chata, were either as a matter of objective fact out of reach, or else deemed too "poverty-stricken and profitless" to be worth effort beyond the creation of fantastic denizens for them.[8] The subversive idea that their inhabitants were too happy to need *imperium* had also occurred to some.[9]

A still narrower understanding of "the whole world" than the one favored by geographers and historians was that contained in Roman imperial titulature, in such expressions as *dominus orbis terrarum* and the others already quoted. The Romans knew full well that there was no such thing as *imperium sine fine*.[10] Admittedly this universalist vocabulary was not entirely conventional: when Eusebius of Caesarea, in full knowledge of the existence of Iran, calls "the whole of the earth" a single "immense body", and Rome its head,[11] an important political point is being made. But when it came to the question of what was strategically indispensable to the existence of empire, the Romans and all the other successful imperial nations of antiquity were complete realists.

The details of Rome's frontier policy do not need to be examined here; but it is important to note that after Constantine founded Constantinople in 324, and especially after the disasters that befell the West in the early fifth century, it gradually came to be accepted that Rome might still be Rome without its western half[12]—as indeed turned out to be the case. The important players in the game of world empire were, after all, in the East. They were Christian Rome with its capital at Constantinople, the Sasanian Empire, and the Islamic Empire. Almost all culture that needed to be taken seriously had arisen in the eastern Mediterranean, Syria-Mesopotamia, or Iran. Even Roman law could now be perfectly well studied at Beirut.[13] Raw materials and manpower abounded in or near these regions. The role models from the past were Cyrus and Alexander. Only Rome had ever consistently behaved as if its existence were tied to control of the Mediterranean in its entirety. But the barbarian threat was now making the western Mediterranean lands—Italy, Spain, and North Africa—an improbable environment for further thoughts of world empire. Augustine knew from experience that the "appetitus unitatis et omnipotentiae" in the things of this world would

[8] Appian pref. 7; Plutarch, *Theseus* I.1; and cp. Miquel, *Géographie humaine* 2.483–513.

[9] *Expositio totius mundi* 5–11.

[10] Rubin, *M.H.R.* I (1986): 15–18, to which add Eusebius, *H.E.* III.8.11; Sozomen, *H.E.* II.6.1; and Chadwick, *History and thought* XI, on use of *oikoumene/oikoumenikos* in the titles of professional associations, etc.

[11] Eusebius, *Vita Constantini* I.26.

[12] Kaegi, *Byzantium and the decline of Rome*, esp. 224–55.

[13] See below, p. 64.

THE WORLD'S TWO EYES

pass as do the shadows.[14] As proved by Justinian's short-lived recon-
quest, and the difference between the knowledge of Western affairs displayed on the one hand by the historian Procopius (under Justinian) and
on the other by his successors Agathias (died circa 580) and Theophylact Simocatta (under Heraclius), the Byzantine *oikoumene* could do
without the Latin world.[15] Iran never controlled it. The Islamic Empire
engrossed North Africa and Spain, then lost them again without great
trauma. And though the heirs of the deposed Umayyad caliphal family
continued to rule Spain as an independent Islamic state from 757 onward, they did not claim the religious title "Caliph" for themselves until
929, knowing that it was inseparable from control of the central Islamic
lands and especially of the Holy Places.[16] Fernand Braudel was right to
emphasize the bipartite character of the Mediterranean, linked only by
the Straits of Messina and the Sicilian Channel. "To claim that the
considerable obstacles between the two halves of the Mediterranean
effectively separated them from each other would be to profess a form of
geographical determinism, extreme, but not altogether mistaken."[17]

How then does the eastern Mediterranean relate to the lands still
further east that are the focus of our story, and in particular to the Fertile
Crescent? Christian Rome (or "Byzantium") would have been inconceivable without Constantinople, the Sasanian Empire without the Iranian plateau, the Islamic Empire without Arabia. But what they all impinged on and fought over was the Fertile Crescent. Our concern in this
chapter is with Rome and Iran up to Constantine, and we cannot understand their relations unless we have a feel for the geographical arena
within which they encountered each other.

"Arena" is indeed the best word to describe this region, physically as
well as functionally.[18] The Fertile Crescent is only the inner rim of its
northern hemicycle. The region we are concerned with is a vast oval

14 Augustine, *De vera religione* XLV.84; and similar skepticism about Rome's aspiration to universal power in *Historia Augusta, Vita Taciti* XV.

15 Ostrogorsky, *Zur byzantinischen Geschichte* 86–87, underlines continuing Byzantine interest in the West until the reign of Constans II, but in the context of an irreversible
shift of gravity eastward.

16 Collins, *Arab conquest of Spain* 127–29.

17 Braudel, *Méditerranée* 1.123 (tr. S. Reynolds).

18 On awareness of the historical role of this Mountain Arena in antiquity, see below,
pp. 102–4, and in the Muslim geographers, Miquel, *Géographie humaine* 2.270–72;
3.3–5, 7–8, 17–23: the "système orographique universel" here described, despite its
North African and Central Asian ramifications, corresponds in its Islamic heart to my
Mountain Arena. Since this region is rarely discussed as an integral whole, cartographic
depictions are few. The best tend to be part of an even larger whole, including Central
Asia: e.g., Brice, *Atlas of Islam* 19; Miquel's map opposite 3.493/4.332; and *The Times
atlas of the world* pl. 27.

whose circumference touches on and interacts with but does not include the Black Sea in the North, the Iranian plateau in the East, the Arabian Sea and the Gulf of Aden—the Indian Ocean's northwestern reaches—in the South, and the Egyptian desert (beyond the Nile Valley) and the Mediterranean in the West. The whole is rimmed by an almost continuous line of mountains, themselves in places of such great extent that they constitute subregions that independently interact with as well as defining the edges of the great expanse of plain and desert that lies at the region's heart.

This is particularly true of the mountain rim's northernmost sector, which, viewed from the Syrian-Mesopotamian plain, is sufficiently defined as the Taurus, but functionally extends as far as the Pontic range fringing the Black Sea, and even the Caucasus. The Taurus flow straight into the Zagros Mountains, which separate Mesopotamia from Iran. The Zagros then fringe the Persian Gulf to the East and, once they have allowed the Gulf waters to slip through the Straits of Hormuz, continue into Oman, the high and rugged southeasterly tip of Arabia surrounded islandlike by sea and sand, whose position has caused its history to be closely bound up with that of Iran. Further along Arabia's southern coast, the mountains rise again from Dhofar westward toward Yemen, the peninsula's southwestern tip; and the Red Sea, like the Persian Gulf, narrows abruptly at its southern end between the mountains of Yemen and Ethiopia's rugged plateau. From Yemen and Ethiopia the mountains tend northward on either shore of the Red Sea—they are the two sides of the Great Rift Valley. And west of the more westerly of these two chains lies another broadly North-South valley, that of the Nile, which, though strictly speaking outside the great mountain rim, is pushed by the Sahara into close interaction with the whole region described here. Beyond the highlands of Sinai at the Red Sea's northern end we descend to the Mediterranean; but along the Mediterranean's eastern edge, behind the narrow coastal plain, there are always hills and eventually mountains again—Lebanon and the Nusayri range of northwest Syria, and then beyond Antioch (Antakya) the Amanus range, which links up with the Taurus and closes the arena. And what this mountain rim contains is Syria, Mesopotamia, and Arabia, a vast expanse not without incident but nowhere broken by heights or (in the case of the Rift Valley) depths such as those that surround it. Only in the northern hemicycle does a Fertile Crescent mediate between the mountains and the desert. In the southern hemicycle the transition is usually abrupt, and civilization is confined to the highlands (Yemen, for example), and the valleys and oases bordering the desert: Najran, Marib, Hadramawt, and many others. The great Marib dam nourished extensive agriculture on runoff from the Yemeni uplands until, at the beginning of the seventh century, the dam finally broke without hope of repair and the area reverted to barren wilderness.[19]

For the purposes of our investigation of Roman-Iranian relations before the emergence of the First Byzantine Commonwealth, which was more or less coterminous with the southwest Asian Mountain Arena just described, it is mainly the Fertile Crescent that concerns us. The Fertile Crescent was the most direct, easiest link between the Greek, Roman, and eventually Byzantine and Ottoman Mediterranean and the Iranian heartland beyond the Zagros. Between these two culturally distinct worlds there had always been informal exchanges. Much that was most elevated in Greek culture was held to have originated in the East; the Iranians for their part appreciated Greek art and Roman technology. Certain basic geographical facts also enmeshed these two worlds. The Mediterranean climate and way of life enjoy only the most precarious of footholds on the southwest Asian landmass, along its coasts and in those river valleys that lead down to them; while the Zagros Mountains are a forbidding rampart dividing Mesopotamia from the Iranian plateau. But between the Mediterranean and Iran, the Fertile Crescent mediates. Though far apart, then, the Mediterranean and Iran are not unrelated; they are equally implicated in Syria-Mesopotamia.

Indeed, Syria-Mesopotamia suffers from a crucial weakness that guarantees the embroilment in its affairs of whoever controls the eastern Mediterranean or Iran. As the sometimes extensive but usually short-lived empires of Sargon of Akkad, the Assyrians, the Babylonians, and later the Seleucids demonstrated, the Fertile Crescent cannot maintain long-term political autonomy, for it is too easily threatened by circumjacent regions whose geography makes them natural fortresses and power centers: in the North and Northwest, Anatolia; in the East, as Herodotus recalls in the very last sentence of his *Histories*, the Iranian plateau; in the South, Arabia; in the Southwest, Egypt; in the West, the Mediterranean.[20] In the period that concerns us, Anatolia and Egypt belonged to the Mediterranean empire of Rome; Arabia was as yet quiescent. Therefore either Rome or Iran had to dominate the Fertile Crescent, or they had to learn to coexist within it, ideally in an equilibrium of mutually recognized power, as two eyes illuminating the world

[19] Müller, *Enc.Is.*[2] 6.564.

[20] See the revealing series of sixteen maps in *Atlas of Israel*[2], sec. IX/1, showing the empires that dominated the Fertile Crescent from the Pharaohs to the British.

together,[21] but in practice either more or less uneasily. Of Palmyra, the caravan city in the Syrian desert, Pliny noted that "it has a destiny of its own between the two mighty empires of Rome and Parthia, and at the first moment of a quarrel between them always attracts the attention of both sides."[22] By the same token, the Palmyrenes' brief independence in the late 260s and early 270s, though it embraced Egypt and much of Anatolia,[23] was doomed because they neither took to the western sea nor scaled the Zagros.

Only in a very limited sense, then, was or is the Euphrates a "geographically imperative" frontier.[24] International frontiers have at times run along both the Euphrates and the Tigris, and have even acquired considerable symbolic force;[25] but they have actually represented nothing more profound than a political and military stalemate, the inability or indisposition of the powers on either side to eliminate the other and so realize the Fertile Crescent's inherent unity. In fact, that unity cannot be realized within the closed context of the Fertile Crescent alone. For the Fertile Crescent is not just a potential unity. It is also a vortex that pulls inward and fuses what lies around it. So not only can the Fertile Crescent never enjoy long-term autonomy, but its unity can only be realized on a secure basis as part of a wider unification of the Iranian plateau with the Mediterranean. And that unification has only twice been achieved, by Cyrus and by Muhammad,[26] who both in doing so created empires that for about two centuries enjoyed the otherwise unparalleled luxury of having no serious competitor on the stage of the

[21] Petrus Patricius fr.13; Theophylact Simocatta, *Historia universalis* IV.11.2. For other expressions of the idea of the parity of the two empires, see Philostratus, *Vita Apollonii* I.27; Herodian IV.10.2; Justin, *Epitoma Historiarum Philippicarum* XLI.1.1,7; Ammianus Marcellinus XVII.5.3, 10; Chabot, *Synodicon orientale* 37 (synod of Church in Iran, 420); Procopius, *Anecdota* II.31; John Malalas 449.19–21; Winter, *Friedensverträge* 112–13, 205–7, 213–15, 224–29; Winter, in *Migratio et commutatio*; Lee, *Historia* 40 (1991). That the two empires routinely notified each other of changes of ruler also implies recognition of parity and of a division of the world into spheres of influence: Theophylact Simocatta, *Historia universalis* III.12.2, 17.1; VIII.15.2. On the legal aspect of this mutual recognition see Chrysos, Κληρονομία 8 (1976): 5–24.

[22] Pliny, *Naturalis historia* V.21.88; though, as E. Will observes, *Syria* 62 (1985): 265, this remark might more appropriately have been made about Armenia (cf. below, pp. 78–79).

[23] See Isaac, *Limits of empire* 220–28; also Graf, in *Eastern frontier*, on Zenobia's "ecumenical" political program and diplomacy.

[24] Pace Frézouls, in *Géographie administrative* 225.

[25] On the Roman period, see Millar, *Britannia* 13 (1982): 19.

[26] Frézouls, in *Géographie administrative* 224, speaks, from the usual Hellenocentric perspective, of Alexander and Muhammad.

"known" world (which for practical purposes excluded China).[27] In short, "world empire" presupposes (in antiquity) control of the eastern Mediterranean basin and the Iranian plateau, and therefore also of what lies between.

IRAN, THE GREEKS, AND POLYTHEIST ROME

This truth was first demonstrated by Cyrus the Great. Cyrus founded the Iranian Empire during his three decades' reign from circa 559 to 529 B.C. He earned his reputation as "the most energetic of the kings in Asia"[28] by merging the Medo-Persian Empire with the Neo-Babylonian and Lydian Empires—that is to say, by conquering the whole of Asia Minor, and southwest Asia as far as Gaza. His successor Cambyses (529–522) added Egypt, Cyprus, and the maritime dimension that the empire seems to have lacked under Cyrus[29]—though control of the coast in effect meant control of the sea, Mediterranean shipping being mostly cabotage.[30] Darius I (522–486) conquered (either more or less superficially) the Indus Valley in present-day Pakistan, Libya, and the greater part of the Aegean, along with Thrace and Macedonia. Iran's further expansion into Greek lands was checked at Marathon (490), while after Salamis (480) and Plataea (479), Iranian rule was thrown back to the coasts of Asia Minor, themselves much disputed by Athens in the decades to come. But for the first time in antiquity the Iranian plateau and the eastern Mediterranean basin had been united in one political entity; and Iran continued, especially in the aftermath of the King's Peace of 387–386, to play an active part in the game of Aegean politics.

The Achaemenids' power base lay on the Iranian plateau. The same was to be true of the Abbasids, while the long rivalry of Iran and Rome was to be essentially a rivalry of land armies in the southwest Asian Mountain Arena. Nonetheless, Darius I's interest in India points forward to and reminds us of the commercial and therefore political importance that the Indian Ocean acquired from the Hellenistic period onward. He who controls the Iranian plateau may also use the Persian Gulf and, to some extent, the southern Iranian coast as an opening onto the

[27] Rome from Hannibal to the mid-third century was never seriously shaken, but neither did it ever eliminate its eventual challengers, the Germans and Iran.

[28] Arrian, *Indica* IX.10. On the formation of the Achaemenid Empire, see Dandamaev, *Achaemenid Empire*.

[29] Herodotus I.143, III.34.

[30] Braudel, *Méditerranée* I.94–98.

sea routes to India. And although India will play only a peripheral role in the present narrative, the importance of the Indian Ocean is increasingly and deservedly emphasized.[31] We should at least bear in mind that the Iranian plateau implies, strategically and commercially, the Indian Ocean, which was a factor in the power play of Romans and Sasanians, and which in the Islamic period became a world of its own, a counterweight to the Mediterranean.

Within the Achaemenids' vast empire there were many inaccessible areas where the king's writ did not run. It was a firmly administered but not a homogeneous realm. There were, especially in later years, innumerable conflicts between center and periphery; the naval arm tended to be in the hands of Levantines, not Iranians, who did not take naturally to the high seas;[32] and the rulers on the whole respected and even drew inspiration from the diversity, including cultural and religious diversity, of their subjects.[33] They did this, though, not out of weakness but because they believed that all gods should be worshipped in their own countries, and that maintenance of order among their many subject races was the mission entrusted to the Achaemenids by God.[34] The Achaemenid Empire had no cultural motive, no mission to Iranize, only the militarily, politically, and economically motivated goals of preserving order and the Iranian elite's domination. What balance Cyrus personally held between traditional Iranian polytheism and Zarathushtra's teaching about the supreme God and creator Ahura Mazda is difficult to discern,[35] but whatever it was, it did not add up to an anticipation of Constantine's attempted or Muhammad's successful conjoining of imperial impetus with missionary monotheism to create cultural as well as political world empire.

Both despite and because of this laissez-faire approach, the

[31] Chaudhuri, *Asia before Europe*; Wink, *al-Hind* 1.45–64.

[32] Wallinga, in *Achaemenid history* 1 68–75.

[33] Herodotus I.135; Nylander, in *Power and propaganda* 353–57; Briant, in *Grandes figures religieuses*; Dandamaev and Lukonin, *Ancient Iran* 292–360.

[34] Dandamaev and Lukonin, *Ancient Iran* 356–60; Frei and Koch, *Reichsidee* 49–109.

[35] In this book I shall use the term "Mazdaism" to denote the religion of Iran in all its mainstream manifestations within Iran, including the teachings of Zarathushtra. Zoroastrianism (as we call it, after the Greek for Zarathushtra) represented a conceptual and ethical advance on Indo-Iranian polytheism; but polytheism persisted until the Islamic conquest, while Zoroastrianism retained Ahura Mazda and also certain other beneficent powers, though not the wicked and violent Daevas. Zoroastrianism was inextricably mixed up with the older polytheism in the beliefs and practices of ancient Iranians; the Zoroastrian creed, the Fravarane, defines those who subscribe to it as "Mazdayasna". For a sympathetic but inevitably (given our lack of evidence) not uncontroversial account of Zoroastrianism's entire history, see Boyce, *Zoroastrians*.

Achaemenid Empire survived until the death in 323 of its final ruler, the Macedonian Alexander.[36] Alexander saw himself as Cyrus's true heir. On campaign he at times followed self-consciously in his great predecessor's footsteps,[37] and he insisted that he had lawfully acceded to the Iranian throne.[38] By adding Greece to Iran, he also realized the dream of Darius and Xerxes; while as a non-Iranian he felt free to move the main capital down from the Iranian plateau to Babylon in the Fertile Crescent,[39] the logical center, as the Abbasids were also to perceive, for a world empire that embraced the eastern Mediterranean as well as Iran. But because, despite his claims to legitimacy, Alexander came as a conqueror from without, he destroyed the system at the same time as he realized the dream. His evanescent empire was too purely the product of military action and almost wholly deficient in administrative structures other than those taken over from the Achaemenids, which had little in common with those of Macedonia. Perceiving, no doubt, that his empire was also, even by antique standards, much too little the fruit of cultural or economic penetration, Alexander began to foster a real mingling of Greeks and Orientals; the interracial marriages he encouraged his soldiers to contract are proof of that. But Alexander died too soon to use the fruit of these marriages, while his Macedonian lieutenants were far more interested, once their leader was gone, in establishing an Aegean power base than in preserving the eastern conquests. Although the Seleucids, who inherited most of Alexander's empire, were already half Iranian by the second generation (Antiochus I), and much more committed to the non-Mediterranean world than has traditionally been admitted,[40] they lost control of eastern Iran in the mid-third century; while competition between the Seleucids and the Ptolemies meant that no single power controlled the eastern Mediterranean basin. Whatever the local continuities between the Achaemenid and post-Achaemenid situations, these rivalries undermined the nearest that antiquity had come to a world empire, and heralded a thousand years of strife between its parts.

One might ask, then, why Alexander is called "the Great". The answer lies not only in his youth and energy, but in the charisma that gave birth to a Hellenocentric dream. By founding new cities throughout his possessions and settling Greeks in them, Alexander inaugurated a tre-

---

[36] Useful accounts of Alexander in Iran are Badian, *C.H.Ir.* 2.420–501; Bosworth, *Conquest and empire.*

[37] Strabo XV.1.5, 2.5; Arrian, *Anabasis* VI.24.2–3.

[38] Briant, in *Idéologie monarchique.*

[39] Strabo XV.3.9–10.

[40] See, e.g., Sherwin-White, in *Hellenism in the East.*

mendous expansion of Hellenism's cultural territory. This was not pro-
grammed into the project from the start; Alexander's most pressing
priorities were reliable garrisons and supply lines protected by his own
veterans. Nor would his new cities have become such cultural dynamos
had there not been an ample supply of educated Greeks whose prospects
at home did not outweigh the risks of emigration. But in part because the
notions of empire and culture had not been too closely linked by Alexander, the culture was able to evolve even as the empire dissolved. With
the culture spread and grew the Alexander legend. In the eyes of the
Greeks and their Roman heirs, Alexander, much more than Cyrus,
stood for world empire, and *imitatio Alexandri* became one of the
themes of their history.

What Alexander came to stand for in the mind of posterity, then, was
not just military glory but also cultural domination—Greek cultural
domination. Because of the chaos into which the Hellenistic world gradually descended, it was only once the Romans had absorbed it, united
the whole Mediterranean, and brought peace again that anyone could
aspire to follow Alexander's road to the East. And though Trajan,
Caracalla, and Julian consciously set out in those fateful footsteps,
while Septimius Severus and Galerius achieved substantial successes
despite humbler aspirations,[41] polytheist Rome never pulled off that
combination of military and cultural impetus that Alexander had, however accidentally and even posthumously. The Roman Empire saw itself
as the antithesis of barbarism and was well aware of its own cultural
distinctiveness; but its rulers thought mainly in the realistic terms of
balance of power and profit. Even when world empire seemed within
their grasp, as when Trajan stood on the shores of the Persian Gulf and
"began to think about the Indians, and was curious about their affairs",
realism soon broke in.[42]

This realism was founded in some measure on self-doubt, not least
cultural self-doubt.[43] The occasional political or military humiliation
such as the capture of the Emperor Valerian by Shapur I in 260, or
Jovian's cession of Nisibis in 363, could be counterbalanced, even
effaced, by successes greater or lesser, running from Septimius Severus's
substantial territorial gains down to the smaller boundary adjustments,

[41] For a lucid account of Rome's eastern frontier, see Frézouls, in *Géographie administrative*. On the dating of and Diocletian's disputed participation in the 297/8 campaign,
see Kolb, *Eos* 76 (1988), and Kettenhoffen's review of Winter, *Friedensverträge*, in *B.O.* 47
(1990): 174.

[42] Cassius Dio LXVIII.29.1.

[43] On fluctuating Roman motives in the East, see Isaac, *Limits of empire* 17, 23–28,
52, 265–67.

1. Shapur I triumphs over the Roman emperor Valerian without even
unsheathing his sword. Cameo, fourth century.

together with plunder and excuses for self-glorification that were the
more usual outcome of eastern (or any other) campaigns. Culturally,
though, the self-doubt ran deeper. In the West, with the exception of
Carthage, Rome had to deal with less-organized societies and less-
sophisticated cultures. There, its achievement was indisputable. But everyone knew that the worthy enemy, the enemy whose defeat would
bring true glory, was Iran, as Julian made clear to those pedestrian
advisers who preferred him to campaign against the Goths on the
Danube.[44] The Iranians were not only a real state and a serious military
power. They were a *Kulturvolk* too. Greeks might feel effortless superiority to them, but Romans were not Greeks; their Hellenism was
secondhand. And even real Greeks might not feel completely sure. If
Constantius II's ambassador, the Platonist Eustathius, had succeeded in
his attempt to convert Shapur II to philosophy in 358, the polytheist
historian Eunapius, for one, would have been very pleased[45]—it would
have been a worthy triumph. As late as the sixth century, experienced
polytheist philosophers visited the Iranian court under the impression

[44] Ammianus Marcellinus XXII.7.8: "hostes quaerere se meliores aiebat". Cp. too the
minimal impact on our sources of Aurelian's abandonment of Dacia, with the scandal of
Jovian's cession of territory to Iran: Millar, *Britannia* 13 (1982): 20.
[45] Eunapius, *Vitae philosophorum* VI.5.

that they might learn something worthwhile about Plato from Khusrau I.[46] To this sense of cultural uncertainty vis-à-vis Iran was added a fear of its otherness. We may doubt, for instance, whether the philosophers who visited Khusrau's court really wanted to admire Iran. Their professed admiration owed not a little to their disenchantment with Justinian's Christian empire, and the disappointments they experienced during their journey will only have intensified an already strong sense of Iran's irreducible cultural otherness. It has even been suggested that Diocletian and Julian, the last two polytheists to rule the whole Roman Empire, regarded this otherness as in itself a casus belli, refusing to accept the relativity of moral codes. According to this view, Diocletian's rescripts against incest (295) and Manichaeism (297—or, as less conveniently dated by many, 302) were meant to justify, at least in part, his campaigns against Iran.[47]

In practice, the Romans confined their expansion in the East to the relatively well Hellenized areas. While we have no reason to suppose that they could have subdued the Iranian plateau even if they had wanted to, the suspicion remains that cultural as well as strategic considerations made Mesopotamia's eastern edge the boundary of what (even at moments of optimism) seemed possible. Alexander's exoticism was not for the Romans. But a certain balance of power was maintained. If occasional glory or even profit could be derived, so much the better.

SASANIAN UNIVERSALISM

The Romans had to become Christians before they discovered a cultural force capable of making significant inroads into Iranian territory—and even then their armies never managed to keep up. I will return to this problem in chapters 4 and 5. But what was Iran's position in this equation of power? A remarkable story about the Emperor Caracalla (211–17) is worth retelling at this point, for the sake of the powerful contrast it makes between what it represents as unabashed Roman militarism on the one hand, and on the other an Iranian perception that something more was needed. The story is carefully told to reflect maximum discredit on its protagonist, but like all such stories, it would have been implausible had there been no truth in it. Our source is the contemporary historian Herodian.[48]

[46] Agathias II.30–31.
[47] Chadwick, *Heresy and orthodoxy* XXI.152–53; Kolb, in *I cristiani e l'impero* 36–44.
[48] Herodian IV.10–11 (tr. C. R. Whittaker, with adjustments).

According to this writer, the Emperor Caracalla "wanted to have the title of 'Parthicus' and to report to the Romans that he had mastered the barbarians in the East." Unfortunately, Rome and Iran were at peace. So Caracalla sent a letter to Artabanus IV, one of two rivals for the Parthian throne, asking for his daughter's hand in marriage. "The two most powerful empires were those of the Romans and the Parthians," he wrote.

If they were united by marriage and no longer separated by a river, he would create one invincible power. For the remaining barbarian peoples would be an easy conquest for them, one by one in their separate national groups and confederacies. The Romans had an infantry force, which was invincible in close-quarter fighting with spears, while the Parthians had a large cavalry force, which was highly skilled in archery. If these forces united and all the agencies for successful warfare cooperated, they would surely have no difficulty in ruling the whole world under a single crown. Furthermore the locally grown spices of the Parthians and their wonderful woven clothes, and on the other side the metals produced by the Romans and their admirable manufactured goods, would no longer be difficult to get and in short supply, smuggled in by merchants. Instead both sides would have shared and unimpeded enjoyment of these things from the unification of their countries under a single rule.

This attractive proposal was coolly received:

The initial Parthian reaction was to say that it was not fitting for a Roman to marry a barbarian since they had nothing in common, they did not understand each other's language, and had different habits of food and dress. The Romans had plenty of patrician families (like the Arsacids in Persia) from whom Antoninus [Caracalla] could choose a daughter. The racial purity of neither should be contaminated.

But Caracalla pressed his suit, and Artabanus gave in. Caracalla rode into Parthian territory to collect his bride, and was enthusiastically received. On the plain before his capital, Artabanus and his unarmed retinue greeted the Roman ruler. "All were anxious to get a view of the bridegroom. This was the moment at which Antoninus gave the signal to order his army to set upon the barbarians and kill them." Artabanus himself was snatched from danger by his bodyguard, but much of the Iranian crowd was massacred. "Antoninus retired unopposed, loaded with booty and prisoners. . . . He sent a dispatch to the Senate and

Roman people announcing the subjugation of the entire East and the submission of everyone in the kingdom east of Mesopotamia." Some of his last coins, in 217, duly celebrate a *vic(toria) Part(hica)*.[49]

Though both compressed and embroidered, Herodian's story makes quite good sense, at least at its core. Artabanus needed Caracalla's help against his brother and rival Vologeses VI. And Caracalla pointedly styled himself "Savior of the *oikoumene*" and *kosmokrator*. Indeed, he seems to have been particularly attached to these titles,[50] and we may assume, as Dio explicitly states, that he intended that he would be the one to rule the united empire.[51] He after all was going to marry and sexually subdue the Iranian king's daughter. But all the time Caracalla had in mind, if we believe Herodian, a quicker and more theatrical—he would have said more glorious—way of making the same point, by massacring his bride-to-be's male entourage and pointedly doing without the subtler dominations of the bed.

Caracalla here seems to parody one of the standard moves in Romano-Iranian propaganda warfare—the deliberate refusal sexually to harass one's opponent's women.[52] Galerius captured but did not violate King Narseh's harem in 297/8,[53] in this imitating Alexander's treatment of Darius's mother, wife, and two virgin daughters.[54] In 359 Shapur II similarly refrained from some Christian virgins discovered in a Roman fort,[55] and in 363 Julian with the same self-consciousness respected captive Iranian beauties.[56] By contrast, the *Historia Augusta*, taking some liberties with the historical course of events, has the Palmyrene ruler Odenathus hand over the captured concubines of Shapur I to his son Septimius Herodianus, who was "wholly Oriental and given up to Grecian [*sic*] luxury".[57] This eagerness of both Romans and Iranians to demonstrate moral superiority contained a tacit recog-

[49] *B.M.C.* 5.465–66.

[50] Mastino, in *Popoli e spazio romano* 91–94, 118, 152, 155.

[51] Cassius Dio LXXVIII.1.1.

[52] This refusal may very well contain a deliberate allusion to Herodotus's view, expressed at the beginning of his book (I.1–4), that woman-stealing was at the root of the hereditary enmity between Greece and Asia. As it happens, a similar story marks Macedonia's first appearance in Herodotus's narrative: V.17–21.

[53] Petrus Patricius fr. 13–14.

[54] Plutarch, *Alexander* XXI. Basil, *Ad adulescentes* VII.9, followed by many later Byzantines, singles out Alexander's treatment of Darius's women as an example of ancient Greek virtue worthy to be imitated by Christians.

[55] Ammianus Marcellinus XVIII.10.3–4.

[56] Ibid., XXIV.4.27. Standards later fell: Procopius, *De bello Persico* II.8.35; John of Ephesus, *H.E.* III.6.7.

[57] *Historia Augusta, Valeriani duo* IV.3, *Tyranni triginta* XV.4, XVI.1–2; cf. Felix, *Aussenpolitik* 1.80.

nition that the other side was more or less on an equal footing. Indeed, in 298 the Iranians are said openly to have admitted that the Romans' behavior had shown them superior: "non modo armis, sed etiam moribus Romanos superiores esse confessi sunt".[58] But Caracalla was determined to give them no such opportunity. In its stark juxtaposition of vacuousness and brutishness with percipience and peaceableness, Herodian's story reads like Iranian propaganda. It would be interesting if Iranians really had held, against Romans, that a successful superpower would have to combine common cultural ground—or at least cultural penetration—with political, military, and economic self-interest. But at least we know that in the Roman Empire such matters were discussed.

Caracalla was one of the Alexander legend's prize victims. So was Julian. But on the other side of the frontier the Achaemenids had not been wholly forgotten, and Alexander was treated as the last of their line or as their odious destroyer, but not as the founder of a new empire.[59] In A.D. 35 the Arsacid monarch Artabanus III laid claim to "the old boundaries of the Persian and Macedonian Empires", and announced that "he planned to invade the territories held first by Cyrus and then by Alexander".[60] But in general the Arsacids were less belligerent, less of a threat to Rome, than their self-assertive Sasanian successors.[61] Herodian records how, not long after Caracalla's expedition, the first Sasanian monarch, Ardashir (mid-220s—239/40),

> refused to be contained by the River Tigris, and crossed the banks which were the boundary of the Roman Empire. He overran Mesopotamia and threatened Syria. Believing that the entire mainland facing Europe and contained by the Aegean Sea and the Propontis Gulf (the whole of what is called Asia) belonged to him by ancestral right, he was intending to recover it for the Persian Empire. He alleged that from the reign of Cyrus, who first transferred the kingdom from the Medes to the Persians, up to Darius, the last of the Persian kings, whose kingdom Alexander of Macedon had destroyed, the whole country as far as Ionia and Caria had been under the government of Persian satraps. So it was his right to restore and reunite the whole empire as the Persians had once held it.[62]

Shapur II maintained the same right in 358, in a letter to the Emperor Constantius: "That my forefathers' empire reached as far as the River

58 Festus, *Breviarium* 25; cf. Winter, *Friedensverträge* 167–68.
59 Yarshater, C.H.Ir. 3.472–73.
60 Tacitus, *Annales* VI.31.
61 For the maximalist view of the Arsacids, see Wolski, in *Archaeologia iranica*.
62 Herodian VI.2.1–2, and cf. 4.5, and Cassius Dio LXXX.3–4.

Strymon and the boundaries of Macedonia even your own ancient records bear witness; these lands it is fitting that I should demand"—
though Shapur well knew that discretion is the better part of valor: "But
at all times right reason is dear to me, and trained in it from my earliest
youth, I have never allowed myself to do anything for which I had cause
to repent. And therefore it is my duty to recover Armenia with Mesopotamia, which double-dealing wrested from my grandfather".[63] Our
source is here Ammianus Marcellinus. In the opinion of this sober
observer, Shapur meant what he said. "The threats of the Persians were
soon brought into effect, as they claimed everything as far as Bithynia
and the shores of the Propontis."[64]

It is tempting and in some quarters fashionable to take a skeptical
view of evidence for Iranian history that comes overwhelmingly from
Greek and Latin sources,[65] and admittedly reflects Rome's calculated
alarmism better than her significant but not dominant role in the Iranian
worldview.[66] It is maintained that the texts just quoted are inventions or
at best elaborations based on knowledge of the Achaemenids' wars not
available to the Sasanians themselves, and that no extant Sasanian
source makes any such claim. In particular the *Res gestae divi Saporis*,
the great inscription on the "Kaaba of Zarathushtra" at Naqsh-i
Rustam in which, not long after 260, Shapur I recorded in Parthian,
Middle Persian, and Greek his victories over the Romans, makes no
unambiguous, permanent claim to those parts of the Roman Empire
west of the Euphrates that had once belonged to the Achaemenid
realm.[67] But the purpose of Shapur I's inscription is to boast how many
provinces he devastated, plundered, and conquered, not to draw attention to his failure to keep them, which he would have done had he gone
on to assert hereditary title to these areas. And while it is true that the
Achaemenid kings personally were virtually absent from Sasanian *literary* memory, whereas readers of Herodotus were copiously informed
about them, it should not be forgotten that Alexander was well known
to the Sasanians, both for good, as heir of the Iranian Empire, and for ill,

[63] Ammianus Marcellinus XVII.5.5–6 (tr. here and elsewhere J. C. Rolfe).

[64] Ibid., XXV.4.24.

[65] E.g., Kettenhofen, O.L.P. 15 (1984); Kettenhofen, B.O. 47 (1990): 164–66, 176–
77, 178; Potter, *Prophecy and history* 370–76 (discussing only the evidence for Ardashir);
Isaac, *Limits of empire* 21–22. For the opposite view see Winter, *Friedensverträge* 26–44,
51–52, 75–77, 122–23, with detailed discussion of the above-mentioned and other
sources, including indications of Sasanid emulation of the Achaemenids preserved by
Muslim writers; also Wiesehöfer, *A.M.Iran* 19 (1986); Panitschek, *Klio* 72 (1990).

[66] Cameron, D.O.P. 23–24 (1969–70): 115.

[67] Thus Kettenhofen, O.L.P. 15 (1984): 184–87; also Chrysos, Κληρονομία 8 (1976):
7–11. For another view see Winter, *Friedensverträge* 37–38.

as its destroyer.[68] While so specific a reference as that to the Strymon may (but need not necessarily) be Ammianus's embellishment, the mere assertion that the Iranians had once held everything as far as the Aegean required no profound knowledge of ancient history.

In general, it is unreasonable to maintain that the Sasanians had no knowledge at all of the Achaemenids.[69] There were, for instance, the visible monuments of the past such as the tombs of the Achaemenids at Naqsh-i Rustam, a place that the Sasanian dynasty too regarded as of central significance, and obviously not by coincidence.[70] Sasanian tales of the Kayanian Empire that Alexander destroyed also seem to contain reminiscences of the Achaemenids.[71] Nor were Greeks unknown in Iran, especially at court, and they had their own stories to tell. Were the Sasanians not clever enough to use what they learned from the Greeks in order to overawe the Romans? It should also be borne in mind that most of what we know of Sasanian literature is preserved at second hand by Iranian and Arab writers who lived long after the Sasanian Empire's demise. The silences of such a tradition are no adequate basis on which to reject repeated and plausible assertions by non-Iranian writers.

Indeed, among the Sasanian texts thus indirectly preserved, the *Letter of Tansar* firmly supports our Greek and Roman authorities. Few scholars currently accept without reserve the *Letter of Tansar*'s claim to date from the reign of Ardashir. Precisely the passage here in question alludes to Khusrau I (531–79), though that could be an interpolation. But we may accept the *Letter* as a statement of Sasanian aspiration, albeit not of the first generation. The sage Tansar is writing to one of Ardashir's subordinate kings:

> Today the King of Kings has cast the shadow of his majesty over all who have acknowledged his preeminence and service and have sent him tribute, and has protected their borders from attack by his own men. Thereafter he has devoted all his thoughts to attacking the Greeks and pursuing his quarrel against that people; and he will not rest until he has avenged Darius against the successors of Alexander, and has replenished his coffers and the treasury of state, and has restored by the capture of descendants [of his soldiers] the cities

---

[68] Yarshater, *C.H.Ir.* 3.377–78, 388–91, 472–73. A Nestorian ecclesiastical document dated 544 calls Khusrau I the "new Cyrus": Chabot, *Synodicon orientale* 69–70.

[69] See above, n. 65.

[70] Meyer, *J.D.A.I.* 105 (1990): 291 (with photograph); and note also Huyse, *A.M.Iran* 23 (1990). Potter, *Prophecy and history* 372–73, both underlines this point and denies its significance.

[71] Yarshater, *C.H.Ir.* 3.470–73. On late Arsacid as well as Sasanian invocation of the Achaemenids, see also Russell, in *Iranica varia* 180–81.

which Alexander laid waste in Iran. And he will impose on them tribute such as they have ever paid our kings for the land of Egypt and for Syria; for in ancient times they had made conquest in the land of the Hebrews. When Nebuchadnezzar went there and subdued them, he did not establish any of our people in that place because it had a bad climate, poor water and chronic sicknesses. He entrusted that region to the king of the Greeks, contenting himself with tribute. So things remained down to the time of Khusrau Anushirvan.[72]

Another text that tells of Ardashir, the probably late-Sasanian *Book of deeds of Ardashir son of Papak*, likewise vaunts the tribute that Rome and India had paid Iran, and claims that "the Caesar of Byzantium, the sovereign and Tab[?] of Kabul and the King of India and the Khagan of the Turks and other chief rulers from every region came to the court in sweet peace".[73]

Whether, regardless of what they said for propaganda, the Sasanians really wanted to reconquer the whole of the Achaemenid Empire is, strictly speaking, another matter. But since, in the early seventh century, they did precisely that (a point not always emphasized by those who deny the historicity of the statements discussed above), let us suppose that so startling an event did not come about purely by accident.[74] Benjamin Isaac has recently maintained that the Sasanians' motive for invading Syria was not to acquire world empire or indeed to occupy permanently anything west of the Euphrates but, more modestly, to distract the Romans from trying to take over in Armenia or expand east of the Euphrates, two moves totally unacceptable at Ctesiphon.[75] This is true in the sense that Septimius Severus's conquest and annexation in the 190s of two new provinces across the Euphrates, Osrhoene and Mesopotamia, became a permanent bone of contention,[76] while the partition of Armenia under Theodosius I contributed to a long period of peace. The borderlands were undeniably a constant headache for both powers.

[72] *Letter of Tansar* p. 42 (tr. Boyce 65). Note also Masudi's view of Ardashir as restorer of the Achaemenid achievement and principal forerunner of Muhammad's Islamic Empire: *Kitab muruj al-dhahab* §504.

[73] *Book of deeds of Ardashir son of Papak* XIII.20–21 (tr. W. W. Malandra, to whom I am obliged for sight of his unpublished translation and discussion of this text).

[74] Attested instances of Iranian skepticism about world empire (Herodian IV.10–11, and see above, pp. 24–27; Theophylact Simocatta, *Historia* IV.13.7–12, partially quoted below, pp. 98–99) are special pleading in difficult or embarassing situations where Rome had the upper hand.

[75] Isaac, *Limits of empire* 17, 28–33, 52–3, 249–51; likewise Drinkwater, *R.S.A.* 19 (1989) [1991].

[76] As frankly acknowledged by Cassius Dio LXXV.3.3.

But Isaac's assertion that the Romans were in general more militarily aggressive than the Iranians will not command universal assent.[77] Counting campaigns is not the only criterion for such judgments. One campaign may have more effect than another, and Shapur I's in the mid-third century were certainly long remembered. If it was to be another three centuries before Iran managed to penetrate Syria again, that was thanks to the success of the Mesopotamian buffer, not for want of effort on Iran's part. Propaganda and the diplomatic offensive also have to be taken into account; the Iranians had a provocatively exalted idea of their place in the world.[78] We may grant Isaac that "in diplomacy and war one must distinguish between words and deeds",[79] but words and the ideologies they reflect still have independent significance. The historian disregards words as an indication of possible future action at his or her own risk. And Isaac knows that eventually, in the 630s, "it was a wholly unexpected war of ideas and religion that brought down the existing order".[80] Though this is a simplistic view of the Arab invasions, the Sasanians did undeniably have a religion.

Isaac is aware that Mazdaism,[81] through its at times close alliance with the ruling elite, helped the Sasanian state acquire a strong religious identity and exercise a degree of intolerance within Iran for which there was no Achaemenid precedent. Likewise, foreign policy acquired a nationalist motivation considerably more focused than anything attempted by the Arsacids.[82] Attributing to the first Sasanian ruler Ardashir what was undoubtedly a longer-term development, Agathias writes:

> He was a devotee of the Magian religion and a practitioner of its mysteries. Consequently the priestly caste of the Magi rose to inordinate power and arrogance. It had indeed existed before, and its name was very ancient, but it had never before been elevated to such

---

[77] Winter, *Friedensverträge* 216, takes the exactly opposite position.

[78] See, e.g., Rubin, *M.H.R.* 1 (1986): 39–42, on Iranian demands for subsidies/ "tribute"; also *Oracula Sibyllina* XIII.99 on the "arrogant Persians", and plate 1.

[79] Isaac, *Limits of empire* 21. Chrysos, Κληρονομία 8 (1976): 6–24, further distinguishes between political or propaganda declarations on the one hand and legal theory (or "legal reality") on the other, and points to the mutual diplomatic recognition that prevailed between Rome and Iran (see above, pp. 17–18 and n. 21) as a counterweight to more aggressive declarations.

[80] Isaac, *Limits of empire* 268.

[81] See above, n. 35.

[82] Isaac, *Limits of empire* 16. On the Mazdean-Sasanian alliance see *Denkard* IV, pp. 412–15 (tr. Shaki, *Arch. Orient.* 49 (1981): 115–21, and Boyce, *Textual sources* 113–14); Bianchi, in *Incontro di religioni*; Chaumont, *Christianisation* 99–120; Choksy, *B.A.I.* 2 (1988); Gnoli, *Idea of Iran* 140–42, 164–74.

a position of privilege and immunity. It had sometimes actually been spurned by those in power. . . . Nowadays, however, the Magi are the object of extreme awe and veneration, all public business being conducted at their discretion and in accordance with their prognostications. In private affairs too they preside over and oversee the proceedings when anyone makes an agreement or conducts a suit, and nothing whatever is held to be lawful or right among the Persians unless it is ratified by a Magus.[83]

And Elishe, an Armenian source also of the sixth century but relying heavily on earlier authorities, represents the Magi as addressing Yazdagird II (439–57) in the following words:

Valiant king, the gods have given you your empire and success. They have no need of human honor; but if you convert to one religion all the nations and races in your empire, then the land of the Greeks will also obediently submit to your rule.[84]

Even the Achaemenids had not gone that far.

Here at last are non-Iranian statements about Sasanian policy whose spirit, if not letter, is confirmed by the Sasanians' own pronouncements. "The gods," Shapur I proclaims on the "Kaaba of Zarathushtra" at Naqsh-i Rustam, "have made us their ward, and with the aid of the gods we have searched out and taken so many lands [i.e., Roman provinces], so that in every land we have founded many Varahran fires [the highest grade of Mazdean sacred fire] and have conferred benefices upon many magi-men, and we have magnified the cult of the gods."[85] And the Mazdean high priest Kirdir, who was "absolute and authoritative in (the matter of) the rites of the gods, at the court and from province to province, place to place, throughout the Magian land"[86] under all the Sasanian rulers from Shapur I (240–72) to Narseh (293–302), describes in a text inscribed at various places, including Naqsh-i Rustam, how he established fire temples and implanted magi both throughout the Sasanian Empire and in Syria, Cilicia, Cappadocia, and the lands south of the Caucasus from the Black Sea to the Caspian (Trans-

---

[83] Agathias II.26.3, 5; cf. Cameron, *D.O.P.* 23–24 (1969–70): 108–9. There were exceptions who confirmed the rule, e.g., Hormizd II (302–9), who according to the *Chronicle of Seert* 12 (*P.O.* 4.255) "se montra indépendant dans ses idées sur l'administration des affaires et n'écouta pas les Mages"; and cf. the same source, 73 (*P.O.* 5.331), on Yazdagird I (399–421).

[84] Elishe, *History of Vardan and the Armenian war* p. 9 (Ter-Minasean; tr. Thomson 63).

[85] *Res gestae divi Saporis* 328–30 (Back).

[86] Inscription of Kirdir (see *Bibliography*) §2.

caucasia), including Armenia, Iberia (Georgia), and Albania (roughly the equivalent of modern Azerbaijan).[87]

Particularly among such groups as the "Magousaioi" of Cappadocia, "numerous . . . [and] scattered throughout almost the whole country, colonists having long ago been introduced to our country from Babylon",[88] Shapur and Kirdir will have aspired to capitalize on the tenacious survival of Iranian tradition and cult, the legacy of the Achaemenids— just as, two centuries later, Peroz (459–84) sent an embassy to Constantinople with a list of complaints, including the allegation that "the Romans, wishing to turn the Magi (who had long lived in Roman territory) from their ancestral customs, laws, and forms of worship, harassed them and did not allow the fire, which they call unquenchable, to be kept always burning as their law requires".[89] Given the fragility and brevity of the mid-third-century conquests, we should take Kirdir's emphasis on making provision for (presumably) already existing fire cults more seriously than Shapur's claim that he founded new ones.[90] Zarathushtra remained a national rather than a universal prophet, and Mazdaism did not evolve into (or even, usually, come to see itself as) a religion for non-Iranians.[91] But what is not in doubt, and most important for us in the present context, is the link between Kirdir's reforming and expansionary zeal and Shapur's conquests and dreams of past Achaemenid glories. Kirdir's inscriptions give us a vivid insight into the practical implementation of what might almost be called Sasanian universalism. On the political level the Sasanians were, we may at least say, aware of Cyrus's world empire and probably prepared to exploit its precedent. On the cultural and religious level they were not missionaries, and even their sporadic persecutions of Manichees, Christians,

---

[87] Ibid., §§14–15; and cf. Chaumont, *Historia* 22 (1973); Gignoux, *C.R.A.I.* (1989).

[88] Basil, *ep.* 258. Philippus (Bardaisan), *Book of the laws of countries* p. 44 (Drijvers) mentions Magians in Egypt and Phrygia; Eusebius, *Praeparatio evangelica* VI.10.17 (reporting Philippus) adds Galatia. On these texts, see further Boyce and Grenet, *History of Zoroastrianism* 3.256, 277–79, 492–93.

[89] Priscus fr. 31 (Müller) = 41.1 (Blockley, whose translation I use, slightly emended).

[90] Cf. Moses Khorenatsi, *History of the Armenians* II.77 (tr. Thomson 225): "Ardashir [I—but probably Shapur I is meant] . . . increased the cults of the temples [in Armenia] and ordered the fire of Ormizd, which was on the altar at Bagavan, to be kept perpetually burning."

[91] See, e.g., Gnoli, *Idea of Iran* 158–59, on Mazdaism's conservatism; Boyce and Grenet, *History of Zoroastrianism* 3.220, on Mazdaism in Asia Minor; Lieu, *Manichaeism* 232, on Mazdaism in China. The Mazdaism of Armenia is not necessarily an exception. That Christian Armenians often though not universally regarded themselves as non-Iranians does not necessarily reflect the self-image, much less the actual identity, of pre-Christian Armenians: Garsoian, *Armenia* X.6–11; Russell, *Zoroastrianism in Armenia* 89–93, 528.

and other non-Mazdean groups did not carry them far or for long beyond the Achaemenid model of cultural pluralism. Kirdir's pronouncements about the intimate relationship between Mazdaism and successive early Sasanian rulers undoubtedly have a streak of idealism in them, and later on, during the fourth to seventh centuries, the relationship was to have many ups and downs, some of them dramatic.[92] But even so, the Sasanians' faith was by and large allied to their Iranian identity in a way that was perceived, by such as Agathias and Elishe, to have political consequences.[93]

The Iranian Empire had at last acquired cultural motive and momentum—and, as often happens in such situations, the history books had to be rewritten. From the tenth-century Arabic writer Masudi we learn how Ardashir, the first Sasanian king, was much exercised by the fact that Zarathushtra had lived about 300 years before Alexander; Alexander had lived 513 years before Ardashir; and Zarathushtra had prophesied that the Iranian Empire and religion would be destroyed after a thousand years. Perceiving that his own dynasty was destined, on this calculation, to last less than two centuries, Ardashir wished to add another two centuries; so he proclaimed throughout his kingdom that he had acceded to the throne in the two hundred sixtieth year since Alexander.[94] In order to mesh Sasanian pretension with Mazdean prophecy, Ardashir excised some two and a half centuries from Iranian history.

Less than a century after Ardashir's accession, and within a generation of Kirdir's disappearance from the historical record, Rome embarked on a similar alliance, but with an unambiguously universalist religion, Christianity. From Constantine to Heraclius, recurrent and at times almost constant military confrontation between Christian Rome and Mazdean Iran sharpened each side's cultural identity and conviction of superiority. Constantine's removal of his capital to Constantinople further contributed to this process. By acknowledging the importance of the Iranian front, Constantine also invested the prestige of his empire in the East, and brought for the first time within the bounds of possibility an Iranian assault on the capital itself. The collapse a century

[92] Gnoli, *Idea of Iran* 164–74.

[93] In an unpublished paper, "The role of the Achaemenids in Sasanid ideology", which she kindly sent me when this book was in its final stages, Patricia Crone argues that Sasanian political universalism was itself culturally motivated—for the purpose not of propagating Iranian values, but of legitimating a program of internal "modernization" involving massive annexation of Greek and Roman wealth, ideas, technology (see the passage from Herodian quoted above, p. 25), and even workers (in the shape of captives from the eastern provinces).

[94] Masudi, *Kitab al-tanbih wa'l-ishraf* pp. 97–98 (tr. Carra de Vaux 140–41); cf. Gnoli, *De Zoroastre à Mani* 37–38.

later of Rome's control of the West and monopoly of Mare nostrum made the neutralization of Iran even more a priority, if the West was to be regained. The balance of power between Rome's Mediterranean empire and Iran had been destroyed—not in the sense that Byzantium was unable to hold its own in a straight fight with Iran, but because all too often it was faced with the impossible task of fighting on two fronts, in the West as well as the East. The growing threat from Huns and Slavs in the North was another reason why Rome and Iran failed to come properly to grips with each other in the fifth and sixth centuries,[95] though relations did become markedly less peaceful as the sixth century wore on.

Then, in the second and third decades of the seventh century, the Iranians conquered nearly the whole Roman East and, significantly, assembled a fleet with which they attacked Cyprus and Rhodes.[96] This was a serious attempt to meet the geographical precondition of world empire—control of the eastern Mediterranean basin as well as Iran. As for the cultural element, our Christian sources represent the Iranian campaign as strongly anti-Christian or at least anti-Chalcedonian in tone.[97] The Christians of the occupied provinces eventually reached a modus vivendi with their new Iranian masters;[98] but Heraclius's counterattack was every bit a crusade, though intended to reestablish coexistence with Iran rather than to destroy the other empire completely.[99] In 626 the Iranians at last arrived, in conjunction with the Avars, before the walls of Constantinople. The experience etched itself deep into the Byzantine mind, which in the later sixth century had become more accustomed to identifying Empire and Church,[100] and by now instinctively saw the confrontation as a direct assault on Christianity as well as on the capital. The Mother of God alone defeated the enemy, whose aim was "not so much to capture the Queen City as to throw down the royal majesty of Christ".[101] In the face of such defining opposition it became clear not only that Iran's aspiration to world empire was real and even

[95] On the Huns, see esp. Isaac, *Limits of empire* 74–75, 229–35, 261, 263, 267.

[96] Foss, *Byzantine Asia Minor* I, esp. 724–25, 730, 732–33, on Cyprus and Rhodes.

[97] *Chronicon Paschale* p. 728; *Chronicon anonymum* ("Khuzistan chronicle") p. 28 (tr. Guidi 24); Theophanes p. 301.21–24; Agapius of Manbij, *Historia universalis* pp. 198–200.

[98] Dagron, *T.&M.Byz.* 11 (1991): 18–28; Kaegi, *Byzantium and the early Islamic conquests* 45, 68n.5.

[99] See below, p. 98.

[100] Cameron, *Continuity and change* XVI.99–102, 106–8.

[101] Germanus I of Constantinople, *Homily on the deliverance of Constantinople* §§9–11, on the Arab siege of 717–18, but elsewhere alluding also to that of 626. (Procopius, *De bello Persico* II.26.2, had already offered this same explanation for Khusrau I's hostility to Rome.) Compare the passages quoted in n. 97 above.

realizable, but also that Christianity was of the essence of Romanity, that empire and religion advanced or fell together. This attitude was highly characteristic of Byzantium; it was the Emperor Constantine's most enduring legacy, even if it took some time to mature. But before Constantine, what of polytheist Rome, which survived the first Christian emperor by half a century at least? The sort of cultural universalism that made Christianity so useful an ally for the Empire of East Rome had not been wholly a Christian invention.

2

POLYTHEIST ROME:
TOWARD CULTURAL UNIVERSALISM
WITHIN EMPIRE

THE OBVIOUS late antique cultural or, more specifically, religious universalisms, those of Christ and Mani, were universalisms from birth.
Mazdaism, though not universalist, had discovered how to present itself
as a focused, coherent national faith that might afford valuable support
to Sasanian imperialism. But the polytheism of the Romans and Greeks
and other peoples who had fallen under Roman rule was almost by
definition not universalist, and certainly not universalist from birth. It
was a phenomenon about which we can hardly talk meaningfully except
in terms of a multiplicity of independent cults. For that precise reason,
though, the study of universalist tendencies within late polytheism is
uniquely useful. By illustrating the evolution and the transformative
power of universalist ideas, it enables us to understand more clearly,
because progressively, what late antique universalism, and in particular
cultural universalism, meant.

SEEDS OF POLYTHEIST UNIVERSALISM

Unlike the Jews, who when they entered their "Promised Land" brutally
eradicated the gods of the peoples they supplanted, all other ancient
states considered that conquered peoples' deities had the right to continued honor provided they recognized their subordinate position. Not
infrequently, they were adopted by the conqueror. But whatever the
origin of the conqueror's gods, they had to be visible and recognizable,
not just at the political center but at the periphery too. This visibility and
recognizability was achieved by both unofficial and official means. Unof-
ficially, syncretism allowed the gods of the center to be manifest at the
periphery in local garb. Officially, at least in the Roman Empire, it was
through the cult of Rome and of the emperor and his family that the
religious system and values of the center were projected to the periphery.
The imperial cult could be seen as more than just a perfunctorily worn
badge of political loyalty. Since it was highly conspicuous, thanks to the
central location of its temples in the provincial cities, and specific in that

it was devoted to a small group of easily recognizable personifications or persons, yet at the same time capable of assimilation to other polytheist cults,[1] the imperial cult could also act as a focus for what one might call a polytheist identity.[2] Typically, it was through refusing participation in the imperial cult that Christians came into conflict with polytheism and the political system that imposed it. The imperial cult, though a part, came to stand for the whole. Recent work has emphasized how the cult of the emperor helped subjects understand their relationship to power;[3] but we should not lose sight of the way in which the center used it to assimilate the periphery and unify the empire. The extreme ease with which one might conform to its requirements made it an ideal common denominator, while the plethora of polytheisms from which it had emerged went on doing what they were best at—expressing the natural variety of human religious behavior by allowing it to direct itself toward many objects.

But the imperial cult was not the only seed of polytheist universalism that was germinating in the Roman world. Christians called the cult of the old gods "paganism", that is, "rusticity", not just because the expression was derogatory but also because it was such a convenient shorthand for this vast spectrum of cults ranging from the international to the ethnic and local, some totally isolated, some richly syncretized with others, but none claiming exclusivity. It was easier to shoot at one target than at many—and the one target was carefully painted in the most lurid possible colors, derived from cults selected for barbarity, not typicality. In self-defense, polytheists sought to explain themselves and rationalize their uncontrollably complex heritage.

Long before Christian monotheism became a serious threat, philosophers had sought the common ground held by the polytheist world's many theological traditions. Hence the symbolic significance attached to Pythagoras's and Plato's studies with Egyptian priests, Chaldaeans, and Magi.[4] This tendency became especially marked in late antiquity, which privileged "the purified philosophy of Plato",[5] but had adopted much that was in origin Aristotelian, Stoic, and in particular Pythag-

---

[1] See, e.g., Ghedini, *Giulia Domna*, esp. 123–84, 188–93.

[2] Cf. *Passio Sanctorum Scilitanorum* 3, Saturninus the proconsul attempting to persuade Christians to conform: "We too are a religious people, and our religion is a simple one: we swear by the genius of our lord the emperor and we offer prayers for his health—as you also ought to do" (tr. H. Musurillo). See also references in Frend, *Rise of Christianity* 274.

[3] Price, *Rituals and power.*

[4] Diogenes Laertius III.6–7, VIII.2–3.

[5] Hierocles, *De providentia* ap. Photius, *Bibliotheca* 214.173a.

orean. The bitter controversies of the old schools were transcended in order to create a united front against Christianity, and a monotheist theology was offered on Plato's immense authority. Those, like Iamblichus, who favored the Pythagorean element in this synthesis sought with special insistence a *rapprochement* between Greek wisdom and that of the barbarians, notably the Chaldeans and Egyptians.

But it was not easy to see how the gods and their less intellectual worshippers might be similarly reformed. The second-century philosopher Celsus recognized common ground between the various polytheisms,[6] but he also took their diversity for granted, and rejected not only Christianity's claim to be a law for all nations, but the very possibility that such a law might exist.[7] A century or so later Porphyry, a leading Platonist and redoubtable polemicist against Christianity, seems to have been less certain. According to Augustine, he admitted "that no doctrine has yet been established to form the teaching of a philosophical sect, which offers a universal way (*universalem viam*) for the liberation of the soul; that no such way has been produced by any philosophy (in the truest sense of the word), or by the moral disciplines and teachings of the Indians, or by the 'elevation' (*inductione*) of the Chaldeans, or in any other way; and that this universal way had never been brought to his knowledge in his study of history."[8] Much of the argument's original texture has clearly been lost in the Augustinian filter. It seems likely that Porphyry was concerned with teachings applicable beyond the narrow circles of philosophers; but did he really believe, as Augustine appears to imply, that there may be a "universal way" of salvation for all mankind? And if he believed that, would he have admitted his failure to find it? Or had Porphyry in fact argued for pluralism, on the ground that there is no uniquely valid way?[9] To Augustine it was self-evident that Porphyry could not have found a universal way among the purveyors of alien wisdoms, "because those nations were especially influenced by a superstitious interest in the doctrine and the cult of angels of various kinds". And his vigorous assertion of Christianity's universality marked a significant advance over Celsus's opponent Origen, who did not disagree in theory, but admitted that mankind was more likely to follow a single doctrine in the next world than in this.[10] As for Porphyry, we can at least assume that the question of universality had posed itself to him, and that

---

6 Celsus ap. Origen, *Contra Celsum* V.41.

7 Ibid., VIII.72.

8 Augustine, *De civitate Dei* X.32 (tr. H. Bettenson).

9 As argued by Vanderspoel, in *Grace, politics and desire* 180–81.

10 Celsus ap. Origen, *Contra Celsum* VIII.72.

he had thought further along these lines than Celsus, just as Augustine found it possible to be less skeptical than Origen about universalism, at least in its cultural form.[11]

For Augustine it was essential to overlook or obscure any progress his opponents were making toward a more coherent self-representation—hence his notorious assumption that Varro is on an equal footing with his own personal observations and experiences as a source for the nature of polytheism.[12] But his correspondent the grammarian Maximus of Madauros knew better. In a letter he wrote to Augustine (circa 390), he asked:

> Who is so foolish, so mentally astray, as to deny the very certain truth that there is one supreme god, without beginning, without natural offspring, like a great and splendid father? His powers that permeate the universe he has made we call upon by many names, since to all of us his right name is of course unknown. For god is a name common to all cults, and so it is that while with differing prayers we pursue, as it were, his members piecemeal, we seem, in truth, to worship him entire.[13]

As he surveyed the temples gathered around the forum of Madauros, Maximus found it natural to see the many local gods as but aspects of one universal god, satraps of a divine King of Kings.[14] This centripetal view of polytheism built on tendencies in Greek thought already detectable in Homer.[15] But they became much more common currency in late antiquity.

Acceptance of such ideas in wider circles was assisted by the habits of syncretizing related deities into single composites, and envisaging gods

---

[11] Note e.g. Porphyry's inclusion on an equal footing of Egyptian as well as Greek material in his *De imaginibus*, which proposes a variety of rational interpretations of cult-symbols. Porphyry's esteem for Christ as distinct from the use made of him by Christians (Wilken, in *Early Christian literature*) is another sign that he may indeed have tried to formulate an inclusive "universal way". Nor was he alone in pursuing this line of thought: Parke, *Oracles of Apollo* 104–5. O'Meara, *Pythagoras revived* 26–28, argues that Porphyry did in fact succeed in finding Plato almost everywhere he looked: he was a "universalizing Platonist". For Augustine's skepticism about political universalism, see above, pp. 14–15.

[12] Augustine, *De civitate Dei* IV.1.

[13] Augustine, *ep.* XVI.1 (tr. J. H. Baxter). Earlier see, e.g., Celsus ap. Origen, *Contra Celsum* V.41.

[14] Ibid., VIII.35; and, on the idea's pedigree, Chadwick, *Origen: Contra Celsum* xvii–xx.

[15] Peterson, *Monotheismus* 47–49; Kenney, in *Classical Mediterranean spirituality*.

as impersonal powers.[16] In the Roman period henotheist ideas were quite widespread in the general population, but it is not always easy to put one's finger on them. When the fourth-century rhetor Libanius remarks that as a dwelling place for the gods Antioch can vie even with Mount Olympus,[17] he intends no more than a boast about the city's many temples. Rhetors who spoke in praise of cities were expected to claim that they had "built very many temples, or (temples) of all the gods, or many (temples) for each god".[18] And in its emphasis, at least, Libanius's understanding of polytheism was the exact opposite of that of Maximus. "Festivals of the gods", he maintained, "are marked off by their geographical location: neighboring peoples can be seen in procession, one to this god, one to that; and the name of the deity to whom sacrifice is offered is mighty in the eyes of the one or the other, but it is never the same for both."[19] For the likes of Libanius, then, the temples of Antioch existed for the sake of the city, and there was no reason why a mere plurality of gods should there evolve into a consciously universal, far less henotheist or monotheist religion. In less strictly conventional situations, though, the frequent dedications "to all the gods (and goddesses)", or Didymean Apollo's command to "honor and reverence all the blessed ones",[20] may betray such a tendency. This is certainly the case at holy places where the worship of a primary god or goddess attracts other divinities, generates a multiplicity of cults, and, eventually, stimulates speculation about their interrelationship. Eleusis, for example, is called the "common sanctuary of the [whole] world" by the rhetor Aelius Aristides, speaking in 171.[21] In principle this need mean no more than that people from all over the world visited Eleusis to be initiated into Demeter's mysteries; but in such a situation syncretisms were inevitable, which is why we read in an aretalogy of Isis discovered on a late Hellenistic inscription at Maroneia in Thrace: "It pleased you [Isis] to dwell in Egypt; in Greece you honored above all Athens. . . . That is why in Greece we hasten to gaze upon Athens, and in Athens, Eleusis, for we deem the city the ornament of Europe, and the sanctuary the ornament of the city."[22]

---

[16] Nock, *Essays* 34–45; Nilsson, *Geschichte* 2.534–43, 569–78; Habicht, *Inschriften des Asklepieions* 12–14; Fowden, *Egyptian Hermes* 75–94.

[17] Libanius, *or.* XI.115.

[18] Menander Rhetor I.362.26–28.

[19] Libanius, *or.* XII.15 (tr. A. F. Norman).

[20] Günther, *M.D.A.I.(I.)* 21 (1971): 99–105 (probably a third-century inscription).

[21] Aelius Aristides, *or.* XXII.2.

[22] Grandjean, *Arétalogie d'Isis* 18.

Possession of a sacred center was not, of course, a precondition of universality. Some of the most popular cults, especially mysteries such as those of Isis or Mithras, had no sacred center, but instead a network of autonomous cult-places, which had the advantage of making the cult accessible to a larger and more diverse public. And no cult could even become a candidate for diffusion until it had something to offer that was of more than purely national or local appeal. If a god formulated a spiritual message to the individual as an individual rather than purely as a member of a social collectivity, his or her adepts were more likely to propagate the cult wherever they might go, and start it on the long road toward universality. The horizontal extension of any cult presupposed a strong vertical axis between the individual believer and his or her god.

Even so, if the universality of a particular cult and eventually of polytheism generally was to be perceived, some focus and definition that was apparent from without was plainly desirable. The statements of theologians and philosophers were all very well, but in practice, and as far as most people were concerned, this external mode of definition was topographical—the sacred center. And in the Maroneia aretalogy we begin to see how syncretism—here, that of Isis and Demeter—could push a holy place that was no longer content with being merely famous toward a claim to universal significance on the theological level.

A much more explicit statement of this view, with reference to the holy land of Egypt, can be found in the Hermetic *Asclepius*, a Latin version of a lost Greek original that was perhaps composed in the third century: "Are you not aware, Asclepius, that Egypt is the image of heaven or, to put it better, the place where everything that is directed and superintended in heaven is transferred and comes down to earth? Indeed, if we are to tell the full truth, our land is the temple of the whole world (*terra nostra mundi totius est templum*)."[23] In the opinion of the fifth-century Platonist Proclus, the same was true of the individual holy places of the Egyptians, with their vast priestly archives full of records stretching back to the beginning of memory. The Egyptian temple was like an icon of cosmic order: "If then the World is the most holy of temples, in which eternally reside the principles that hold together the All, then the registering of ancient deeds in the temples must represent the image of the constitution of these principles."[24] But it was firmly believed that the image *is* the god;[25] so the final logical step was to make the stability of the universe dependent on the correct performance of the temple cults: "All things remain immobile and everlasting, because the

[23] *Asclepius* 24.
[24] Proclus, *In Timaeum* 38d.
[25] Funke, *R.L.A.C.* 11.714–16.

42

sun never halts in its course; all things remain perfect and whole, because the mysteries of Abydus are never revealed."[26] This view was formulated with unique clarity in Egypt, which had been less Hellenized than other parts of Alexander's empire and still regarded itself as an especially holy land; but the polytheists of Greece believed no less strongly in the universal significance of their mysteries. When in 364 the Emperor Valens banned nocturnal sacrifice, they petitioned that the mysteries, "which maintain in security the human race", be exempted; and when in the 390s the temples of Greece were destroyed, there were not a few who committed suicide rather than witness the inevitable cosmic catastrophe.[27]

The precise mechanisms by which a holy place acquired such a universal or even cosmic role, and became a sacred center, can still be grasped at Didyma or Epidaurus, where a profusion of altars and dedications to different gods turns what started out as a temple of Apollo or Asclepius into a veritable pantheon.[28] At the Pergamene Asclepeum, the dedication to "Zeus Asclepius" of the Hadrianic round temple that so resembles the Roman Pantheon reflects a recognition, at least in intellectual circles, that God was one and all-embracing.[29] Such sanctuaries offered a possibility, at a particular point on the earth's face, for the worshipper to feel in contact, like Maximus in the forum at Madauros, not just with the gods of that place, but with the whole divine world, whether conceived of as syncretistic or merely symbiotic, more pluralistic or less. This was not a new perception in late antiquity, and the authors of the illustrative texts of various dates just quoted did not see themselves as innovators. But it took a long time for such ideas to seep into wide circulation, for which some would have held that they were anyway not suited. Proclus, for example, continuing the passage just referred to, argues that cities can never aspire to the symbolic clarity of temples, because their nature partakes too much of the temporal and partial.[30] Nonetheless, two later Roman cities, Alexandria and Rome, were widely held to play a universal role in the worship of the gods. Both preserved the public rituals of the old religion when elsewhere they had already been abandoned.[31] Both therefore offered the Church an oppor-

---

[26] Iamblichus, *De mysteriis* VI.7.

[27] Zosimus IV.3.2–3; Eunapius, *Vitae philosophorum* VIII.1.10–11.

[28] Rehm, *Didyma* 2 no. 504 (πάνθεος περιβωμισμός; Diocletianic), and Günther, *M.D.A.I.(I.)* 21 (1971): 99–105; *I.G.* 4².380–588 (Epidaurus); and cf. Herodian V.5.8 (temple of Elagabalus, Rome) and 6.8.

[29] Habicht, *Pergamon* 11–14.

[30] Proclus, *In Timaeum* 38e.

[31] Libanius, *or.* XXX.33, 35.

tunity of exceptional validity and consequence to disprove the old religion, by attacking it in its sacred centers.

Alexandria

For the polytheist historian Eunapius of Sardis, writing around the year 399, Alexandria had been, "on account of the sanctuary of Serapis, a whole sacred world".[32] Writing a few decades earlier, before the temple's destruction, the author of the *Expositio totius mundi* says of Alexandria that "the gods are worshipped most assiduously; and the temple of Serapis is there, a spectacle unique in the whole world. For nowhere in the world is there to be found such a building, nor a temple of such a plan, nor such devotion."[33] And the historian Ammianus Marcellinus is only slightly less ecstatic: "Next to the Capitolium, with which revered Rome elevates herself to eternity, the whole world beholds nothing more magnificent."[34] Alexandria was "a whole sacred world" in several interrelated senses: because pilgrims came in large numbers and from faraway places to visit the Serapeum; because through that shrine and through Serapis's association with other gods, such as Isis and her son Harpocrates, they found a way into the whole exotic world of Egyptian religion (or what passed for such in non-Egyptian circles); and because Serapis and his companions had so successfully transcended the particularity of their Egyptian origins, to become gods for all mankind.

Since Serapis was also, at least for those of Greek culture, the lord of the River Nile, Alexandria became the center for those rites in honor of the river on which Egypt's prosperity (and its very survival) depended.[35] It was in this capacity that the Christians first attacked him—Constantine disbanded the group of priests responsible for the Nile cult, and removed the "sacred cubit", by which the annual flood was symbolically measured, from the Serapeum to a church.[36] But sacrifices to the Nile continued,[37] until Bishop Theophilus destroyed the Serapeum in 391. With reference to each stage in this assault—the disbanding of the priests, the removal of the Nile cubit, and the destruction of the

[32] Eunapius, *Vitae philosophorum* VI.10.8 (ἱερά τις ἦν οἰκουμένη).

[33] *Expositio totius mundi* 35.

[34] Ammianus Marcellinus XXII.16.12. Note also *I.G.U.R.* 1191, an epigram in which "a pure handmaid of all the blessed ones" calls her native Alexandria and adopted Rome "the metropolises of the cosmos and the earth"; and the assertion by the first century B.C./A.D. P. Berl. 13045.28–30 (Kunst, *Rhetorische papyri* 17) that Alexandria stands out among the other cities of Egypt as the only one that belongs truly to the *oikoumene*.

[35] Bonneau, *La crue du Nil* 319–24, 353–54, 426–35.

[36] Sources and discussion in Hermann, *Jb.A.C.* 2 (1959): 30–35.

[37] Libanius, *ep.* 1183 and *or.* XXX.35.

Serapeum—one or another of the sources preserves the story of how, immediately afterward, all waited in suspense to see whether or not the Nile would rise, until the Christians were rewarded with a superabundant flood, to the dismay of the polytheists. The story may be legendary, but it underlines the palpable disproof, which shook the world, of what had until then been axiomatic: that the land of Egypt would be destroyed if the old gods ceased to be worshipped, above all in Alexandria.[38]

Rome

Despite its cosmopolitanism and the native Egyptians' hostility, Alexandria was enmeshed in the egocentricity of Egypt.[39] Only Rome could aspire to be a truly universal city. The cult of "Dea/Urbs Roma" may have been more a cultural and political metaphor than a "religious experience", but it was nonetheless fostered with special zeal in the second, third, and fourth centuries: "She is worshipped with blood after the fashion of a goddess, the name of the place is reckoned as a divinity, the temples of the City and Venus rise to the same high top, and incense is burned to the pair of goddesses together." Thus Prudentius, not later than 402–3, used the historic present to describe a freshly remembered past.[40]

By diplomatic guile or right of arms, the Romans had also made their city "a place meet to be the resort of every god", "Rome the place of empire and the gods."[41] Later in the *Contra Symmachum*, Prudentius has this to say:

As her valor conquered cities and won her famous triumphs, Rome got herself countless gods; amid the smoking ruins of temples the victor's armed right hand took her enemies' images and carried them home in captivity, worshipping them as divinities. One figure she seized from the ruins of Corinth by the two seas, another she took for booty from burning Athens; the defeat of Cleopatra gave

[38] Fowden, *Egyptian Hermes* 13.

[39] Cf. Severus of Antioch, *ep.* 46, p. 146: "It is the habit of the Alexandrians to think that the sun rises for them only, and towards them only the lamp burns, so that they even jestingly term outside cities 'lampless' " (tr. E. W. Brooks).

[40] Prudentius, *Contra Symmachum* I.219–22 (tr. H. J. Thomson). On the cult of Rome, see Gagé, *A.I.Ph.O.* 4 (1936); Knoche, in *Prinzipat und Freiheit*; Turcan, *A.N.R.W.* II.16.2, 1069–71.

[41] Ovid, *Fasti* IV.270 (tr. J. G. Frazer), *Tristia* I.5.70 (tr. A. L. Wheeler). Cf. also, e.g., Lucan III.91 ("deum sedes"), Claudian, *Panegyricus dictus Honorio Augusto VI cos.* 185 ("urbem . . . deorum").

her some dog-headed figures, and when she conquered the sands of Ammon there were horned heads among her trophies from the African desert.[42]

The accumulation of sacred works of art at Rome by Augustus and his immediate successors had largely aesthetic motives,[43] but the gods did not cease to be gods in their new environment. From the time of the Severans onward, when Rome began to be ruled by emperors from outside the traditional Western elite, foreign divinities came in the guise of conquerors as well as captives—one thinks particularly of Caracalla's innovative establishment of a temple of Serapis within the city limits. Elagabalus succeeded only in alienating the Romans when he imposed on them the uncompromisingly Oriental sun-god of his native Emesa. But fifty years later, Aurelian captured Palmyra (272–73), carried off to Rome statues of the Sun and Bel to adorn his magnificent new temple of Sol,[44] and knew how not to offend Roman taste, while preserving the cult's Syrian connections. The concept expressed by Hadrian's Pantheon was being consciously enriched; and the idea of Rome as the whole earth's "communis patria", the "common town" (*asty koinon*), the "acropolis" where all the "demes" of the world assemble,[45] was increasingly linked with the idea of Rome as a "holy city".[46] With Prudentius, one could then draw the conclusion that the capital was the "one single home for all earthborn divinities",[47] the focus of all the sacred forces within the empire, "an assembly of gods", as the Constantinopolitan rhetor Themistius put it in a speech delivered to the Roman senate in 376, "a deme of heroes, a tribe of guardian spirits. . . , the ocean of beauty",[48] "the temple of the whole world".

[42] Prudentius, *Contra Symmachum* II.347–56. Similarly Claudian, *De consulatu Stilichonis* III.169–73.

[43] Dio Chrysostom, *or.* XXXI.147–48, 151; Pausanias VIII.46.

[44] Zosimus I.61.2.

[45] *Digesta* XXVII.1.6.11, XLVIII.22.18(19), L.1.33; Athenaeus, *Deipnosophistae* I.36.20bc; Aelius Aristides, *or.* XXVI.61; Rutilius Namatianus I.66. Cp. Sozomen, *H.E.* VII.4.5, on the New Rome as "citadel of the whole world".

[46] Apuleius, *Metamorphoses* XI.26; Themistius, *or.* XIII.178b.

[47] Prudentius, *Contra Symmachum* I.189.

[48] Themistius, *or.* XIII.177d–178b. For other expressions of this idea by polytheists, either directly preserved or reported in Christian polemic, see Minucius Felix, *Octavius* 6 (each people worships its own gods, but the Romans worship them all); Arnobius, *Adversus nationes* VI.7 ("civitas maxima et numinum cunctorum cultrix"); *Historia Augusta, Vita Aureliani* XX.5 ("templum deorum omnium"); Claudian, *De consulatu Stilichonis* III.135 (Rome "septem scopulis zonas imitatur Olympi"); Rutilius Namatianus I.49–50 ("genetrix . . . deorum, / non procul a caelo per tua templa sumus"); Gelasius I, *Adversum Andromachum* (*Collectio Avellana, ep.* 100) 14.

This last phrase occurs not in Themistius but in the account by Ammianus Marcellinus of how Constantine removed from the temple of Amun in Egyptian Thebes (Karnak) the mighty obelisk that today stands in the Piazza San Giovanni in Laterano: "Constantine . . . tore the huge mass from its foundations, and rightly thought that he was committing no sacrilege if he took this marvel from one temple and consecrated it at Rome, that is to say, in the temple of the whole world (*in templo mundi totius*)."[49] This seems to have been the emperor's present to Rome on the twentieth anniversary of his accession—his *vicennalia* (326). And Ammianus's phrase perhaps comes from the declaration Constantine himself made on that occasion to announce the intended gift, which was finally delivered by his son Constantius, thirty-one years later. *Templum mundi totius* is precisely what Egypt is called in the passage already quoted from the Hermetic *Asclepius*. This text circulated widely in Constantine's time and milieu, and it seems likely that in his speech the emperor quoted it in order to underline the significance of the object he was giving to the old and still substantially polytheist capital. Constantius eventually set it up on the central barrier of the Circus Maximus, where it joined a collection of art that made many allusions to the empire's varied religious traditions,[50] and could be seen by the whole population gathered to watch the chariot races. The Circus Maximus was considered an image of the cosmos,[51] and over it presided the emperor, himself "the metropolis of all pieties",[52] whose "sacred precinct is the whole earth",[53] but whose home was the Eternal City: "Of a truth no other city could fitly be the home of the world's rulers; on this hill is majesty most herself, and knows the height of her supreme sway; the palace, raising its head above the forum that lies at its feet, sees around it so many temples and is surrounded by so many protecting deities."[54] Constantine's compliment, so perfectly attuned to these ways of thought, nonetheless signified their impending redundancy. It was merely a palliative for his already apparent intention to relieve Rome of the two functions, as capital of the empire and residence of the emperor, that explained her accumulation of gods.

Nevertheless, half a century or so was to pass before any emperor could feel free of the need to mollify the powerful polytheist element in the

---

[49] Ammianus Marcellinus XVII.4.13; and, for the interpretation here offered, Fowden, *J.H.S.* 107 (1987).

[50] Humphrey, *Roman circuses* 175–294.

[51] Dagron, *Naissance d'une capitale* 330–38.

[52] Eusebius, *H.E.* IX.7.6 (rescript of Maximin Daia against the Christians, 312).

[53] Dio Cassius LII.35.5.

[54] Claudian, *Panegyricus dictus Honorio Augusto VI cos.* 39–44 (tr. M. Platnauer).

old capital's senatorial aristocracy. It was the Emperor Gratian (375–83) who took the fateful steps of repudiating the title "Pontifex Maximus", withdrawing state subsidies to the cult of the old gods, and removing from the Senate House the altar of Victoria,[55] by whose favor the city had become the universal temple. In all probability he acted at the bidding of Ambrose, the powerful and aggressive bishop of Milan. Ambrose well knew that the gods of Rome still enjoyed enough prestige to render their disproof an urgent necessity. In the evil times that had now fallen on polytheism in many parts of the empire, Rome was seen as a bulwark of the old ways—even in the Greek East, which had nothing to learn about religion from the Latin West. None other than the patriotic Antiochene Libanius conceded, in a speech probably composed in 386, that "the gods in Rome grant greater blessings. . . . The stability of empire depends on the sacrifices performed there."[56]

With this continued affirmation, at least in certain circles, of the Eternal City's role as "temple of the whole world", we may also connect the well-known cultic eclecticism of the senatorial aristocracy. The often-quoted inscription on the tomb of one of the polytheist senatorial circle's leading lights, Vettius Agorius Praetextatus (d. 384), proclaims him "augur, priest of Vesta, priest of Sol, *quindecemvir, curialis* of Hercules, consecrated to Liber and in the Eleusinian [mysteries], hierophant [of Hecate at Aegina], *neocorus* [i.e., priest of Serapis], initiate of the taurobolium [of Cybele], Father of Fathers [i.e., initiate of Mithras]"; while his wife, Fabia Aconia Paulina, was "consecrated at Eleusis to the god Iacchus, Ceres and Cora, consecrated at Lerna to the god Liber, Ceres and Cora, consecrated to the goddesses at Aegina, initiate of the taurobolium [of Cybele] and of Isis, hierophant of the goddess Hecate and consecrated to the Greek goddess Ceres [i.e., Demeter]."[57] Though never unknown, multiple priesthoods and initiations probably became more common in late antiquity.[58] They are attested especially often in Rome, where a circle of which Praetextatus and Paulina are only the best-known representatives self-consciously espoused and proclaimed the universal polytheism, Roman, Greek, and Oriental, that is so comprehensively abused in the *Carmen contra paganos*.[59] The em-

[55] Cf. Croke and Harries, *Religious conflict* 28–51.

[56] Libanius, *or.* XXX.33; and cf. Themistius, *or.* XIII.177d–178b, with Dagron, *T.&M.Byz.* 3 (1968): 160–61, 191–98.

[57] *I.L.S.* 1259–60; cf. Bloch, *H.Th.R.* 38 (1945): 242–44 and table. Macrobius, *Saturnalia* I.17.1, calls Praetextatus 'sacrorum omnium praesul'.

[58] Nock, *Essays* 38; Bloch, *H.Th.R.* 38 (1945): 211–13; Reynolds and Ward-Perkins, *Inscriptions of Roman Tripolitania* nos. 567–68, on which see Lepelley, *Cités de l'Afrique romaine* 2.347–48; Libanius, *or.* XIV.5–7; Eunapius, *Vitae philosophorum* VII.3.1–4.

[59] On this, see Barnes, in *Grace, politics and desire* 167–68.

peror was now a Christian; Gratian had recently abandoned the title "Pontifex Maximus"; and the imperial cult, once one of the most omnipresent and (at least implicitly) universalist aspects of polytheism, was so conducted that Christians could participate and even hold priesthoods in it.[60] Under these circumstances, someone else had to stand for the unity of the old religion.

Rome as a sacred center was destined to have a new lease on life under the Christian dispensation. In the period here in question some Christian writers were content to adopt the old vocabulary—Ausonius, for example, happily calls Rome "first among cities, the home of the gods".[61] Others qualified it, but did not doubt that what had once been a great pagan city would become a great Christian city, as soon as it was cleansed of its ancient pollution: "Rome, thou ancient mother of temples, now given up to Christ."[62] Because of Rome's importance, its purification had to be exemplary. Hence Ambrose's insistence on the removal of the Altar of Victory, and hence Theodosius's insistence on the role of both Rome and Alexandria as touchstones of Christian orthodoxy,[63] rather in the same way that churches were built over temples to efface memories of the old gods. Now that polytheism has been struck in its head, Augustine argued in a sermon delivered at Carthage in June 401, it must also be attacked in its limbs, the provincial cities. "Si in capite gentium res praecessit, membra non sunt secutura?"[64] Augustine's allusion is vague, but foremost among the events he had in mind must have been the Battle of the River Frigidus, at which Theodosius I had eliminated Eugenius and his backers among the polytheist elite of Rome. In his *De civitate Dei* Augustine gives an account of this battle that carefully underlines both sides' invocation of divine support—polytheist by Eugenius's followers, Christian by those of Theodosius. So do several of the other Christian accounts, while the polytheist Zosimus omits this aspect out of embarrassment rather than ignorance.[65] For Christian writers the battle by the Frigidus was the most convincing disproof of Roman polytheism, especially because the capital's fall to the Goths in 410 admitted no such easy explanation. The old

[60] Chastagnol, *Evolution politique* 174–82; Lepelley, *Cités de l'Afrique romaine* 1.362–69; Bowersock, in *Jewish and Christian self-definition* 3 176–82 (on distinctively Christian elements introduced into the cult after Constantine's death); Clover, *B.C.T.H.* 15–16B (1984).

[61] Ausonius, *Ordo urbium nobilium* I.

[62] Prudentius, *Peristephanon* II.1–2.

[63] *Codex Theodosianus* XVI.1.2.

[64] Augustine, *sermo* XXIV.6. On the date, cf. Lambot's edition, 324–25.

[65] Zosimus IV.58, and Paschoud's edition, 2(2).488–500, for the text of the other accounts.

gods had already been banned, so they could hardly be blamed; but the Church, despite a growing self-identification with Rome, was not yet ready to accept full responsibility for the fortunes of a city so burdened by its past. Zosimus, discerning that here at least polytheism had not suffered a clear-cut defeat, squeezes what consolation he can from the situation—the dilemma of Pope Innocent, forced to allow invocations of the old gods but insisting they be kept private; the success of certain Etruscan diviners in saving the town of Narni, even if not Rome itself, from Alaric.[66] But Augustine's mind was not tempted by this sort of pettiness. Realizing the impossibility of the situation, he turned his eyes from the earthly city to the City of God.

This was a natural enough reaction, granted that Christianity was a monotheism at once universal and transcendent. Since its kingdom was not of this world, it was easy for Christianity to extract itself from the rough-and-tumble of history—though that was not destined to be its most usual reaction, and indeed it was quite soon to be proclaiming Rome greater as Peter's see than it had ever been as the seat of empire.[67] The many gods of polytheism, by contrast, had allowed themselves to be defined too much in terms of their function here below in time and space, and in particular in relation to imperial Rome, city and empire. The late polytheist universalism we have been looking at was still at heart a locally or at best nationally based universalism, fully within the traditions of a religion that had always lacked central authority. One focused the many gods in one place, to the glory of that place; then one might or might not go on to wonder whether the many gods were really one. Christianity, by contrast, aimed to embrace all places in one universal Church, and did not think to be confined by the bounds of the Roman or any other empire. But the inherent limits of polytheist universalism and the challenge from Christianity do not exhaust the catalogue of problems faced by polytheists attempting to come to terms with the changing world of late antiquity.

THE THIRD CENTURY

Not long after he murdered his brother and co-emperor Geta, Caracalla declared to the Roman senate that "just as Zeus alone of the gods holds power, so he gives it to one among men".[68] The element of special pleading here will have escaped no one. But at least Caracalla's divine

---

[66] Zosimus V.41.1–3.

[67] See the passages in Leo and Prosper of Aquitaine discussed by Markus, in *Inheritance of historiography* 37–39.

[68] Herodian IV.5.7.

analogue needed no introduction. When Elagabalus presented his Syrian Baal to the same august audience, and sought to subordinate all other gods to him, he went too far. The Severans were well aware of the political applications of subordinationist theology—perhaps they were even au courant with Christian discussions of this problem.[69] But they were also a little ahead of their times.

In the aftermath of the last Severan's death, in 235, Rome's chaotic political situation and the lack of dynastic continuity severely undermined the imperial cult's effectiveness. It probably seemed decreasingly meaningful to offer divine honors to the ephemeral rulers spawned by the crisis of the mid-third century; certainly the evidence for the conduct of an imperial cult dwindles rapidly. But some attempt continued to be made to find an alternative, by privileging a supreme god whose reflection or representative the emperor had long been held to be by those political thinkers who espoused the Hellenistic tradition that the king was the "living law".[70] Aurelian's cult of Sol, the Sun, is the obvious example.[71] Aurelian (270–75) worked desperately hard and with much success to restore the cohesion of the Roman world after the disastrous 250s and 260s. He seems to have felt that the earthly autocrat needed a heavenly mirror image: once this heavenly autocrat was accepted, his earthly counterpart might expect to be still further magnified. Aurelian was no longer "like god" but "born god", just as his divine protector, with whom he communicated in personal visions, had been raised above the other gods. These ideas were not without echo among Aurelian's successors, and they are an important stage in the prehistory of the Christian doctrine of empire forged by Constantine and formulated by Eusebius: one god, one empire, one emperor. But in the meantime the tetrarchy attempted something slightly different: the combination of a personal relationship with the gods with a bureaucratic type of dynasticism that privileged the office rather than its holder.

Diocletian's idea[72] was to split the empire with a second Augustus, assimilating himself to Jupiter and his colleague to Hercules. The Augusti made no claim to personal divinity, though we may wonder

[69] Momigliano, *Ottavo contributo* 318–19; dal Covolo, *Severi* 61–73; Buraselis, Θεία δωρεά 52–64.

[70] Dvornik, *Early Christian and Byzantine political philosophy* 245–77, 453–557. Versnel, *Ter unus* 37, remarks: "the growth of henotheism . . . and the development of . . . monarchical forms of rulership in the . . . Hellenistic empires . . . are more than sheer chronological coincidences". He develops this point in ch. 1. As to which was the model and which the imitation, see the pointed remarks of Veyne, *Latomus* 45 (1986): 282–83.

[71] Halsberghe, *Sol invictus* 130–71; Turcan, *A.N.R.W.* II.16.2, 1064–73; Štaerman, in *Mélanges Lévêque* 4.374–79.

[72] Kolb, *Diocletian*, esp. 88–114, 168–72.

whether many of their subjects noticed. Both were assisted by Caesars, who were adopted as sons, married to daughters of the Augusti, referred to as "Iovius" or "Herculius", and perhaps, more or less officially, protected respectively by Mars and Sol-Apollo. The raw materials of this system were impeccably Roman. As far as its theological aspects are concerned, Jupiter, Hercules, and Mars were central to Rome's "veterrima religio", while Sol had long been naturalized. Even the idea that particular gods might occupy privileged positions in the official pantheon was by now familiar. But the politico-religious synthesis implied by the tetrarchic system was newer. It may even be that Jupiter and his son Hercules were calculated to steal some of the Christians' thunder. Certainly they did not get their jobs just because Diocletian felt full of ancestral devotion toward them, or was suddenly overwhelmed by visionary enthusiasm. They both have a rather premeditated air; and when the tetrarchic system that they mirrored collapsed, they too were condemned, sooner or later, to hang separately.

JULIAN AND HELIOS-MITHRAS

Of all the late polytheist rulers and thinkers, the Emperor Julian best understood the contrast between and differing consequences of Christian universalism that flowed from the unicity of God, and polytheist universalism that had to be painstakingly constructed, by process of addition, from an overpopulated Olympus or even from local particularisms. Julian went to some pains in his polemical treatise against Christianity (*Contra Galilaeos*) to emphasize the firm bonds that united the different races of men with their national gods. But he also evolved a theology strongly influenced by the philosophers, a theology of basically henotheist character that started from "the common father and king of all peoples";[73] and he aspired to build an integrated and centralized polytheist Church Militant, on the Christian model, in order to propagate his theological vision.[74]

In his attempt to restructure polytheism along more universalist lines, Julian appears to have seen a powerful ally in the cult of the Sun—Sol in Latin, Helios in Greek—identified with Mithras. At the end of his satirical work the *Caesars*, in which he imagines a contest before the Olympians to find who had been the best emperor of Rome, Julian has Hermes turn to him and say: "As for thee, I have granted thee knowledge of thy father Mithras. Do thou keep his commandments, and thus secure for thyself a cable and sure anchorage throughout thy life, and

[73] Julian, *Contra Galilaeos* fr. 21.115d; id., *or.* XI on Helios, esp. 131c and the clear statements of henotheism at 138b and 151 ab.

[74] Julian, *ep.* 84, 89; Sozomen, *H.E.* V.16.1–4.

when thou must depart from the world thou canst with good hopes adopt him as thy guardian god."[75] Julian's special attachment to Mithras, which at the end of the *Caesars* is directly paralleled to Constantine's attachment to Jesus, certainly owed something to the remarkable coherence of a cult that in the second to fourth centuries united males of all races, though mainly soldiers and officials, across the length and breadth of the empire, organized at least the more dedicated of them in a firmly defined seven-grade hierarchy, and gathered them in sanctuaries whose iconographic program is uniform to a degree unusual in the polytheist tradition, to worship a god regarded as superior to other gods and everywhere the same. Mithras did not, as Isis for example so often did, depend on local syncretisms for his specific identity. His was "an omnipotence which tends to put all the other gods in the shade or marginalize them and subordinate them to his action. . . . Although Mithraism belongs iconographically to polytheism, it in practice resembles . . . a cultic monotheism".[76] This is not the place to examine the reasons for the Mithras cult's wide dissemination and appeal. But one or two aspects of this in almost every way problematic and controversial religion should be singled out for their relevance to our discussion of late antique universalism.

Mithras was not originally a Greco-Roman but an Iranian god, and one of the grades of initiation through which adepts passed continued to be called "the Persian". Writing around the year 346, Firmicus Maternus bitterly attacks Mithraists as self-conscious Iranizers: "You then who claim that in these temples you celebrate your mysteries in the manner of the Magi, according to the Persian ritual, why is it only these customs of the Persians that you praise? If you think it worthy of the Roman name to follow Persian rituals and Persian laws. . . ."[77] But in reaction to Franz Cumont's view of the Mithras cult as a religion with

[75] Julian, *Caesares* 336c (tr. W. C. Wright); and cp. *or.* XI.130bc, 155b. On Julian and Mithraism, see Simon, in *Etudes Mithriaques* 470–75.

[76] Turcan, in *Knowledge of God* 260. See also the recent syntheses on Mithraism by Merkelbach, *Mithras*, with Beck's review, *Phoenix* 41 (1987); Turcan, *Cultes orientaux* 193–241; Clauss, *Mithras*. The exclusion of women partially undermines the Mithras cult's universalist credentials, though in practice it cannot be isolated from the wider context of polytheism, which certainly did not exclude women; compare the initiations of Praetextatus and his wife, above, p. 48.

[77] Firmicus Maternus, *De errore profanarum religionum* V.2. It has been supposed that the two pages missing at this point from our only manuscript dealt at greater length with the Mithras cult (see the note ad loc. in Turcan's edition); but the context indicates that Firmicus Maternus went on to list, in time-honored fashion, the abominable habits of the Persians, and to ask why Mithraists did not follow them too, as well as the Magian ritual. The Iranian origin of Mithras and his cult was uncontroversial in antiquity: Lucian, *Deorum concilium* 9; Celsus ap. Origen, *Contra Celsum* VI.22; Proclus, *In Rempublicam* 2, p. 345 (Kroll).

deep and specific roots in Iran, as, in effect, a Romanized Mazdaism, and therefore essentially an import into the Roman Empire, the 1970s revival of Mithraic scholarship tended toward a "Western" view of this god and reduced the direct Iranian contribution to Mithras's name and little (if anything) more.[78]

The Roman cult of Mithras certainly was unrecognizably different from the Iranian cult of Mithra. But Firmicus Maternus was not fooled, and in any case religions do change, even unrecognizably, in transmission. The Greeks (and Romans) notoriously recast alien cultures in their own image, or at least in digestible form—Zarathushtra is scarcely more recognizable in Greco-Roman garb than Mithra.[79] We know that the Iranian communities established by the Achaemenids in Asia Minor, western as well as eastern, persisted through the Hellenistic and Roman periods,[80] while in western Asia Minor Mithra's fellow Iranian divinity Anahit acquired a virtually independent cult, partly merged with that of Cybele.[81] Mithra himself is attested in Armenia, Commagene, Cappadocia, Pontus, Phrygia, and perhaps Lycia.[82] This was the natural and unsurprising counterpart—in fact, the predecessor—of Alexander's implantation of Hellenism in Iran. Common sense suggests, and there is now a tendency for scholarly opinion to accept,[83] that Greco-Roman worship of an originally Iranian god must have evolved where Iranians, Mithra(s), Greeks, and Romans were all to be found together, in an atmosphere of religious syncretism but also of adaptation of the Iranian tradition even by those who were closest to it, the communities of Magians or "Magousaioi".[84] James Russell's recent study *Zoro-*

[78] Beck, *A.N.R.W.* II.17.4, surveys the field.
[79] Beck, in Boyce and Grenet, *History of Zoroastrianism* 3.
[80] Boyce and Grenet, *History of Zoroastrianism* 3.197–308; and above, p. 33.
[81] Boyce and Grenet, *History of Zoroastrianism* 3.252.
[82] Merkelbach, *Mithras* 43–72; Russell, *Zoroastrianism in Armenia* 261–87; Boyce and Grenet, *History of Zoroastrianism* 3.259–61, 272–73, 301–3, 325–26, 476. With the mountain, rock-cut staircase tunnel (or "cave"?), and Mithra-cult at Pekeriç some 90 km. west of Erzurum (Russell, *Zoroastrianism in Armenia* 264; Sinclair, *Eastern Turkey* 2.250 and pl. 69–70), compare all the same at Arsameia in Commagene (Dörner and Goell, *Arsameia am Nymphaios*, esp. ch. 8 and pl. 29–33). These are not Roman-style Mithraea, but may represent a development in that direction, in which an element of Mazdean hilltop worship is still preserved.
[83] Beck, *A.N.R.W.* II.17.4, 2071–74; Ries, *A.N.R.W.* II.18.4, 2769, 2772–74; Boyce and Grenet, *History of Zoroastrianism* 3.468–90.
[84] On these see above, p. 33; and on their unorthodoxy Chaumont, *Historia* 22 (1973): 681–83. Cp. also the transmission of Mithra-worship eastwards into the Kushan sphere, where the god is identified with Helios and there is (1) a strong Greek element in the cultural mix and (2) an indisposition to adopt the dominant gods of contemporary Iran, e.g., Ahura Mazda: Rosenfield, *Dynastic arts of the Kushans* 77, 81–82; Colpe,

astrianism in Armenia traces in detail the gradual transformation of the Mazdean tradition as it passed through the Armenian filter. Though Russell underlines the fully Iranian character of the Armenian Mihr,[85] what becomes clear from his book is that those who accept some evolutionary connection between Mazdean Mithra and the Mithras of the Rhine camps have harmed their case by ignoring the middle ground of cultural interaction across which Mithra slowly travels from East to West. Among the many and varied carriers were Plutarch's famous Mithraic pirates of first-century B.C. Cilicia,[86] and Tiridates, the Parthian king of Armenia, who amidst immense publicity traveled to Rome to receive his crown from Nero, and declared at the coronation ceremony that he did obeisance to Nero "even as I do unto Mithras".[87] We still do not know how the Roman Mithras cult acquired the complex and distinctive doctrine, iconography, and ritual that characterize its maturity, from the second century A.D. onward. But Christianity is our best witness that such evolutions are possible.

Reinhold Merkelbach has rightly pointed out that the collapse of native Oriental milieus in the aftermath of Alexander had much to do with the uprooted, universalizing style not only of the Mithras cult but of all those other mystery religions from the East that went beyond the usually quite narrowly local appeal of the more traditional Greco-Roman gods.[88] In particular, the whole vast liminal zone on the marches of the Iranian world, where the Romano-Iranian and later the Byzantine-Arab frontier ran, especially the ancient cultures and gods of the Tigris-Euphrates region, once convinced of their universal vocation, now dominated by superpowers whose center of gravity lay far away, provided fertile ground for the genesis of universalizing religions that saw the whole world as potentially theirs[89]—and might well, as Mithras did, shed almost all evidence of their ultimate origin. With the incorporation of Anatolia into the Roman Empire, its religions gained access to a

---

C.H.Ir. 3.850–51; Staviskij, *Bactriane* 196–97; also Gonda, *Mitra* 131–36, on relations with the Indian Mitra.

[85] As does Waldmann, *Der kommagenische Mazdaismus*, esp. 36, that of the Commagenian Mithras.

[86] Plutarch, *Pompeius* XXIV.5.

[87] Cassius Dio LXIII.5. For the accuracy of this report, see Garsoian, *Armenia* X.35–40.

[88] Merkelbach, *Mithras* 39, 75–6. Compare, e.g., the known client cities of even the famous oracle of Apollo at Claros (map: Lane Fox, *Pagans and Christians* 174) with the distribution of Mithraea (maps in Vermaseren, *Corpus*, esp. at the end of vol. 2).

[89] See, e.g., the articles by Westenholz and Steiner in *Power and propaganda*; Irmscher, *Klio* 60 (1978) 178–79; and below, p. 122, on the Nestorian Church's universalist claims.

political continuum that allowed the Mithras cult, for example, to spread from the Euphrates to Hadrian's Wall,[90] and, supplementing polytheism's internal dynamic, encouraged the more general universalist tendencies that already existed within it. The role of the city of Rome in these developments was particularly significant, as transmitter and perhaps also as generator. It is at least possible that the Roman Mithras's evolution received significant impetus there.

But still more important to Mithras was his identification with the Sun, which allowed him to draw on the considerable reserves of Solar piety throughout the Roman Empire. The Emperor Aurelian's attempt to advance Sol to cultic primacy had considerably increased these reserves, and Julian planned to capitalize on them by placing Sol-Helios-Mithras at the heart of his polytheist restoration. Through his initiation in the mysteries of Mithras, Julian had gained an intimate personal relationship with the god; but his *Hymn to King Helios* also makes clear from its opening lines the universal role of the Sun, under the Good, as ruler of all beings including the gods, who are subordinated to his beneficent "hegemony". By underlining that it was Helios who caused him to be born into the House of Constantine, and that he himself represented the fourth generation of the family that had been attached to worship of the Sun, Julian also drew special attention to the link between earthly and heavenly monarchy. To Mithras he made only passing allusion, sensing that a mystery cult that had not disseminated itself indifferently through all social categories and was associated with Rome's hereditary enemy was not the ideal standard-bearer for his campaign. On the other hand, the Mithras cult did provide a uniquely structured and appealingly personal approach to the worship of the Sun. Examining it in the light of its solar connections, Julian probably found it the most radical and convincing manifestation of such universalist tendencies as were then at work within polytheism. No wonder he espoused it with such warmth. But just as the Christians' disproof of polytheism in its most ambitious settings, Alexandria and Rome, echoed around the world with special resonance, so too Julian's failure did unique harm to his cause because his aims were so visibly universalist. He had given the Christians what they had previously been obliged to invent for themselves—an incarnation of polytheism, a single target to shoot at.

---

[90] See, e.g., the remark of Aelius Aristides, *or.* XXVI (*Regarding Rome*). 105: "When were the times more suitable or when did the cities have a greater portion? The grace of Asclepius and the Egyptian gods now has experienced the most extensive increase among mankind" (tr. C. A. Behr).

UNIVERSALISM AND ROME'S IDENTITY

Despite Aurelian and Julian, the universalist tendencies implicit and increasingly explicit in polytheism did not cohere into a political and historical force to be reckoned with. Polytheism was inchoate enough as a religion without being expected to turn into a political philosophy as well; while the cities genuinely needed their local gods, and wanted them to be satraps, not Roman provincial governors here today and gone tomorrow.[91] Although until Constantine the Roman Empire was ruled by polytheist emperors, polytheist universalism did not impart motive or expansive force to empire even to the limited extent that Christianity would. Rather, polytheism used the symbol and reality of Rome as a core around which to crystallize its own identity. Polytheist universalism remained cultural universalism *within* empire, without significant political motive beyond the preservation of that empire. As late as the fifth century the Platonist sage Proclus devoted himself to the regular worship of a thoroughly ecumenical selection of the old gods, and maintained that "it befits the philosopher not to observe the rites of any one city or of only a few nations, but to be the hierophant of the whole world in common".[92] Yet his was a purely private initiative, which many polytheists would have regarded as invalid, at least as public cult, on the grounds that worship of the gods benefited the state only if paid for by the state.[93] Meanwhile the Egyptian Nonnus was composing his epic poem the *Dionysiaca*, celebrating the travels both within the empire and as far afield as India of the god whose legend and iconography had long symbolized Rome's universalist political and even, in the imagination of some, cultural-religious aspirations, especially in the East.[94] But these last manifestations of polytheist universalism—and Nonnus was in fact, it seems, a Christian—remain confined to the personal religious or literary sphere.

Even granted the limitations of polytheist universalism, though, we have now seen enough to be able to claim some understanding of what cultural universalism meant in late antiquity. What we are dealing with could be described, in the broadest terms, as the emergence of the

---

[91] See above, p. 40.

[92] Marinus, *Vita Procli* 19 (tr. L. J. Rosán, with adjustments). Proclus's example was perhaps imitated by the long-lived polytheist community at Harran: see next chapter, and Tardieu, in *Simplicius*, esp. 57.

[93] Zosimus IV.18.2, 59.3; V.41.3.

[94] Nonnus, *Dionysiaca* XIII.1–34; Turcan, *Sarcophages romains* 441–72; plate 2.

2. Triumph of Dionysus. Sarcophagus, circa 170–80.

imperial Roman identity,[95] expressed from the fourth century in the use of the word Romania to denote the empire.[96] The emergence of this identity was an extremely slow process—even the city of Rome could hardly play the universal assembly and acropolis without the kaleidoscopic but complicating and retarding variety of its visiting and resident provincials, both gods and men. "Cette hétérogénéité est la rançon de l'universalité"[97]—polytheist universalism is additive, and therefore inherently pluralistic. The process of identity formation is more readily apparent once one gets out into the provinces and watches the evolution and spread, especially in the second century, of the typical Roman city with its standardized buildings, the imperial cult, and even the Oriental religions that by this time were so widely accepted throughout the empire. Among the most influential patrons of these Oriental religions were the Severans, the first imperial family of non-European origin. And it was Caracalla who gave legal expression to the ideal of a united and egalitarian empire with a firmly Roman identity by extending Roman citizenship to the great majority of his subjects (Constitutio Antoniniana, 212/13). On the cultural level, Hellenism performed a similar role, providing a common frame of reference, or at least allowing those

[95] For an excellent brief sketch of this process, see Millar, *Roman Empire and its neighbours* 1–12.

[96] Irmscher, in *Popoli e spazio romano*.

[97] Turcan, in *Popoli e spazio romano* 60.

rooted in local cultures to express themselves in terms comprehensible to those rooted in other local cultures.[98] For provincial identities persisted: provincial law, for example, did not sink without trace in the wake of the Constitutio Antoniniana.[99] If a homogeneous Roman identity was the ideal, a more dynamic and coherent force seemed to be needed to underpin it—not myth that explains but revelation that exhorts, speaking directly through a charismatic prophet to a human condition that is the victim of circumstance as well as history's one constant. Perhaps Constantine was in part responding to this perceived need when he accepted Christianity for himself and by implication for his empire.

One point remains to be made. If the sort of cultural universalism that made Christianity appear so useful an ally of Romania was not wholly a Christian invention, we must modify the fashionable assumption that polytheist Rome was ideally pluralist and tolerant. This assertion is often made in order to point a contrast with a monolithic and intolerant Christian Rome. Much of the rest of this essay will argue how little monolithic Christian Rome was, in no small part precisely because it espoused monotheism. That it also became less and less tolerant of polytheists, Jews, and heretics is beyond dispute; but it is not helpful to make this point by trying to construct an ideally pluralist and tolerant polytheism that never existed. This is what Arnaldo Momigliano did in a late article oddly entitled "The disadvantages of monotheism for a universal state".[100] Between his *Fragestellung* ("whether and how plurality of gods was related to the pluri-national character of the Empire") and the conclusion that "pagans never managed . . . to produce a consistent case for the interdependence between polytheism and political pluralism in the Roman Empire", there is a significant terminological slippage, for plurinationalism is not the same as political pluralism, which in any case the Roman Empire never espoused. Momigliano apparently thought that since Christians paralleled the Empire's unity with that of the Church, polytheists ought not to have been content with the polytheism-plurinationalism equation (as Celsus and Julian were), but to have evolved a polyarchic political philosophy too. The polyarchy of polytheism is indeed a theme of Christian apologetic—but, quite rightly, with

---

[98] Such is the argument of Bowersock, *Hellenism*, e.g., 13: "It was Greek culture that allowed the infinite multiplicity of . . . far-flung and diverse cults to exist as part of a loosely-defined common enterprise that we call paganism and that the Greek-speakers of the time quite rightly called Hellenism."

[99] See, e.g., Seidl, *Rechtsgeschichte Ägyptens* 237–39.

[100] Momigliano, *Ottavo contributo* 313–28.

reference to the whole world, not the Roman Empire's internal arrangements.[101] When the Christian Procopius, invited to pour a libation to the tetrarchs, quoted back Homer's line, "It is not good to have many lords; let there be one lord, one king", he was alluding to a specific and transient political reality. Before he had time to explain that he was only joking, he had become the first of Eusebius's Palestinian martyrs.[102] The search for a systematic polytheist justification of polyarchy ends in failure; and we know that an increasing body of late antique opinion regarded monotheism as theoretically advantageous for the universal state. Hence Momigliano's disillusioned (and correct) conclusion: that exponents of "enlightened pluralism" are better sought in the eighteenth than the second, third, or fourth century.

[101] Tatian, *Oratio ad Graecos* 28–29; Eusebius, *Praeparatio evangelica* I.4.2, and *De laudibus Constantini* III.6, XVI.2–7; and cp. Celsus ap. Origen, *Contra Celsum* VIII.72, on the impossibility of "uniting under one law the inhabitants of Asia, Europe and Libya, both Greeks and barbarians even at the furthest limits" (tr. H. Chadwick).

[102] Eusebius, *De martyribus Palestinae* I.1.

3

THE FERTILE CRESCENT:
CULTURAL UNIVERSALISM
BETWEEN AND BEYOND
EMPIRES

BEFORE TACKLING Constantine's Christian empire, we must look more carefully at the Fertile Crescent. It was in the Fertile Crescent that Christianity acquired its potential coherence, by being born not of the sedimentation of myth but as a historical revelation; and it was in the Fertile Crescent that Christianity manifested much of its early dynamism. It was also in the mountainous fringe of the Fertile Crescent, in Commagene and Cappadocia but also farther north in Armenia and Pontus, that we glimpsed Mithra(s) on his way from Iran to Rome. Besides being the arena of diplomatic and military confrontation between Rome and Iran, the Fertile Crescent was the scene of complex cultural interactions and evolutions.

The Fertile Crescent was a high road that linked the priests of Egypt at one end to the Chaldeans and Magi at the other, not to mention the sages of India beyond. Among the Greeks and Romans, there had long been those who stood in awe of the wisdom of this Orient; and Alexander's campaigns, followed by the foundation of the Hellenistic monarchies, pulled Hellenism's center of gravity sharply eastward. Alexandria took on the mantle of Athens; by the imperial Roman period Syria too had become part of the Greek landscape. Even the source of the Styx could conveniently be visited not far south of Damascus.[1] No one was more quintessentially Greek in the second century than Lucian of Samosata by the Euphrates. Plotinus, the third century's most original Platonist, was an Egyptian. When he set off from Alexandria (ca. 242/3) to visit the sages of Iran and India as a passenger with the Emperor Gordian III's army,[2] he proclaimed as an individual of outstanding intellect and broad sympathies what we have already posited as the precondition of world empire: the unification of Iran and the

---

[1] Damascius, *Vita Isidori* fr. 195, 199 (*Epitoma Photiana*); Tardieu, *Paysages reliques* 38–69.

[2] Porphyry, *Vita Plotini* 3.

Mediterranean. Plotinus's two most influential successors, Porphyry and Iamblichus, were Syrians. The theurgical doctrines of Iamblichus, so central to late polytheist Hellenism's search for identity, were derived from the *Chaldean oracles*, purportedly composed by Babylonian sages. The list might go on, not forgetting the enormous numbers of Roman subjects deported to Mesopotamia during the campaigns especially of Shapur I and II—a significant channel of Greek cultural influence and technical skill behind the Sasanian frontier, which was in any case never an obstacle to human intercourse.[3] No wonder that the Fertile Crescent, at the conceptual as well as the actual center of the Mediterranean and southwest Asian world, produced religions of real or imagined universal appeal. I shall concentrate on four examples: the Sabians of Harran, Judaism, Manichaeism, and Christianity. Each represents a phase in the evolution of late antique universalism.

THE SABIANS OF HARRAN

The city of Harran (Carrhae) lay at the center of the Fertile Crescent's arc, exposed on the plain, athwart the road from Antioch to the Iranian frontier. Some forty kilometers to the northwest, Edessa is built where the Syrian plain meets the Kurdish hill country, the Mountain Arena's rim. Edessa was to be as important in the history of Christianity in this area as Harran was to the history of polytheism.[4] For precisely that reason, Julian avoided Edessa but stopped at Harran as he marched toward the Iranian frontier.[5] Perhaps it was the Edessenes who spread the wicked story that Julian had a woman hanged and disemboweled in the temple of the Moon, seeking to divine what was to befall him.[6] Still, in those days Harran's polytheist sympathies were far from unparalleled. By the sixth century, though, the determined adherence of a section of its inhabitants to their traditional astral cults, particularly to that of the Babylonian moon-god Sin, seemed distinctly idiosyncratic. That, together perhaps with the presence there of a group of Platonist philosophers who had fled Justinian's intolerant Christian empire, invoked Khusrau II's aid, and gained special protection under the terms of the Romano-Iranian treaty of 532,[7] earned it exemption from attack

[3] Chaumont, *Christianisation* 56–84, 88–89.

[4] On Harran and the Sabians, see Cramer, *R.L.A.C.* 13.634–50; Tubach, *Im Schatten des Sonnengottes* 129–83; Tardieu, *J.A.* 274 (1986): 1–29.

[5] Ammianus Marcellinus XXIII.3.1–2; Sozomen, *H.E.* VI.1.1. Contra, Zosimus III.12.2, on whose confusion see Paschoud ad loc.

[6] Theodoret, *H.E.* III.26.1.

[7] Agathias II.30–31; Tardieu, *J.A.* 274 (1986): 22–27; Tardieu, in *Simplicius* 40–57; Tardieu, *Paysages reliques*.

during Khusrau's campaign of 544.[8] As is clear from their handling of the Monophysites, the Sasanians appreciated the possibilities of disruption offered by religious diversity on the Roman side of the frontier.[9] The polytheists of Harran were a small group compared to the Monophysites, but their city was sensitively positioned close to the frontier[10]—in effect, between the two great rival empires.

It was again closeness to the frontier, this time the Byzantine-Arab frontier, that earned them their next and best-known appearance on the stage of history, when the Caliph al-Mamun visited Harran on his way to campaign against the Byzantines in 830.[11] Struck during an audience by the unconventional appearance of the polytheist community's representatives, "whose mode of dress was the wearing of short gowns and who had long hair with side bangs", he inquired about them and, discovering that they were not People of the Book,[12] ordered them to become so before he got back, or face death. Many of the polytheists immediately complied, but the cannier took legal advice and were told to call themselves Sabians, "for this is the name of a religion which Allah, may his name be exalted, mentioned in the Quran". So they adopted this name as a cover for their continued adherence to the old ways, and their descendants are still attested as polytheists as late as the eleventh century.

Harranian polytheism was a collage of Aramaic, Greek (including Platonist), and Babylonian elements. Given the facts of geography, it could hardly have been otherwise, and we do not have to consider a consciously universalist tendency, even of the most elementary additive variety.[13] Sabianism never became a missionary faith, nor did it even spread, as a popular religion, beyond its traditional territory. Nonetheless, one does not live at the center of the world and remain unaware of it. At Edessa, the court philosopher Bardaisan (154–ca. 222) had set out to disprove the power of the stars and the doctrines of astrology by arguing from the diversity of national customs, which compel people to behave in ways that could not possibly be predicted from their stars. The range of examples Bardaisan is represented as drawing on in his disciple

[8] Procopius, *De bello Persico* II.13.7.

[9] See below, p. 123.

[10] Ammianus Marcellinus XXIII.3.4 ("vicino limite"), 5, and Frézouls's map, in *Géographie administrative* 195.

[11] Al-Nadim, *Kitab al-fihrist* 9, pp. 320–21 (Flügel)/385–86 (Tajaddod; tr. Dodge 751–53). On the date, see Chwolsohn, *Ssabier* 1.140.

[12] See below, p. 158.

[13] Note though that in earlier times "the cult of Sin at Harran [had] implied the notion of a kingdom of the totality of the land, which was given to the rulers at Harran" (Drijvers, *Cults and beliefs at Edessa* 141–42). No doubt this was an attraction for emperors who visited Harran before (Julian) or in the course of (Caracalla) campaigning against Iran.

Philippus's *Book of the laws of countries* is tremendous, from China to Britain.[14] Perhaps he got a lot of them from books. But Edessa, caught between Rome and Iran, was the perfect place for information gathering;[15] and many of Bardaisan's examples cluster around the Fertile Crescent itself, for there was quite simply the greatest variety and concentration of human traditions, if we except such artificial concentrations of variegated but uprooted humanity as were to be found at Rome, for example. Likewise the mid-fourth-century author of the *Expositio totius mundi*, though he describes the cities, customs, and curiosities of all mankind, has a firm sense that Syria is the world's hub. He describes it at length and with affection. Antioch is for him the residence of the *dominus orbis terrarum*, while Rome is a city of memories that emperors embellish but do not live in, and Constantinople is barely mentioned.[16] From Beirut and its law schools emanate the lawyers who, by applying Roman justice throughout the provinces, ensure the empire's stability—"civitas per quam omnia iudicia Romanorum stare videntur".[17] Apart from Syria, the author of the *Expositio* presents no other region as being of such universal significance. And still in the fifth century, when the empire was divided, Simeon the Stylite brought its peoples together. Among the crowd come to admire that most Syrian saint and "great wonder of the *oikoumene*" might be found pilgrims from the eastern provinces, but also "Ishmaelites, Persians, Armenians, Iberians, Himyarites, Spaniards, Britons, Gauls, and Italians".[18]

Syria was, precisely, that part of the world where the distance between local and universal history was the shortest. Thus it is not wholly surprising that the Sabian scholar Thabit bin Qurra (834/5–901), reflecting on the origins and history of his community, could pen the following words:

> Whereas many submitted to the false doctrine under torture, our ancestors held out with the help of God and came through by a heroic effort; and this blessed city has never been sullied by the false doctrine of Nazareth. Paganism (*hanputa*), which used to be the object of public celebration in this world, is our heritage, and we shall pass it on to our children. Lucky the man who endures hardship with a well-founded hope for the sake of paganism! Who was it that settled the inhabited world and propagated cities, if not the outstanding men and kings of paganism? Who applied engineering

[14] Philippus (Bardaisan), *Book of the laws of countries* pp. 38–62 (Drijvers); cf. Drijvers, *Bardaisan* 90–92.

[15] Porphyry, *De abstinentia* IV.17; Porphyry ap. Stobaeus, *Anthologium* I.3.56.

[16] *Expositio totius mundi* 23, 50, 55.

[17] Ibid., 26.

[18] Theodoret of Cyrrhus, *Historia religiosa* XXVI.11.

to the harbors and the rivers? Who revealed the arcane sciences? Who was vouchsafed the epiphany of that godhead who gives oracles and makes known future events, if not the most famous of the pagans? It is they who blazed all these trails. The dawn of medical science was their achievement: they showed both how souls can be saved and how bodies can be healed. They filled the world with upright conduct and with wisdom, which is the chief part of virtue. Without the gifts of paganism, the earth would have been empty and impoverished, enveloped in a great shroud of destitution.[19]

It seems then that the Sabian elite, those who had a view of history and the possibility of generalizing about their tradition, were convinced that as survivors, if not in any more dynamic sense, the Sabians could indeed claim a role of universal significance. They were the people from whom everyone else had acquired culture, and Harran stood not at the edge of an empire but at the focus of human history. Being so conspicuously "the other", and caught as they were between two expanding world religions, Christianity and Islam, Thabit and his circle found in their community's history not just an explanation of themselves but also a strategy for survival.

JUDAISM

Such problems were not unfamiliar to the Jews. But their ancestors, the ancient Israelites, had been unique, and not just in the Fertile Crescent,

---

[19] This passage is preserved by Bar Hebraeus, *Chronicon syriacum* 168–69, who guarantees the integrity of his quotation by adding: "We have cited this passage from the work of this man to demonstrate his ability in Syriac literary composition." The translation was kindly supplied by Andrew Palmer, together with the following note: "Thabit not only uses the word *ḥanpūtā*, derogatory in most Syriac authors, in a positive sense [indeed, Faris and Glidden, *Journal of the Palestine Oriental Society* 19 (1939–41): 8–9, followed by Montgomery Watt, *Enc.Is.*[2] 3.166, suggest this was the Harranian polytheists' standard designation for their own culture, by analogy with Muslim use of Arabic *ḥanif*, itself derived from the Syriac term—G.F.] but also uses positive words in a derogatory sense or else turns derogatory words usually used of paganism against the 'Nazarenes'. 'False doctrine' (*ṭu'yay*) is an example of the latter: 'destitution' (*msam'lūtā*)—usually meaning 'asceticism'—of the former. He hijacks the title of the 'blessed city' from Edessa and portrays paganism as a source of light, a saviour of souls, whereas the Christian Edessenes had always portrayed Ḥarrān as the black opposite of their sacred pole. He mimics the style of the Beatitudes, substituting 'Lucky' for 'Blessed', and he describes his pagan ancestors as Christians described confessors of the Faith." This whole celebratory passage may in fact be a deliberate inversion of the theme "ubi sunt qui ante nos in mundo fuere?", so much beloved of Christian and Muslim moralists, and of which Becker, *Islamstudien* 1.501–19, provides abundant examples. Cp. also the view, expressed by certain Muslim writers, that Christianity's triumph spelled the doom of ancient Greek science: Miquel, *Géographie humaine* 2.468–70.

for believing in one god who transcended and excluded all others. The question naturally arose: Was Yahweh for the Jews alone, the "chosen people", or might others too enjoy access to his favor?

The Jews themselves had become widely scattered, partly because of deportations imposed by the Assyrians and Babylonians and later by the Iranians, and partly through emigration.[20] The important and intellectually influential Jewish community in Babylonia continued to flourish right through late antiquity, and it provided yet another channel of cultural contact across the political frontier between Rome and Iran. Other Jewish communities were to be found throughout the Roman Empire. Unlike the Harranians, who were caught between empires, the Jews spread across the territory of both Rome and Iran. Geographically speaking, they were already universalists. And they were dynamic too. They benefited from the *pax Romana* to develop their communities, build impressive synagogues, and assert a claim to social esteem. They had had a long tradition of political independence too, so no one doubted their ability to form and run a state if left to their own devices. "The two great Jewish revolts, of 66 and 132, were religious and nationalist movements of a strikingly modern kind; they were almost unique instances of state-formation within the Roman Empire."[21]

As for the Jewish religion, there were obvious difficulties in claiming that God had disinherited the vast majority of mankind; in that sense, at least, Jewish monotheism implied universalism. In addition, a strong Hellenizing school of interpretation had for centuries expounded Judaism in the light of Greek thought, offering a spiritualized and universalized version of the Hebrew faith that is often assumed to have been directed toward interested outsiders. Some Jews presented their One God as the god of the whole *kosmos*, and themselves as priests on behalf of all mankind.[22] They looked forward to the coming of the Messiah, the gathering of the dispersed of Israel, and the establishment of God's kingdom, which was to embrace all gentiles as well as Jews.[23] Gentile interest was manifest at various social and intellectual levels.[24] Magicians, for example, might be impressed by the Jewish god's exoticism and by his reputation for hitting back effectively at his enemies. Henotheism was widespread among worshippers of the old gods, and monotheist tendencies were not unknown. Here too, then, was possible common

---

[20] Schürer, *History of the Jewish people* 3(1).1–86.

[21] Millar, *J.J.S.* 38 (1987): 147.

[22] Philo, *De Abrahamo* 98; *De specialibus legibus* I.97, II.167. But see Will, in *Hellènika symmikta*, for a skeptical view of Philo's alleged missionary intention.

[23] Schürer, *History of the Jewish people* 2.514–37.

[24] Post-Holocaust scholarship has tended to emphasize evidence for interest in and integration of Jews: Gager, *Origins of anti-Semitism* 35–112; Rutgers, *A.J.A.* 96 (1992).

ground. And some Jewish congregations approved of gentile interest, assigning sympathetic outsiders a certain status within their community, and the title of "God-fearer" (*theosebes*).[25] One could also convert fully to Judaism by being circumcised and observing the entire Law to its full extent, in which case one was called a "proselyte" and might even, depending on time and place and the mood of those concerned, be deemed "like (an) Israel(ite) in all . . . respects".[26] Between Judaism and Christianity in particular there was also an extensive grey area made up of people who, had they been pushed, might have jumped one way or the other, but in the meantime found there a milieu that, they no doubt considered, gave them the best of both worlds.[27] Within the Church, too, Judaizers were a constant presence and problem: one has only to recall, for example, the disruption caused by disagreements over whether or not Easter should be celebrated according to the Jewish computation.[28]

It seems, though, that some "God-fearers" worshipped the many gods and Yahweh indifferently.[29] For these people, Judaism had a legitimate claim to universal validity, as a religion contributed by one *ethnos* among many to the symphony of polytheism.[30] Although there was not much a Jew could do about such common-sense attitudes, he could not accept this view of his faith. In a world that expected religions to cohabit, Jews, like pre-Constantinian Christians, were often compelled to affirm the distinctiveness of their monotheism and reinforce the boundaries of their communities. The inclusiveness and universality of Yahweh himself was not denied; some Jews even went so far as to welcome proselytes. But Jews made no serious active effort to proselytize. Outsiders were expected to find the truth by their own labors, and when they had done so were unblinkingly informed that "the world was created only for the sake of Israel, and only Israel were called children of God, and only Israel are dear before God".[31] Not surprisingly, we have little evidence for a Jewish apologetic against polytheism.[32]

[25] Trebilco, *Jewish communities* 145–66.

[26] A second- or early third-century Palestinian conversion formula, quoted by Cohen, *J.J.S.* 41 (1990): 180; see also below. Religious profession rather than birth came to be accepted as proof of Jewish identity by the state too: Goodman, *J.R.S.* 79 (1989).

[27] Kinzig, *V.Chr.* 45 (1991).

[28] Eusebius, *Vita Constantini* III.5.

[29] Reynolds and Tannenbaum, *Jews and God-fearers* 62–64; cf. Williams, *J.Th.S.* 39 (1988): 104–5, 110–11; Goodman, *J.J.S.* 40 (1989): 177–78.

[30] Cp. Julian, *Contra Galilaeos* 100c, 148bc.

[31] A second- or early-third-century Palestinian conversion formula, quoted by Cohen, *J.J.S.* 41 (1990): 180.

[32] Lieberman, *Hellenism in Jewish Palestine* 127; Goodman, *J.J.S.* 40 (1989): esp. 178, 184: "the evidence for rabbinic approval of the winning of converts is . . . extremely indirect and allusive . . . implicit and occasional".

If only for what it tells us, by contrast, about Christianity, Judaism's frequent lack of enthusiasm for proselytism needs to be emphasized in the present context. The Jews proclaimed themselves the "chosen people" not only because they were circumcised and worshipped Yahweh but because they could show Jewish descent; they had been born, that is, from the wombs of Jewish mothers. And so the *Mishnah* declares:

> There are (those who) bring (the) firstfruits (of the produce of their land) and recite (the confession, 'I declare this day . . .' [*Deut.* XXVI.3–10]). . . . These (people) bring (firstfruits) but do not recite: a proselyte brings but does not recite, because he is not able to say, '(I have come into the land) which the Lord swore to our fathers to give us' [*Deut.* XXVI.3]. But if his mother was an Israelite, he brings and recites. And when he [the proselyte] prays in private, he says, 'God of the fathers of Israel'. And when he prays in the synagogue, he says, 'God of your fathers'. (But) if his mother was an Israelite, he says, 'God of our fathers.'[33]

Such discriminatory statements are not infrequently encountered among the sayings of the rabbis:

> R. Hama b. R. Hanina [third century] said: 'When the Holy One, blessed be He, causes his divine Presence to rest, it is only upon families of pure birth in Israel, for it is said, "At that time, saith the Lord, will I be the God of all the families of Israel" [*Jer.* XXXI.1]— not unto all Israel, but unto "all the families of Israel", is said— "and they shall be my people".' Rabbah [d. 322] son of R. Huna said: 'This is the extra advantage which Israel possesses over proselytes. . . .' R. Helbo [third to early fourth century] said: 'Proselytes are as injurious to Israel as a scab.'[34]

Once reborn in the waters of Christian baptism one was in the fullest sense a member of the Church community, but not so in the synagogue. "R. Eliezer b. Jacob [second century] says: 'A woman who is the daughter of proselytes may not marry a priest unless her mother was an Israelite.' The same (law) applies to proselytes and freed slaves, (and holds) even to the tenth generation."[35] The charitable assumption that

---

[33] *Mishnah, Bikkurim* I.1, 4 (tr. M. W. Rubenstein and D. Weiner in Neusner [ed.], *Mishnah*); cf. Schürer, *History of the Jewish people* 3(1).175–76. Others not allowed to make the Avowal included persons of doubtful sex and androgynes: *Mishnah, Bikkurim* I.5.

[34] *Babylonian Talmud, Kiddushin* 70b (tr. H. Freedman).

[35] *Mishnah, Bikkurim* I.5 (tr. Rubenstein-Weiner). For further evidence that proselytes were regarded by Jews as something different, see Cohen, *H.Th.R.* 82 (1989): 29–30; also

such rules were never applied in all their rigor does not survive perusal of the Talmud. The rabbis made it their business to catalogue exactly where the ravages of intermarriage had rotted the community: "R. Papa the Elder [d. 376] said on Rab's [d. 247] authority: 'Babylon is healthy; Messene [in southern Mesopotamia] is dead; Media is sick, and Elam is dying. And what is the difference between sick and dying?—Most sick are [destined] for life; most dying are for death.'"[36]

The historical background against which all this needs to be seen is the aftermath of the revolts of 66–74 and 132–36. Ever thereafter, a suspicion of disloyalty clung to the Jews, particularly in view of their extensive ties of kin and religion beyond the Roman frontier, in Mesopotamia. The Jewish community now entered a period of defensive consolidation. Abandoning the Greek voice of the Hellenizers, they readopted the old Hebrew and Aramaic voice we hear once again in the legal writings of the rabbis, which began, at least as oral publications, to reach their present form from the early third century onward.[37] Some rabbis were well versed in Greek culture, but "their fundamental work was that of Judaizing the foreign elements".[38] "[Eleazar] Ben Damah [early second century] the son of R. Ishmael's sister once asked R. Ishmael, 'May one such as I who have studied the whole of the Torah learn Greek wisdom?' He thereupon read to him the following verse: '"This book of the law shall not depart out of thy mouth, but thou shalt meditate therein day and night" [*Josh.* 1.8]. Go then and find a time that is neither day nor night and learn then Greek wisdom.'"[39] Like Syriac and Coptic, Hebrew gave birth to a new literature in late antiquity. But there was an important difference: the models were not Greek. And as the synagogue and learned culture of the Jews changes, albeit

---

L. Bodoff's article enquiring "Was Yehudah Halevi racist?", *Judaism* 38 (1989), with particular reference to Halevi's assertion that those who become Jews do not take equal rank with born Israelites: "There is an interesting question as to whether Halevi believed that the progeny of converts were similarly disqualified. If they are not disqualified, Halevi's alleged 'racism' affects only one generation, which hardly makes Halevi into the kind of racist to which our modern sensibilities so severely object"(181). By this standard, R. Eliezer b. Jacob and any others who thought like him were indisputably racists— unless, of course, one follows the now fashionable view that race is color, as, e.g., Lewis, *Race and slavery* 17, esp. n.4, against Bowersock, *Roman Arabia* 123–24, who rightly points out that in ancient terms race is what distinguishes one *ethnos* ("ethnic group") from another.

[36] *Babylonian Talmud, Kiddushin* 71b (tr. Freedman); cf. Cohen, *J.J.S.* 41 (1990): 195–96.

[37] Goodman, *Roman Galilee* 9–12.

[38] Lieberman, *Greek in Jewish Palestine* 92.

[39] *Babylonian Talmud, Menahoth* 99b (tr. E. Cashdan).

gradually and unevenly, from Greek to Hebrew,[40] the God-fearers disappear from our records.

The emergence of an individual and universal cast of thought, and its elevation to the transcendental, resulted in an aspiration for the replacement of the politico-national hope by one that was essentially religious. But it amounted to no more than a powerful start in that direction. The national expectation still carried greater weight. It was modified in various ways; it was enriched with elements essentially different from its own; but it remained firm throughout the changes of the years. In cosmopolitan Christianity, it was superseded by a supra-national vision.[41]

This period of defensive consolidation from the second century onward also saw the emergence of a new Jewish political identity. "Certain fundamental conditions", Fergus Millar has recently pointed out,

allowed the re-emergence of a semi-independent Jewish local authority, whose effective powers extended to the exercise of the death penalty. In brief, these conditions were the possession of a text, the Bible, which was both a national history and a source of law; a national language, Hebrew; a system of law, regulating (for instance) marriage and divorce; social institutions, such as schools, synagogues and Sabbath worship; recognised interpreters of the law, the rabbis; and finally by the end of the second century a communal leader, for whom Jews used once again the title *nasi*, 'prince', and whom Greeks called *ethnarches* or *patriarches*.[42]

---

[40] Tcherikover, Fuks, and Stern, *Corpus papyrorum Judaicarum* 1.101–2, 106–9; Reynolds and Tannenbaum, *Jews and God-fearers* 82–84.

[41] Schürer, *History of the Jewish people* 3(1).547; likewise Frend, *Rise of Christianity* 272. Ruether's assertion, *Faith and fratricide* 57 (and cp. 26), that Judaism was more universalist than Christianity, and that "Rabbinic learning was a pathway open to all men" (in Hebrew and Aramaic?), is willfully unhistorical; cp. Goodman, *Roman Galilee* 76–78, on the esoteric atmosphere of the rabbinic schools. And although Boccaccini, *Middle Judaism*, believes that "one of the worst stereotypes of the Christian theological tradition is that of a 'universalistic' Christianity emerging from a 'particularistic' Judaism" (251), he admirably demonstrates how the Jewish literature sympathetic to proselytism presupposed strong resistance to it, already in the period before the revolts (252–66). Boccaccini prefers to blame Christian competition for the eventual demise of Jewish proselytism (265), a position that even the eminent author of his book's foreword finds impossible to reconcile with Boccaccini's view that Christianity was and is just another Judaism (xviii).

[42] Millar, *J.J.S.* 38 (1987): 148.

But Origen exaggerated when he remarked that the Patriarch, with his seat in Galilee, "differs in nothing from a king of the nation".[43] Neither he nor the Exilarch in Babylonia[44] was negligible, locally or indeed anywhere there were Jews; but even under these arrangements the Jews remained enclosed in the frame of alien empires, which they could seriously aspire neither to secede from nor to replace.

In the context of the present argument, Judaism provides an important warning: that monotheism does not of itself suffice to generate a proselytizing, actively rather than merely potentially universalist religion. This warning in turn underlines the novelty of Christianity, which did proselytize and proclaim itself universally, and even exclusively. That this difference between Judaism, an ethnic monotheism, and Christianity, a proselytizing monotheism that had cut loose from the ancestral ways, was clearly understood in late antiquity is apparent from Julian's polemical treatise *Against the Galilaeans*. To underline his point, Julian undertook to rebuild the Jewish Temple in Jerusalem. Had this brilliant plan been realized, it would have simultaneously embarrassed Christianity amid its holiest places full of pilgrims from the four corners of the earth, and underlined the distance that separated the Jewish diaspora (and a fortiori Christianity) from its Palestinian roots, for the Temple was unique in Judaism and could not be replicated on earth. It was more convenient for Jews to carry it with them in their hearts, wherever it suited them to take it. By preferring the vertical to the horizontal aspect of their religion, their personal relationship with Yahweh to the spatial and political extension of the faith, the Jews hoped to preserve their distinctiveness and uniqueness while maintaining, through the diaspora, the appearance of universality. But Julian, with exquisite accuracy, drew attention to the impossibility, not only in Judaism but also, he implied, in its offspring Christianity, of turning an ethnic into a universal god, however widespread his cult might be. Only by recognizing all the ethnic gods, but also a higher god above them, "the common father and king of *all* peoples",[45] not just of the Jews, could the world empire solve the problems posed by the plurality of national religious traditions. Needless to say, this was much too neat a solution. Judaism

[43] Origen, *Epistola ad Africanum* 20(14), and note the cautionary remarks of Strobel, *Klio* 72 (1990): 488–89. For an entertaining account of the Patriarch's court and the activities of one of his ubiquitous agents or "apostles", see Epiphanius, *Panarion* I.2.30.4–11 (best taken as illustrating the situation in the late fourth century: Goodman, *Roman Galilee* 117).

[44] Neusner, *C.H.Ir.* 3.917–20.

[45] Julian, *Contra Galilaeos* fr. 21.115d.

may have been ethnic, and Christianity an ethnic apostasy, but both were revealed religions, with a scripture and an impetus that made them much more durable than polytheism. The future lay with revealed religions, and in particular with revealed religions that either proselytized or (in the case of Islam) created political situations in which conversion seemed expedient.

MANICHAEISM

If the Harranians' problem was that they were unrepentant polytheists, while the Jews, though themselves monotheists, ignored and thereby perpetuated polytheism, the Manichaeans were undeniably effective rivals of polytheism and proclaimed themselves Christians, though their dualist dichotomy between spirit and matter compromised God's omnipotence, at least in this world. Manichaeism was one of only two religions we shall encounter in this study that were conceived in late antiquity, and were fully products of that unique conjuncture. Both arose in the Fertile Crescent; both rapidly attained vast geographical extent; and Mani's was even more universalist than Muhammad's, in the sense that it was not even at its inception linked to a particular nation. As Mani himself wrote:

> He who has chosen [i.e., founded] his Church in the West, his Church has not reached the East; the choice of him who has chosen his Church in the East has not come to the West. . . . But my Hope [as Mani was wont to call his teaching] will go towards the West, and she will go also towards the East. And they shall hear the voice of her message in all languages, and shall proclaim her in all cities. My Church is superior in this first point to previous Churches, for these previous Churches were chosen in particular countries and in particular cities. My Church shall spread in all cities, and its Gospel shall reach every country.[46]

Mani (216–76) grew up a member of a Judaizing Christian baptist sect in Mesopotamia. His deeply dualist doctrine shows clear traces of its origin in this "heretical" Christian milieu—Marcion, Bardaisan, and in general gnosticism stand behind it. Nor are Judaic influences suppressed with complete success. Mazdaism and Buddhism also made their contribution as Manichaeism was carried eastward by a mission-

[46] *Kephalaia* 154, cited in Schmidt and Polotsky, *S.P.A.W.* (1933): 45, 87 (Eng. tr. Stevenson, *New Eusebius* 266 [emended]).

ary effort that was already well under way in the founder's lifetime.[47] But Manichaeism was more than just the sum of its parts. It was the final revelation of a doctrine already taught by a whole line of perfect men, and now directly imparted to Mani for the benefit of the whole world: "Wisdom and deeds have always from time to time been brought to mankind by the messengers of God. So in one age they have been brought by the messenger called Buddha to India, in another by Zaradust [Zarathushtra] to Persia, in another by Jesus to the West. Thereupon this revelation has come down and this prophecy has appeared in the form of myself, Mani, the envoy of the true God in the Land of Babylon."[48]

Mani was a conscious imitator throughout his life of the apostle Paul, and never underestimated the importance of mission. With the help of disciples he spread his teachings across Iran and even in India, and around the Fertile Crescent's familiar cultural highway into the Roman Empire. Before long, Manichaeism had spread as far as Roman Africa in the West, while in the East it eventually reached China, where it remained a significant presence until the fourteenth century. With its multicultural background, Manichaeism was a typically appealing and dynamic product of the Fertile Crescent's pluralist environment, fully identified with neither the Mediterranean nor the Iranian world, but adaptable to both. In its beginnings it was a characteristic example of the sort of universalism that grows up between political and cultural blocs; and its growth rapidly took it beyond confinement within any one empire. There is no mission, of course, without translation, and the books of Mani were soon translated from Aramaic into Greek and Middle Persian, and eventually into many other languages. The polyglot "Elect", apostles of Manichaeism who throve on public debate wherever they went, were often merchants by profession, characteristically streetwise products of this frontier world. And their message was one that caught on easily. As Samuel Lieu has pointed out:

> Because Manichaeism was based on a cosmic drama which is largely unrelated to human history and certainly not to the history of a particular people, it lends itself to evangelism across cultural boundaries. This was especially effective in relation to polytheistic

[47] Lieu, *Manichaeism* 51–69 (gnosticism), 248–57 (Mazdaism, Buddhism); Klimkeit, in *Synkretismus*; and the remarkable study by Tardieu, *Stud.Ir.* 17 (1988), emphasizing the role of Iranian and Kushan rather than Indian Buddhism.

[48] Mani, *Sabuhragan*, quoted by al-Biruni, *Kitab al-athar al-baqiya* 207 (Sachau) (tr. Sachau 190, and cf. Lieu, *Manichaeism* 86); and the text from the Dublin *Kephalaia* now published by Tardieu, *Stud.Ir.* 17 (1988): 163–64.

3. Mani (?) and his disciples. Fresco, 1.68 × 0.88 meters, probably eighth or ninth century, from Koço (eastern Turkestan), for a time the capital of the Uighur kingdom.

systems as Manichaean missionaries readily assimilated local deities and demons with those of their own pantheon. Their literal interpretation of the myth also set strict limits to these cultural adaptations and ensured a high degree of doctrinal uniformity among the far-flung communities of the sect.[49]

If by the "Church in the East" Mani meant Mazdaism, his estimate of it was accurate enough.[50] But Christianity, the "Church in the West", he underestimated, as he did Buddhism. Why did his Church fail to hold its own against these two religions and, eventually, Islam? Various possible reasons come to mind. Although the wide diffusion of Manichaean texts, from North Africa to China, is amazing, we should not automatically deduce a firmly articulated ecclesial structure, or any clear sense on the part of the individual Manichaean that he belonged to a universal movement. Richard Lim has recently offered a view of Manichaeism somewhat more nuanced than that of Lieu. He sees Mani's doctrine as "an overarching ideology of unity that served as the binding fiction for the growth of diverse local traditions and practices . . . in a way that preserved the perception of the fundamental unity of the Manichaean church and mission."[51] Certainly Roman Manichaeism's network of

[49] Lieu, *Manichaeism* 32.
[50] See above, p. 72.
[51] Lim, *R.E.Aug.* 35 (1989): 249.

local cells without formal church buildings and dependent on visits from the peripatetic Elect can have afforded relatively little sense of structure or horizontal extension. One also wonders whether the exceptional and elevated position assigned to the Elect, who were the only ones able to observe injunctions such as those against tilling the soil or harvesting, meant in practice that life-and-soul commitment to the doctrine was not fully shared by the wider circle of "Hearers". Even Judaism was for all Jews. It is easy to imagine that the fate of Christianity would have been different had those who worked on the land been excluded from full membership in the Church.

The ultimate failure of Manichaeism also has something to do with its relationship to political power. Sabianism was a classic case of polis polytheism, at once nurtured, empowered, and limited by the sociopolitical organism of the city, in this case Harran. Judaism was similar but bigger. The religion first of a tribe, then of a nation-state, it lost an element of its identity, perhaps even its vital impetus, when Jerusalem fell in A.D. 70. Here was yet another reason why it could not achieve universalist status, for identification with a dynamic, expanding state is essential to the dissemination of a universal religion. As for Mani, he was well aware of the importance of good relations with political authority.[52] He sought to propagate his ideas in the highest places, even at the court of the King of Kings. It seems that for a time he exercised considerable influence over Shapur I himself. But in the last years of his life Mani was opposed by the Mazdean religious hierarchy, not least by Kirdir, and he ended his days a martyr. His followers continued to be persecuted after his death, and not just in Iran: the Roman emperor Diocletian condemned Manichaeism in the strongest terms. In the Roman Empire Manichaeans were often seen as subversive aliens and forced underground. No Manichaean missionary ever troubled, so far as we know, to present himself at the court of a Roman emperor. Justinian extirpated them and their doctrine entirely.

Manichaeism's multicultural background had turned out to be a burden as well as an advantage. The religion was the victim as well as the beneficiary of its origin on the frontiers of empire, amid the manifold stimuli and opportunities of the Fertile Crescent. Spreading too fast, perhaps, and with ambitions too immoderately universalist (although Mani was haunted by the certainty that his successors would lack his

---

[52] *Cologne Mani Codex* 103–4; Klimkeit, in *Documenta barbarorum* 225–27. Tardieu, *Stud.Ir.* 17 (1988): 171, shows that Mani was aware of precedents offered by Zarathushtra and the Buddha; but Jesus did not yet in Mani's day belong in this list, as Mani himself clearly recognizes in the text published by Tardieu (163–64).

own extraordinary energies),[53] Manichaeism had never fully identified even with the Iranian Empire in which it arose. Mazdaism had a less contemporary or compelling gospel, and despite Kirdir's attempt to propagate it beyond the borders of Shapur's empire it was not universalist enough to see itself as a religion for non-Iranians. But its Iranian nationalist credentials were not in doubt, nor its ability to serve as a civic religion, nor the intimacy of its priesthood's alliance with the powerful landowning nobility. Manichaeism was all too obviously and threateningly a religion of cities and merchants for the taste of the traditional Iranian elites.[54] In the world of Iran and Rome into which it was born, Manichaeism fell politically between two stools.

Later in its long history, in the eighth and early ninth centuries (762–840), Manichaeism became the state religion of the Uighur Turks on the northern frontiers of China;[55] and that goes far toward explaining its flourishing condition in Central Asia until the rise of Genghis Khan. But despite the impressive monastic organization that Manichaeism acquired in the Uighur kingdom, it remained the faith of an elite. The mass of the people continued to be adherents of the traditional Turkic religion, Buddhists, or Nestorian Christians. Even under the favorable conditions created by Manichaeism's capture, at last, of the apparatus or at least the support of a powerful state, it did not capture the hearts of the people, much less become the stable and durable world religion its founder had intended and its early dissemination foreshadowed. It was too exactly the antithesis of Judaism: nonethnic and vigorously proselytizing, it ended up so adaptable that some Chinese found it difficult to distinguish from Buddhism.[56]

CHRISTIANITY

Where Manichaeism failed, Christianity succeeded when Constantine espoused it and then, almost as importantly, united the whole Roman Empire under his single rule. The Christian Empire of Rome will be the subject of the next chapter. But even before Constantine gained control of the eastern provinces from Licinius and founded Constantinople (324), Christianity had become either the favored or the official religion of the rulers of two states near or between the Romano-Iranian frontiers.

[53] See the Middle Iranian text published by Andreas and Henning, *S.P.A.W.* (1933): 295.

[54] Gnoli, *Idea of Iran* 157–62.

[55] Klimkeit, in *Documenta barbarorum* 228–41; Mackerras, in *Cambridge history of early inner Asia.*

[56] Bazin, *Turcica* 21–23 (1991); Lieu, *Manichaeism* 256–57, 298–304.

These events were early steps in the evolution of what I shall call the First Byzantine Commonwealth.

The Harranians well illustrate, in this precise region, the propitiousness of borderlands to cultural nonconformity. Again, Jews were to be found throughout the Fertile Crescent; but it was the kingdom of Adiabene, on the Romano-Parthian frontier, whose royal house converted to Judaism in the first century A.D.[57] Likewise, in another area of intense competitiveness between Rome and Iran, the Jew Dhu Nuwas became king of Himyar (Yemen) in the early sixth century.[58] So it does not surprise us to find that the first ruler in the Fertile Crescent who is represented as particularly sympathetic to Christianity is Abgar VIII, ruler from circa 177 to circa 213 of Harran's neighbor Edessa.[59] Edessa's native dynasty had balanced uneasily between the Parthian and Roman Empires from the 130s B.C. until in the 160s A.D. it came definitively within the Roman sphere.[60] Eventually, Caracalla fully incorporated Edessa in the Roman Empire by making it a *colonia*. Two contemporary Christian writers appear to have spoken of Abgar VIII as a "holy man", a "believer";[61] and though there is no certainty that he formally embraced the new faith, Christianity was both an early and a vigorous growth at Edessa. According to a well-known story told by Eusebius with one eye on Constantine, the Gospel was first preached at Edessa as the result of an exchange of letters between Jesus and the Edessene king, an earlier Abgar.[62] This tale and its wide dissemination at least illustrates Edessene Christianity's influence and sense of its own importance. Despite the emphasis in the *Acts of the Apostles* on Christianity's westward spread, the highways of the Fertile Crescent were no less obvious lines of mission than the Mediterranean sea-lanes. And just when the Edessene ruling house was beginning to take an interest in Christianity, an African of Semitic extraction, Septimius Severus, and his Syrian wife

[57] Schürer, *History of the Jewish people* 3(1).163–64.

[58] See below, pp. 114–15.

[59] On Christianity at Edessa, see Millar, *J.J.S.* 38 (1987): 159–62; Chaumont, *Christianisation* 1–8; Palmer, in *Sacred centre*.

[60] See, e.g., Cassius Dio LXVIII.18.

[61] Sextus Julius Africanus, but reported only by later writers: (1) Eusebius-Jerome, *Chronicon* p. 214 (Helm) ("ut vult Africanus"), and (2) George Syncellus, *Ecloga chronographica* p. 439 (Mosshammer); Philippus (Bardaisan), *Book of the laws of countries* p. 58 (Drijvers)—but the crucial phrase in the Syriac is missing from Eusebius's Greek version, *Praeparatio evangelica* VI.10.44. Conceivably it was a later interpolation into the Syriac, but it may equally well have been suppressed either by the pre-Eusebian translator into Greek (Eusebius, *H.E.* IV.30.1) or, more probably, by Eusebius himself in order to make Constantine look more original; in fact, none of his works mentions Abgar VIII's conversion. See also Epiphanius, *Panarion* LVI.1.3.

[62] Eusebius, *H.E.* I.13.

Julia Domna seized the Roman throne and founded a dynasty that was to be noted for its universalist orientation.[63] The Fertile Crescent was remote from the center of Roman power, but it was neither behind the times nor without influence on policy.

If an Edessene king's sympathy for Christianity rapidly became the stuff of legend, so a century later did that of an Armenian king.[64] But the kernel of historical fact was bigger. Like Edessa, with which it had close links, Armenia was caught between Rome and Iran. As Tacitus remarks:

> That country, from the earliest period, has owned a national character and a geographical situation of equal ambiguity, since with a wide extent of frontier conterminous with our own provinces, it stretches inland right up to Media; so that the Armenians lie interposed between two vast empires with which, as they detest Rome and envy the Parthian, they are too frequently at variance.[65]

Armenian ambiguity was intensified in the 220s when the Sasanians displaced the Arsacids in Iran, while Armenia continued to be ruled by Arsacids until 428. The Sasanians did what they could to assert themselves and their religion in Armenia, which became a mission-field for Manichaeism too. But the Christian presence was constantly growing,[66] and offered better ground and hope for national cohesion than could the traditional combination of polytheism and Iranian Mazdaism.

The earliest evidence we have for Christianity in Armenia seems to underline the traditional links between this mountainous land and Mesopotamia to whose rivers it gives rise. Through the haze of legend, it is perhaps possible to identify Edessa as a center from which some of the earlier missionaries set forth.[67] But the conversion of the ruler of Armenia, Tiridates IV (ca. 298/9–ca. 330/1), was the result of an initiative

[63] On links between Edessene Christians and the Severans, see dal Covolo, *Severi* 57.

[64] Chaumont, *Recherches*; Chaumont, *A.N.R.W.* II.9.1; Hewsen, *J.S.A.S.* 2 (1985–86); Russell, *Zoroastrianism in Armenia* 113–52. With the Armenian king's conversion I. Shahîd has associated that of another border potentate, Abgar's descendant the Arab ruler Imru'l-Qais: *B.A.FO.C.* 31–35. But the evidence is questionable: Bowersock, *C.R.* 36 (1986): 113–15; and cf. Shahîd, *B.A.FI.C.* 543–44.

[65] Tacitus, *Annales* II.56 (tr. J. Jackson).

[66] Sundermann, *Mitteliranische manichäische Texte* 45–49.

[67] Klein, *Constantius II.* 170 and n. 15. Note that Moses Khorenatsi (eighth century), *History of the Armenians* II.26–33 (tr. Thomson 163–74), makes the Abgar of Edessa who corresponded with Jesus ruler of Armenia too. Eusebius, *H.E.* VI.46.2, refers to Christians in mid-third-century Armenia under a bishop called Merouzanes. Some have suggested this may indicate "early conversion" of the autonomous satrapies of southern Armenia (e.g., Garsoian, *Armenia* III.345–46); but their argument is based on unverifiable speculation about Merouzanes's name and local connections (Chaumont, *Recherches* 83).

which seems to have emanated not from the Syriac milieu but from the Greeks of Cappadocia. Gregory the Illuminator appears to have been raised at Caesarea, and Caesarea retained authority over the Armenian Church until the 370s. Tiridates's acceptance of baptism at the hands of Gregory, which must have occurred by the year 314 at the latest, had a clear political implication: Armenia was now aligned with Rome. But this was only the beginning of a relationship between Christian Armenia and (soon to be) Christian Rome that was quite as tormented as the Armenians' relationship with Iran. Was Armenia, or was it not, part of Christian Rome? The power play between center and periphery was to become the dominant problem in the history of both the First and the Second Byzantine Commonwealth. In any case, with the conversion of Armenia the First Byzantine Commonwealth had begun to emerge in the Fertile Crescent just as the Roman Empire was switching from persecution to toleration of Christianity, and a full decade before Constantine gained control of the eastern provinces and founded Constantinople.

4

CONSTANTINE: CHRISTIAN EMPIRE AND CRUSADE

THAT THE THEME of the Byzantine Commonwealth should have emerged before—albeit narrowly before—we reach the Christian empire of Constantine is an omen. Commonwealth will turn out to be a more natural state of affairs than the attempted combination of cultural and political universalism—that is, missionary monotheism and imperial impetus—into world empire in the fullest sense. But at the same time commonwealths do not form without imperial stimulus, and the seat of empire may remain a powerful focus of sentiment long after the rejection, reduction, or retreat of its active political authority.

ANTECEDENTS OF CHRISTIAN ROME

Although in chapters 2 and 3 the discussion of cultural universalism's evolution within, between, and beyond empires was treated primarily as an autonomous theme, certain aspects of the process have helped link it to the pursuit of world empire, the subject of chapter 1. Polytheism was groping its way toward a universalizing self-definition that had a mixed ancestry in directions as diverse as philosophy and local cultic practice, but was most plainly apparent where all the gods of Rome and its subjects were gathered together in the imperial center on the banks of the Tiber. Judaism had a much clearer identity as a religion, was a monotheism, and could claim adherents everywhere. Though too ethnic to be fitted for universality, it evolved politically after the trauma of the two revolts, under the guidance of its Patriarch and, in Iran, under the Babylonian Exilarch. The language and manner of synagogue worship was standardized, and the community's law was fixed in Mishnah and Talmud. The sudden rise of Manichaeism almost resulted in the capture of the Sasanian state, and even the somewhat furtive Manichaean community that survived Mani was extensive, centrally guided, and scripturally based. Meanwhile Christianity was pursuing that consolidation of its local organization without which its eventual recognition as the religion of empire might have turned out to be less permanent. The gradual formalization of the scriptural canon and the liturgy, the organization of dioceses, and the growing habit of consultation among bishops in provincial councils all contributed to the creation of a more integrated community.[1] Mazdaism, too, became an increasingly visible part of the picture after the Sasanians took control of Iran in the 220s; the dynamic high priest Kirdir imposed orthodoxy, purged cult, and smote the heterodox;[2] and eventually, probably in the fourth century, an effort was made to counteract the prestige of the Torah, Gospels, and Manichaean scriptures by collecting, systematizing, and writing down the hitherto orally transmitted scriptures of the national religion in a single collection called the *Avesta*.[3] The alliance of throne and altar in the Sasanian state is the most obvious precedent for Constantine's policies. But the Sasanian state was a good deal more universalist in disposition than its adopted religion,[4] which was also rent by doctrinal dissension.[5] Hence, no doubt, the relatively sympathetic attitude toward Christianity, Manichaeism, and even Judaism shown by Shapur I[6] and several of his successors.

In short, Constantine grew up in a world many strands of whose religious life reveal common tendencies: toward the integration of community, the centralization of authority, the formulation of scriptural canons and its corollary, the definition and imposition of orthodoxy. Developments such as these might or might not be associated with universalist aspirations on the part of the religion concerned; but they would have been impossible outside the framework provided by the political universalisms of Rome and Iran—even the suppression of the Jewish revolt of 132–36 ended up stimulating that gradual consolidation of the Jewish community we can observe from the second century onward. Also gaining ground was the inverse idea that a state might derive a much more substantial part of its identity from a religion than had earlier been the case. The Sasanians emphasized how they represented the rule of Ahura Mazda over the earth;[7] while under Aurelian and then Diocletian even polytheist Rome, which had traditionally treated religion more as handmaid than as guide, sought heavenly models for earthly rule.[8] The inhibitions of Roman tradition, with roots

---

[1] Frend, *Rise of Christianity*, e.g. 250–51.

[2] Inscription of Kirdir §§11–38.

[3] *Denkard* IV, pp. 412–15 (tr. Shaki, *Arch.orient.* 49 [1981]: 115–21, and Boyce, *Textual sources* 113–14); Kellens, *Enc.Ir.* 3.35–36. Note also the remarks of Russell, in *Iranica varia* 181–83, 188.

[4] See above, pp. 24–34, 76; below, p. 123.

[5] Morony, *Iraq* 286–91.

[6] Cf. Chaumont, *Christianisation* 84–89.

[7] Choksy, *B.A.I.* 2 (1988).

[8] See above, pp. 50–52.

far back in the republic, had now weakened sufficiently for the tired conventions of the emperor cult, which were, up to a point, dependent on the quality and fate of the individual ruler, to be replaced by the idea that the emperor enjoyed ex officio an especially intimate relationship with divinity. But neither Aurelian's Sun nor Diocletian's Jupiter made a strong enough impression; nor, in a religion as heterogeneous and un-Bookish as Greco-Roman polytheism, could there be any sanction at all for the emperor to exercise authority over belief as well as practice. In the face of Christianity and Manichaeism though, to mention only external threats, it was necessary for someone to speak with authority about what was licit, and not just appeal to the *mos maiorum*—whose *maiores*? When Constantine became a Christian he created a golden opportunity to unite a wholeheartedly universalist religion and its abundance of scriptural authority and missionary impetus with an empire's forces of political, military, and economic expansion in order to create a genuine world empire.

For Constantine's coup there was another precedent, much earlier but no less interesting than those so far mentioned. Among the rulers of the first great Indian empire, that of the Mauryas (324–187 B.C.), which embraced all but the subcontinent's southern tip, the mighty Ashoka (ca. 272–231 B.C.) had already presided over just such an alliance with Buddhism, a vigorously prosleytizing religion whose founder had died about one or just over two centuries (depending on which of the ancient chronologies one accepts) before Ashoka's accession, and which had achieved quite substantial dissemination within India but not beyond.[9] The Buddha was conceived of as the ruler of a universal spiritual empire, king of the *dhamma*. As S. J. Tambiah has put it:

> The Buddhist scheme . . . in stating that the universal cosmic law (dhamma) is the root and fountainhead of kingship, raised up the magnificent *cakkavatti* world ruler as the sovereign regulator and the ground of society. By virtue of this grand imperial conception the way was made open for Buddhist monarchs actually to found 'world empires' on a scale hitherto unknown in India or, in face of an inability to found them for logistical reasons, at least to stake imperial claims. The rhetoric of kingship reached a high point in the Buddhist kingdoms.[10]

[9] On Ashoka, see Tambiah, *World conqueror* 54–72; Lingat, *Royautés bouddhiques* 18–60.
[10] Tambiah, *World conqueror* 52. Dhamma is the Pali form of Sanskrit *dharma* = "piety", εὐσέβεια in Ashoka's Greek inscriptions (see next note).

The Buddha's spiritual empire was extended by the devoutly Buddhist Ashoka pari passu with the political authority of the Mauryan dynasty. Buddhism did not become the state religion, nor was it imposed by force; but with Ashoka's help it penetrated southward into Ceylon and westward into the Greco-Iranian world. Throughout his empire Ashoka had inscriptions cut, usually on rocks or pillars, in order to proclaim his ideals of peacefulness, piety, tolerance, abstinence from animal flesh, and so forth. Most were in Prakrit, but in the northwestern parts of his empire inhabited by Iranians and Greeks the inscriptions were set up in Aramaic and Greek too.[11] Though Ashoka claimed that his emissaries reached various Hellenistic courts in the eastern Mediterranean basin,[12] Buddhism was never a continuous presence that far west. But in eastern Iran it became a force to be reckoned with, and in the later first or earlier second centuries A.D. the Kushan ruler Kanishka gave it considerable further impetus.[13] To judge from a recently published passage from the Dublin version of the late-third-century Manichaean *Kephalaia*, Buddhism was at that time as much the state religion of the Kushans as Mazdaism was of Iran.[14] Kirdir's inscription lists Buddhists among the non-Mazdean groups whose influence in early Sasanian Iran the high priest opposed;[15] but he certainly did not succeed in eliminating them.[16]

Ashoka saw himself as a paradigm of moral Buddhist kingship; he became a legend in his lifetime, and his example still lives on in south Asia. That it became known in the Hellenistic world too is virtually certain given the contacts between the Greek "Far East" and the Mediterranean homeland, not to mention the embassy sent by a ruler of Ceylon to the Emperor Claudius, on which occasion each side took a strong interest in the other's political system.[17] That the good king should listen to sages or be one himself was already a familiar idea in the Greek world, and Alexander had made the connection with India (and its wise men) before the Mauryan dynasty came into being. Alexander is the model for Philostratus when he has Apollonius of Tyana visit Phra-

[11] Allchin and Norman, *South Asian Studies* 1 (1985); Mukherjee, *Aramaic edicts.*

[12] Ashoka, Rock Edict XIII. Itō, *Stud.Ir.* 8 (1979); Mukherjee, *Aramaic edicts* 11; and Staviskij, *Bactriane* 106–7, dispute A. Dupont-Sommer's view that Palmyra is referred to in an Ashokan inscription in Aramaic from Afghanistan.

[13] Litvinsky, in *Kushan studies in U.S.S.R.*; Staviskij, *Bactriane* 201–15. On the Kushan Empire, see above, p. 13 and n. 3.

[14] Tardieu, *Stud.Ir.* 17 (1988): 163–64, 169–71, 179. Scholars had previously emphasized that Buddhism was one among several religions tolerated by the Kushans.

[15] Inscription of Kirdir §11.

[16] Stavisky, *B.A.I.* 4 (1990).

[17] Pliny, *Naturalis historia* VI.24.84–91; Romanis, *Helikon* 28 (1988).

otes, king of Taxila, and admire his philosophical life-style and close links with sages. Apollonius also visits Hindu wise men, the Brahmans, whom the local ruler regularly consults just as if they were an oracle. The Brahmans, true universalists, worship the gods of the Egyptians and Greeks as well as their own Indian deities.[18] Since Philostratus wrote his famous biography of Apollonius at the command of Septimius Severus's empress Julia Domna (d. 217), we can assume interest in these matters in high places, though unfortunately the work makes no clear allusion to Buddhism.[19]

But Buddhism was not unfamiliar in the Fertile Crescent, at least to intellectuals curious enough to ask and listen.[20] Bardaisan of Edessa knew from Indian ambassadors whom he met on their way to the court of Elagabalus (218–22) that the king of India was accustomed to visit and venerate Buddhist sages (*Samanaioi*), believed "that peace in his realm depends upon their prayers", and built them residences and sanctuaries.[21] The reference is almost certainly to the Kushan Empire, whose most notable ruler, Kanishka, passes for a "second Ashoka". And the Dublin *Kephalaia* now reveal that Manichaean missionaries regarded Buddhism as the state religion of the Kushans. The papyrus in question comes from Egypt, is written in Coptic, and has been dated before 350.[22] Constantine too was in diplomatic contact with Indian rulers.[23] We are not forced to suppose that he was aware of having, or needed, stars this far in the East to guide him as he set Rome's ship of state on its new course. But if we keep in mind the role of Buddhism as one of Asia's most universalist religions, the widespread awareness of the Ashokan model, and the international standing of the Kushan Empire, we will at least inject some depth and perspective into a picture whose foreground will inevitably be dominated by the relations of Rome and Iran. Iran, of course, was deeply involved in the Buddhist world, and part of the Kushan Empire ended up being reabsorbed into the Iranian sphere of influence under Shapur I and his successors.

The parallel and the distance between Ashoka and Constantine together provide keys to an assessment of Constantine's achievement. In both the Roman and the Iranian spheres, but also in India, where

---

[18] Philostratus, *Vita Apollonii* II.25–41; III.10, 14.

[19] See, though, Christol, *J.A.* 278 (1990): 48.

[20] Dihle, *Antike und Orient* 78–88, 98–101; Colpe, in *Festschrift Theodor Klauser*.

[21] Bardaisan ap. (1) Jerome, *Adversus Jovinianum* II.14 (*P.L.* 23.317); (2) Porphyry, *De abstinentia* IV.17–18. On the name *Samanaioi*, see Christol, *J.A.* 278 (1990): 45–70.

[22] See n. 14 above.

[23] Publilius Optatianus Porfyrius, *Carmina* V.13, XIV.20–22; Eusebius, *Vita Constantini* IV.7, 50. "India" might also mean Arabia: Shahîd, *B.A.FO.C.* 53–56.

Ashoka's empire foundered but his inspiration remained, history's dynamic does indeed seem to have been moving toward an integration of religion and empire founded on the universality of both. Polytheism was vulnerable because, despite certain universalist tendencies of its own, it could truly claim neither unity, catholicity, nor (for want of historical origins) apostolicity—all attributes that the Christian Church accurately identified as de rigueur in a world religion. But even if Constantine had heard of Ashoka, there would be no need to suppose "influence". Both acted on personal initiative born of practical experience in empire building; the career of neither was "inevitable". The proof of this is that the Mauryan Empire disintegrated just half a century after Ashoka's death. Although Ashoka's influence remained, India continued to be a pluralistic as well as a universal civilization. Unlike Christians and Muslims, with their revealed religions, Hindus could not fall into the habit of addressing truth in the singular;[24] and India, along with the central Asiatic regions it influenced, remained fundamentally different from the European and southwest Asiatic world, in the sense that religions accepted a horizontal rather than a vertical relationship to each other—overlay rather than juxtaposition. As for Constantine, the vision he espoused and his biographer Eusebius expounded was only imperfectly realized. Before we ask, in the next chapter, how what set out to be a world empire ended up as a commonwealth, we must understand more exactly what was the vision—or better, perhaps, the strategy—of Rome's first Christian ruler.

CONSTANTINE'S STRATEGY

It has already more than once been implied that there was no sudden Constantinian revolution. Not only were Constantine's ideas and policies in the wind; not only was Constantine in many respects the continuator of Diocletian. It is also the case that to depict Constantine's reign as a revolution is to do no justice to the suspensefulness of the rest of fourth-century history. Constantine saw dynasty, not a continuation of the tetrarchy (despite its obvious dynastic tendencies), as the guarantee of his legacy; but Constantius was an Arian and Julian a polytheist. Nicaean Christianity triumphed indisputably only under a second dynasty, the Theodosian, in the aftermath of legal measures that, as far as polytheism was concerned, even Theodosius I postponed until his last years. Ecclesiastical historians from Eusebius onward did indeed depict Constantine's reign as a turning point, but such recognition may have

[24] Chaudhuri, *Asia before Europe* 53.

come more slowly among those who focused on Rome rather than the Church. There is little sign that Eusebius's *Vita Constantini* was read in the fourth or fifth centuries, except by ecclesiastical historians.[25]

These are all notes of proper caution. When Constantine was laid to rest in 337 nothing (despite Eusebius) was so cut and dried as it may seem to us now. But it is precisely the longer-term dynamic of late antique history, the striving for world empire and the slow emergence of commonwealth, that is our concern here. From this point of view, Eusebius the political thinker deserves more attention than he probably got in his own day or for a long time to come,[26] while Constantine may be allowed to have sown a revolution even if he did not reap it.

As the bishop of Caesarea Maritima in Palestine, Eusebius had significant but only occasional opportunities to correspond with Constantine and meet him personally.[27] Despite his interest in the affairs of Empire and Church and his fascination with Constantine's personality, most of Eusebius's time was taken up with the administration of his important diocese on the Palestinian coast, at the precise point where the world of the Fertile Crescent touched the world of the Mediterranean. Both in his *Vita Constantini* and in other works, Eusebius reveals a detailed knowledge of the affairs of the Roman East. He is every inch a man of the Fertile Crescent, embroiled in its local complexities but aware of the broad horizons to which it offers access, not least toward Iran.[28] The role of Iran in the *Vita Constantini* will obtain our close attention; but before that, two of the *Vita*'s other themes need to be examined: the identity of Empire and Church, and mission both within and without.

Empire and Church

If we examine the development of Constantine's and indeed of Constantius's titulature we will observe a much-increased variety and originality of universalist themes compared to their predecessors.[29] Constantine took a maximalist view of the emperor's job; in fact, he aspired to conquer the world. Even Cyrus and Alexander pale by comparison, according to Eusebius, for they both died unhappily, whereas Constantine, who like them conquered nearly the whole world, died in bed and

[25] See the introduction to Winkelmann's edition, XXVII–XXXIII; also Dagron, *T.&M.Byz.* 3 (1968): 88 n. 25.

[26] See Cameron, in *Tria Corda.*

[27] Barnes, *Constantine and Eusebius* 265–67.

[28] Though see also below, p. 94.

[29] Mastino, in *Popoli e spazio romano* 108–12.

confident in his heirs.[30] Eusebius was a panegyrist, and similar claims
had been made for or by many of Constantine's predecessors, with
sometimes less but sometimes more objective justification. Constantine,
though, was unique in that he alone among the rulers of Rome had also,
as Eusebius puts it, become a "friend of God the sovereign of all".[31]

According to Eusebius, Constantine had a particular weakness for
public preaching: "He usually divided the subjects of his address, first
thoroughly exposing the error of polytheism. . . . He then would assert
the sole sovereignty of God, passing thence to His providence, both
general and particular."[32] In his passionate monotheism, Constantine
took after his father Constantius Chlorus, of whose beliefs Constantine
knew no more than that they centered on "the one supreme God".[33]
"Accordingly, he called on Him with earnest prayer and supplications
that He would reveal to him who He was, and stretch forth His right
hand to help him in his present difficulties."[34] And Constantine was
duly rewarded with his famous vision of the Cross, and the command to
"conquer by this". The implication of this inquiry, especially if taken in
conjunction with Julian's assertion that Constantius Chlorus remained
a polytheist,[35] is probably that Constantine was brought up in an ab-
stractly monotheist rather than concretely Christian environment. And
the principled character of Constantine's monotheism, capable of sus-
taining itself, perhaps even without the Gospels' support, is confirmed
by his relatively tolerant attitude toward Judaism. Constantine took
active steps to limit polytheist cults, but imposed no such restrictions on
Jews,[36] and indeed gave the Jewish hierarchy privileges similar to those
he granted to Christian priests and bishops.[37] Constantine did not like
Jews; but at least they were not polytheists. We shall find a similar but
more clearly articulated attitude in the Quran. We have no reason to
question its sincerity. But Constantine's prayer shows plainly enough
that the political helpfulness of monotheism was appreciated. And when

[30] Eusebius, *Vita Constantini* I.7–9, IV.50–51.

[31] Ibid., I.3.4; I.52.

[32] Ibid., IV.29.3 (tr. here and elsewhere E. C. Richardson); and cp. IV.55.

[33] Ibid., I.27.2: τὸν ἐπέκεινα τῶν ὅλων θεόν.

[34] Ibid., I.28.1.

[35] Julian, *or.* X.336b.

[36] Avi-Yonah, *Jews under Roman and Byzantine rule* 161–66. Jews came to be seriously penalized only in the more narrowly Christian empire of the fifth and sixth centuries: Linder, *Jews in Roman imperial legislation* 67–90. Barnes as usual retrojects this
atmosphere to Constantine's reign, partly on the basis of anecdotal evidence: *Constantine
and Eusebius* 252.

[37] *Codex Theodosianus* XVI.8.2; and cp. XVI.2.2–3, 7.

it came to politics, the Christian Church had an organization and an impetus that no one could rival.

Constantine saw himself as a sacral king, on whose relationship with and right worship of God the Father and God the Son depended not only the prosperity of his people but also the balance of creation generally.[38] But monotheism had a more specifically political payoff too.

> [Constantine] openly declared and confessed himself the servant and minister of the supreme King. And God forthwith rewarded him, by making him ruler and sovereign, and victorious to such a degree that he alone of all rulers pursued a continuous course of conquest, unsubdued and invincible, and through his trophies a greater ruler than tradition records ever to have been before. So dear was he to God, and so blessed; so pious and so fortunate in all he undertook, that with the greatest facility he obtained authority over more nations than any who had preceded him, and yet retained his power, undisturbed, to the very close of his life.[39]

Constantine does not just Christianize the Roman Empire; he unifies it too. And he expounds a worldview to which, though it was not absolutely original, he gave new force: one god, one empire, one emperor.[40] It was this politico-religious universalist program that provided the nascent Christian empire's motive energy. Shortly after the passage just quoted, Eusebius declares that he will concentrate on what made Constantine beloved of God and a paradigm of piety rather than on wars, laws, and the like;[41] while in the oration that he delivered on the thirtieth anniversary of Constantine's accession he offers a "virtual redefinition of the empire itself as a 'school' gathered around a charismatic royal teacher".[42] But from the *Life* it emerges with clarity that precisely by his wars and laws Constantine became the model Christian king, and,

---

[38] Cp. the story of the conversion of Constantine's clone, the king of Iberia, after nature had become disordered (by an eclipse) on account of his lack of interest in the Gospel: Rufinus, *H.E.* X.11; Thelamon, *Païens et chrétiens* 102–5 (with further bibliography on Eusebius's political conceptions; cf. also Mazza, *Maschere del potere* 224–37).

[39] Eusebius, *Vita Constantini* I.6.

[40] Ibid., I.5, 24; II.19; Eusebius, *De laudibus Constantini* III.3–6 and, especially, XVI.3–7. See also Frend, *Monophysite movement* 55–60, and the hymn sung at the Orthodox Church's vespers of the Nativity (25 December): "When Augustus reigned alone upon earth, the many kingdoms of men came to an end: and when Thou wast made man of the pure Virgin, the many gods of idolatry were destroyed. The cities of the world passed under one single rule; and the nations came to believe in one sovereign Godhead" (tr. Mother Mary and Ware, *Festal Menaion* 254).

[41] Eusebius, *Vita Constantini* I.11.

[42] Williams, *Arius* 88.

conversely, that it was through his piety that he won wars and made good laws.

Eusebius particularly emphasizes that God intended Constantine to revive Rome's fortunes not only by reuniting and even expanding the previously divided empire, and by delivering it from polytheist error, but also by setting straight the doctrine and conduct of the Church. Accordingly, Constantine called himself a bishop,[43] and had himself buried amid monuments to the apostles, as if he himself were the thirteenth.[44] These allusions were not understood in any narrowly ecclesiastical sense.[45] They had been transferred onto the spiritual plane, to the extent that Constantine's role could be compared to that of Christ himself.[46] The sacralization of empire inherited from the tetrarchy is reinterpreted by Eusebius in the light of the Gospels and of ecclesiastical history. The *Vita Constantini*, written just after its subject's death, presupposes everything that the *Historia Ecclesiastica* had already explained about the converging forces of universal Empire and universal Church.

Before Eusebius, conventional history had treated Christianity as an occasional intrusion. But some Christian writers had known that Christ's foundation of the Church in the same generation in which Augustus installed the *pax Romana* was no coincidence. Origen, for example, had observed how "Jesus was born during the reign of Augustus, the one who reduced to uniformity, so to speak, the many kingdoms on earth so that he had a single empire. It would have hindered Jesus's teaching from being spread through the whole world if there had been many kingdoms"[47]—and it would also, of course, have made Rome's transition from polytheism to monotheism seem an apostasy, or at least an inexplicable break in the empire's continuity, had Christianity not already been incubating since the time of Augustus. As the intellectual heir both of Origen and of Sextus Julius Africanus, who a century before had written a synchronic history of the Jews and their gentile neighbors,[48] Eusebius intertwined ever more intimately the separate histories of Empire and Church—albeit adopting the Christian viewpoint, as Africanus had the Hebrew—until the point when Constantine, guided by God, presided over their marriage. Just as the Sasanians rewrote history to make Zarathushtra the prophet and guarantor of the

---

[43] Eusebius, *Vita Constantini* IV.24.

[44] Ibid., IV.60, 71.

[45] Cf. ibid., I.44 (οἷά τις κοινὸς ἐπίσκοπος—"just as if he were a general bishop").

[46] Eusebius, *De laudibus Constantini* II.

[47] Origen, *Contra Celsum* II.30 (tr. H. Chadwick); cf. Melito ap. Eusebius, *H.E.* IV.26.7–8.

[48] Sextus Julius Africanus ap. Eusebius, *Praeparatio evangelica* X.10.1–2.

national renaissance they aspired to bring about,[49] so Eusebius united universal Church and universal Empire in a single historical narrative.[50] Whatever the incongruity between the Empire's *aeternitas*—an important constituent of its universalism—and the Church's eschatological expectation, both could henceforth enjoy the symbolic payoff of a shared diachronicity.

Mission

"All authority in heaven and on earth has been given to me", Jesus proclaimed when he appeared to his disciples in Galilee after the Resurrection. "Go, therefore, make disciples of all nations; baptize them in the name of the Father and of the Son and of the Holy Spirit, and teach them to observe all the commands I gave you."[51] Whether or not Jesus actually pronounced these or similar words, the Gospel-writer draws a direct and fateful link between the conjunction of heavenly and earthly power and the obligation to propagate Christianity through mission. This is the foundation text of Christian universalism, and one of Eusebius's favorite quotations.[52] The reality it foreshadows in the context of the New Testament story is brought nearer when Paul imposes the view, frequently stated in the Gospels,[53] and confirmed at the first Pentecost, that the Church is for gentiles and circumcised alike. Once this view was accepted, there was no inherent reason why Christianity should not become an actually universal faith. It proclaimed not just one god—the Jews too did that—but one Church for all men; and its teaching was encapsulated in Scriptures written in an accessible idiom. A new idea of mission—less selective than philosophical recruitment, less passive than Jewish proselytism—was a natural development from these features of Christianity, as Paul demonstrated with paradigmatic vigor. The systematic propagation of revealed truth by traveling teachers was Paul's great contribution on the level of religious organization. He found a brilliant imitator in Mani; but the history of Christian mission could not really be said to have begun until Constantine rescued the Church from semilegality and made tangible its claim to authority on earth as well as in heaven. Constantine, living up to his aspiration to be numbered among the apostles, gave mission a dimension Paul never dreamed

[49] See above, p. 34.
[50] For Eusebius's influence on following generations, see Peterson, *Monotheismus* 82–93.
[51] *Matt.* XXVIII.19–20; cf. *Mark* XVI.15, *Luke* XXIV.47, *Acts* I.8.
[52] Green, in *Making of orthodoxy* 125.
[53] E.g., *Matt.* VIII.10–12.

of and Mani dreamed of but could not bring about, when he conjoined religious self-propagation with the political, military, and economic expansionism of empire.

As emperor of Rome, but also a sort of bishop, Constantine is presented by Eusebius as propagating Christian belief and practice as well as molding the institutions and public doctrine of a new empire. He could not do everything himself, but he could set an example to the bishops who were charged with the Church's local administration. Constantine convenes and plays a leading role at the Council of Nicaea, the central doctrinal and ecclesiological act of his reign; and he writes in person to the Palestinian bishops instructing them how to deal with the holy place of Mambre, having been apprised of superstitious defilements there by his mother-in-law.[54] He likewise supervises the suppression of polytheism, even issuing orders for the closure of specific temples judged especially offensive: the sanctuaries of Asclepius at Aegeae in Smooth Cilicia, and of Aphrodite at Aphaca and Heliopolis (Baalbek) in the Lebanon.[55] This is Constantine the new Moses,[56] leading the chosen people and inspired by a vision of the unity and integrity of people, faith, and land. Kirdir the Mazdean high priest had had something similar in mind; but the Christians of Iran, and for a time the Manichaeans too, went from strength to strength in his day. Only the ancient Israelites had systematically purged their land of gods and cults other than their own.[57] Establishing the Ark of the Covenant in Jerusalem, they had also given themselves a sacred territorial center[58]—another direct precedent for Constantine.

But this time God had chosen all nations, not just one, and not even just the Roman Empire. In the *Vita Constantini* the emperor's mission toward the *ethne*, the "nations", the polytheists within the empire, is balanced by a responsibility for the *ethne* without. Constantine is not just a bishop, but "bishop of those outside".[59] Eusebius takes this as an allusion to Constantine's responsibility for Rome's subjects, but Constantine's own interpretation was more generous. He sought to suppress polytheism and spread Christianity beyond as well as within his own frontiers—an entirely new understanding of the Roman emperor's role,

[54] Eusebius, *Vita Constantini* III.52–53.

[55] Ibid., III.55–58. (Perhaps these are singled out because of Eusebius's special knowledge of the region.)

[56] Ibid., I.12, 20, 38; II.11–12; Eusebius, *H.E.* IX.9.5–9.

[57] E.g., *Exod.* XXIII.23–24, XXXIV.13–16; *Deut.* VII.2–6, XX.15–18; *2 Kings* X.18–27.

[58] *2 Sam.* VI.

[59] Eusebius, *Vita Constantini* IV.24. There will never be agreement about the exact meaning of this phrase: see, e.g., de Decker and Dupuis-Masay, *Byzantion* 50 (1980).

4. Constantine and the 318 bishops at the Council of Nicaea, 325.
Fresco, dated 1512, in the refectory of the
Great Lavra, Mount Athos.

92

inconceivable except within the context of allegiance to a universalist religion. Constantine pursued this end, with regard to the Germanic nations across the Danube, through war, diplomacy, and support of ecclesiastical mission. By piety he vanquished the Goths and Sarmatians, claims Eusebius's continuator Rufinus; the more he subjected himself to God, the more God subjected to him the whole world (*universa*).[60] In a letter to the bishops assembled at the Council of Tyre in 335, Constantine himself claimed that through him the recently defeated Goths and Sarmatians had come to know God and learn piety;[61] while it has recently been suggested that Ulfila was consecrated "bishop of the Goths" at the Council of Constantinople in 336, amid the strenuously imperialist atmosphere of Constantine's *tricennalia* celebrations.[62]

Iran

On the eastern frontier, Rome had to deal with polities less fluid, more like itself, and Constantine could hope for a closer imitation of his new Church-state alliance. Indeed, Armenia and perhaps Edessa too had anticipated Rome, and the ecclesiastical historian Sozomen asserts that they encouraged, at least indirectly, the Christianization of adjoining lands.[63] In the North, the Iberians—the inhabitants, that is, of eastern Georgia—became Christian toward the end of Constantine's reign or at the beginning of Constantius's,[64] and sent the emperor a request for priests. Some of the ecclesiastical historians allege that they sought a political alliance too,[65] but the change of faith carried that implication anyway. The emperor, we are told, was delighted at this turn of events. But ever since his conquest of the East in 324, Constantine had also been looking at Iran itself, and claiming guardianship over the substantial Christian community that had emerged there since the latter half of the second century.[66] In a letter he addressed at that time to Shapur II, and parts of which Eusebius included in his *Vita Constantini*, the Christian emperor made a famous statement of this claim. After underlining at length how God is on his side, Constantine innocuously observes in his final paragraph that the numerousness of Christian congregations in

---

[60] Rufinus, *H.E.* X.8.

[61] Athanasius, *Apologia contra Arianos* 86; Gelasius of Cyzicus, *H.E.* III.18.1–13, esp. 10; and cp. Eusebius, *Vita Constantini* IV.5–6.

[62] Philostorgius, *H.E.* II.5; Barnes, *J.Th.S.* 41 (1990). Heather and Matthews, *Goths* 141–43, incline toward a slightly later date; but 341 is the latest possible.

[63] Sozomen, *H.E.* II.8.

[64] Rufinus, *H.E.* X.11. On the Armenian connection, see Klein *Constantius II.* 178–79; Thelamon, *Paiens et chrétiens* 94; also 96 on the date of the conversion.

[65] Socrates, *H.E.* I.20; Sozomen, *H.E.* II.7.12.

[66] Chaumont, *Christianisation*.

Iran rejoices his heart, and calls down blessings both on them and on their pious and benevolent ruler. "Cherish them in accordance with your usual humanity, for by this gesture of faith you will confer an immeasurable benefit on both yourself and us."[67]

Admittedly, no reader of Eusebius's *Historia Ecclesiastica* would guess that Sasanian Iran even existed, except as the source of Mani's disgusting heresy.[68] Whereas Tertullian had taken the existence of "places inaccessible to the Romans, but subject to Christ" ("inaccessa Romanis loca, Christo vero subdita") as cause for pride,[69] the bishop of Caesarea attached little importance to Churches that did not fall into his one god—one empire—one emperor schema. Christianity and Rome were for him essentially coterminous, and so the existence of the Christians of Iran is let slip, in the *Life of Constantine*, only at the moment when Constantine decides to do something about them. The letter to Shapur was a first warning; its allusions to divinely assisted conquests starting at the western ocean and proceeding eastward were a prelude to war. Constantine no doubt discussed the state of Christianity in Iran with bishop John "of Persia", who attended the Council of Nicaea;[70] while the presence of a bishop from Iran at the Council of Tyre and at the dedication of the Anastasis basilica in Jerusalem (both in 335)[71] illustrates how these major ecclesiastical events could be used to underline Constantine's claim to patronage of the Church Universal. At the ceremony in Jerusalem, Eusebius declared that the Roman Empire heralds God's kingdom, "has already united most of the various peoples, and is further destined to obtain all those not yet united, right up to the very limits of the inhabited world".[72] Additional motive or pretext for the impending campaign was supplied by Shapur's own aggressiveness now that he had reached manhood, not to mention the usual conflict of interests in Armenia.[73] In 337 Constantine was in the midst of preparations to "kindle the Parthian fires"[74] that had lain mostly dormant for almost four decades. He had recently been campaigning on the Danube in a manner calculatedly reminiscent of Trajan, who had come nearer than any other Roman emperor to imitating Alexander.[75] And just as

[67] Eusebius, *Vita Constantini* IV.8–13 (tr. Barnes, *J.R.S.* 75 [1985]: 132).
[68] Eusebius, *H.E.* VII.31.2.
[69] Tertullian, *Adversus Iudaeos* 7.
[70] Chaumont, *Christianisation* 147–54.
[71] Eusebius, *Vita Constantini* IV.43.
[72] Eusebius, *De laudibus Constantini* XVI.6 (tr. H. A. Drake).
[73] Matthews, *Ammianus* 135–36.
[74] Ammianus Marcellinus XXV.4.23.
[75] Barnes, *Constantine and Eusebius* 250; Barnes, *J.R.S.* 75 (1985): 132.

Trajan had played the kingmaker at Ctesiphon,[76] so now Constantine gave his half-nephew Hannibalianus responsibility for Pontus, Armenia, and neighboring areas, and the title "King of Kings", which he would presumably have kept for himself or at least for one of his designated heirs had he intended it as a direct challenge to Shapur,[77] but which nonetheless indicated a claim to suzerainty over Armenia and other supposedly independent kingdoms in the area such as Lazica, Iberia, and Albania. Iran could hardly ignore such a provocation.

On the campaign against Licinius that had made him lord of the East, Constantine had been accompanied by priests and had put the sign of the cross at the head of his army.[78] Now again he took bishops into his confidence, and persuaded them to march alongside him and do battle with infidel Iran through prayer. He even took with him a special tent constructed in the shape of a church.[79] Furthermore, the sixth-century writer John Lydus asserts that the reason Constantine created a Praetorian Prefect of the East was "because he was considering, as the emperor himself says in his own works, a surprise attack upon the Persians. For Constantine knew well, being notable for literary education and constant practice in weaponry . . . that it was not easy to overcome the Persians in war, otherwise than by an assault which poured over them out of the blue."[80] That Constantine remained a busy author until his death we know from Eusebius.[81] And Lydus here alludes to an otherwise unknown work in which Constantine discussed his campaign against Iran[82]—another indication of the importance he attached to it.

The care with which Constantine planned this expedition, at the culmination of a career each step of which had been carefully thought out,[83] compels the conclusion that his aim was indeed to make the whole world Christian and Roman. He perceived that Christian Rome possessed a cultural impetus vis-à-vis Iran that polytheist Rome had lacked. The crusade for world empire, for a practical realization at last

[76] Cassius Dio LXVIII.30.3.

[77] Pace Barnes, *Constantine and Eusebius* 259 (with the references).

[78] Eusebius, *Vita Constantini* II.3–4, 6–9.

[79] Ibid., IV.56. Part of the text is an unknown Renaissance scholar's attempt to plug a half-page lacuna in our MSS (Winkelmann, *Klio* 40 [1962]: 232), but the tent is mentioned in the chapter heading. The *Vita*'s chapter headings were probably not written by Eusebius, but seem nonetheless to be early, so presumably this one reflects what Eusebius wrote: see Winkelmann's edition, XLVI–XLIX.

[80] John Lydus, *De magistratibus* III.33 (tr. T. F. Carney, emended).

[81] Eusebius, *Vita Constantini* IV.55.1.

[82] Kaegi, *Army, society and religion* IV.

[83] Cf. Eusebius, *Vita Constantini* III.29, on Constantine's foresightedness in another context; and Barceló, *Roms auswärtige Beziehungen* 80–82.

of politico-cultural universalism, was on. If Aphrahat can be taken as speaking for them, Shapur's Christian subjects welcomed the new turn of events and identified with the Roman emperor.[84] But just as he was setting out, Constantine died, in May 337. The Christians of Iran realized too late the error of letting themselves be seen as Rome's allies,[85] and paid for it with bloody persecution in the decades to come.[86] This must be part of the reason why they eventually began to distance themselves from Rome, though it was not until 424 that they formally declared independence from the see of Antioch,[87] and even then there was as yet no theological break.

Considering the extraordinary character and inner logic of his career viewed as a whole, there is nothing inherently implausible about this picture of Constantine the universal crusader.[88] Posterity certainly saw him in that light, and so greatly needed his example that the story of his last days had to be rewritten. An important group of mainly early and non-Christian sources relates how Constantine died at Nicomedia, on the road to the East, having already set out against Iran—it was May, the beginning of the campaigning season.[89] There were those, too, who maintained that it was Constantine who was the aggressor. Ammianus, for example: "Since his [Julian's] detractors alleged that he had stirred up the storms of war anew, to the ruin of his country, they should know clearly, through the teachings of truth, that it was not Julian but Constantine who kindled the Parthian fires."[90] Understandably, though, the ecclesiastical historians preferred not to present their hero Constantine as an aggressive old man who died just at the wrong moment. Accordingly, they say nothing, in this context, of the Iranian campaign, and assert that the reason Constantine died at Nicomedia, not Constantinople, was that,

[84] Aphrahat, *Demonstrations* V.1, 10, 24; cf. Barnes, *J.R.S.* 75 (1985): 133–35, 136.

[85] Sozomen, *H.E.* II.9.1; cf. Brock, *Syriac perspectives* VI.7–11.

[86] Decret, *Rec.Aug.* 14 (1979): 140–49. The same cultural fallout from political hostility can be seen in Firmicus Maternus's attack on the Iranian religion of Mithras: *De errore profanarum religionum* V.2, with XXIX.3 (probably alluding to the siege of Nisibis in 346). That both Roman and Iranian imperialism had cultural as well as political aims only intensified the problem.

[87] Selb, *Orientalisches Kirchenrecht* 1.120–21.

[88] I prefer, in other words, Barnes's interpretation to Matthews's view (*Ammianus* 499 n. 14) that Shapur was planning a major strike against the Romans, and Constantine was merely preparing to meet it.

[89] Libanius, *or.* LIX.71–72; Eutropius, *Breviarium* X.8.2; Festus, *Breviarium* 26 (without explicit reference to Constantine's death); Aurelius Victor, *De Caesaribus* XLI.16; *Anonymus Valesianus* 35. Similarly *Chronicon Paschale* p. 532; Theophanes p. 33. On Zonaras's "Leoquelle", see Bleckmann, *Historia* 40 (1991): 356–58.

[90] Ammianus Marcellinus XXV.4.23.

having already fallen ill, he had gone to take the warm baths near Helenopolis.[91] This is the *Life of Constantine*'s version too, except that Eusebius does not omit the campaign against Iran. Instead, he brings it to an abrupt and rather improbable end before Constantine has even set out, apparently in response to an Iranian embassy.[92] How exactly Eusebius explained this we do not know, because at this point our manuscripts of the *Life* have a half-page lacuna for which we should probably thank the later ecclesiastical historians who seem to have been the *Life*'s main readership,[93] and who provide an account of Constantine's last days significantly different, at this particular point, from that of Eusebius.[94] The bishop of Caesarea's problem was that he wrote soon after Constantine's death and in ignorance of the subsequent dismal history of Romano-Iranian relations. He could not see the long-term context that compelled later ecclesiastical historians to adjust the record. We may be sure that Constantine's crusade, albeit interrupted by the emperor's death, would have kept an honored place in Byzantine historiography had the next two generations not been so burned by the Parthian fires.

As it was, Constantine remained a crusader. Trusting in God's protection of the empire, and taking Constantine as its model, Byzantium often felt called to be more than just the container of Christianity.[95] When this vocation conflicted with political prudence, awkward dilemmas had to be faced. One of the first acts of the Emperor Marcian (450–57) was to refuse aid to the Armenians in their life-or-death struggle with Iran—"this ignoble man", an Armenian historian later observed, "thought it better to preserve the pact with the heathen [Iran] for the sake of terrestrial peace, than to join in war for the Christian cove-

[91] Philostorgius II.16; Socrates I.39; Sozomen II.34.1; Theodoret I.32.

[92] Eusebius, *Vita Constantini* IV.57 (title: see above, n. 79).

[93] See above, p. 86.

[94] If in fact Eusebius originally had Constantine die on active campaign, like the other early sources, we would have to suppose extensive recomposition of the *Vita*'s subsequent chapters, which contain the Helenopolis episode. Such suppositions about the *Vita* are not so popular as they used to be, but nor are they inherently unlikely. Libanius, *or.* LIX.72, for example, provides a perfectly respectable solution to the problem of how to reconcile Constantine's ill-timed death with the *Vita*'s encomiastic mood, and in particular with the sentiments about the succession expressed at I.1–2 and IV.72.

[95] Mazza, *Maschere del potere* 237–54. For similar disagreement in the West about whether the empire should be Christianity's fortress or its springboard, see Markus, in *Inheritance of historiography* 37–39. But the Western Empire was in no position to play a dynamic role after the fourth century. Kaegi, *Byzantium and the decline of Rome* 190–204, 210–23, traces Eusebian attitudes in the Greek ecclesiastical historians. Who read ecclesiastical histories we cannot know, but they seem to reflect Establishment attitudes.

nant".[96] Justinian, by contrast, strove not only to extinguish polytheism and heresy, nor just to restore the Roman Empire's former extent, but also to press on further and Christianize those who had never been Romans.[97] But in so doing he made excessive demands on both the economy and the army. The power and authority of the center was irreversibly weakened, as became plainly apparent under Justinian's successors, in whose reigns has been observed

> a drift away from the symbolism of the heaven-endowed earthly empire—the imperial cult and hierarchies of state and Church—towards embodiments of heavenly power of a less fallible nature: the cults of saints, the cult of the Virgin, the icon. . . . Ordinary people were transferring their attention away from the worldly and physical authority of the emperor and the state, distant and ineffective as it often was, towards a more immediate and tangible power, a power and authority invested in heavenly guardians and intercessors directly by God.[98]

Heraclius kindled a brief hope that the emperor might regain something of the immediacy of Constantine's relationship with God, and with it the power to restore the Roman Empire. Though the "new Constantine"[99] may not have wanted to eliminate Iran altogether, he apparently did plan to put it under Byzantine tutelage.[100] George of Pisidia paints Heraclius as a true crusader,[101] and lauds him for recovering the True Cross from the Iranians, comparing him with his "father" Constantine who first discovered the Cross at Jerusalem.[102] Such ideas are also reflected in the speech Theophylact Simocatta attributes to Iranian ambassadors sent to beg Maurice to help their master Khusrau (II) in his struggle for the throne (590). "It is impossible for a single monarchy to embrace the innumerable cares of the organization of the

---

[96] Elishe, *History of Vardan and the Armenian war* p. 73 (Ter-Minasean; tr. Thomson 124).

[97] See below, pp. 101–2, 116; also Procopius, *Aedificia* III.6.6–7.

[98] Haldon, *Byzantium* 37–39, and cp. 58–59, 355–64.

[99] Shahîd, *D.O.P.* 26 (1972): 310 n. 65.

[100] Nicephorus, *Breviarium* 15: note that Heraclius calls the Iranian king his "child"; Mango, *T.&M.Byz.* 9 (1985): 105–17; Kaegi, *Byzantium and the early Islamic conquests* 154–55.

[101] George of Pisidia, *Expeditio Persica* I.139–51; Mango, *T.&M.Byz.* 9 (1985): 105–17. An anonymous Nestorian writer in the 670s reports a rumor that Heraclius had been ordained to the priesthood: *Chronicon anonymum* ("Khuzistan chronicle") p. 28 (tr. Guidi 24). I owe this reference to Peter Brown.

[102] George of Pisidia, *In restitutionem S. Crucis* 47–63.

universe, and with one mind's rudder to direct a creation as great as that over which the sun watches. For it is never possible for the earth to resemble the unity of the divine and primary rule, and to obtain a disposition corresponding to that of the upper order."[103]

Theophylact was writing between 628 and 638, in which case this may be a specific reference forward to the short-lived success of Heraclius's counterattack against Khusrau.[104] Others cast Heraclius in apocalyptic light as herald of Christ's universal kingdom.[105] His reign and the gloomy decades that followed saw the birth of such texts as the Syrian Alexander-legend and the *Apocalypse of Pseudo-Methodius*, which asserted that the Christian empire had been founded by a believing Alexander the Great, and nourished expectations of a crusading savior-king to come at the imminent end of time.[106] Through the annexation of pre-Christian past and eschatological future, Christian Rome's centrality to human history was firmly reasserted against the transitoriness of Iran and Islam alike. In the workaday world, though, the dream of world empire, of missionary monotheism backed by imperial impetus, had long since been translated, step by step, into the reality of commonwealth.

[103] Theophylact Simocatta, *Historia universalis* IV.13.7–8 (tr. M. and M. Whitby).

[104] For a similar reference forward, see ibid. V.15.3–7. On the date, see Whitby, *Emperor Maurice* 39–40.

[105] E.g., Theophylact Simocatta, *Historia universalis* V.15.3–7, on which see the previous note, and the notes to the Whitby translation.

[106] Reinink, in *Use and abuse of eschatology* 108–10.

5

THE FIRST BYZANTINE
COMMONWEALTH: INTERACTIONS OF
POLITICAL AND CULTURAL
UNIVERSALISM

JUST AS Eusebius was Constantine's political theorist, so Themistius was Constantius's. The one was a Christian, the other a polytheist, but their understanding of the relationship between empire and emperor was close.[1] Though we cannot prove that the *Life of Constantine* was read by Themistius, or very much at all at this period,[2] Eusebius's general ideas were in the wind.[3] Whether Constantine had been at his most realistic in planning his crusade against Iran is, though, another question; and under Constantius such ideas, though played with by Themistius,[4] were definitely no longer in the realm of practical possibility. The Roman Empire was as yet far from being unshakably Christian, and to begin with Constantius controlled only its eastern part;[5] the parochialism of a Libanius of Antioch had to be balanced against the universalism of a Themistius;[6] while Sasanian Iran (about which Antiochenes were through bitter experience considerably better informed than Constantinopolitans) had entered one of its most expansive phases under the now mature Shapur II.

For Constantius, security, not external mission, was paramount.[7]

---

[1] Dagron, *T.&M.Byz.* 3 (1968): 85–89. For an attempt to reevaluate Constantius's reign, see *E.A.C.* 34 (1989) (*L'Eglise et l'Empire au IVᵉ siècle*). The danger inherent in such exercises, of underestimating continuity and overestimating (or imagining) novelty, is avoided more successfully by C. Pietri than by L. Cracco Ruggini, for example.

[2] See above, p. 86 n. 25.

[3] See above, p. 90 n. 50.

[4] Themistius, *or.* I.12b.

[5] Barceló, *Roms auswärtige Beziehungen* 82–83.

[6] Dagron, *T.&M.Byz.* 3 (1968): 90–92.

[7] This is one of the main points made by Klein, *Constantius II.*, e.g., 265–69. Meslin, *Archives de sociologie des religions* 18 (1964), argues that, despite its theoretically universalist ideology, official Christianity was throughout the fourth century uninterested in mission to populations outside the privileged bounds of Romania. His evidence is mainly Western, but a similar if weaker case might be made about the East—though the situation changed, as we shall see, in the fifth century, especially in the aftermath of Chalcedon.

Christianity continued to spread beyond Rome's frontiers, but the dream of imposing it by force of arms had proved elusive. The mission narratives preserved by ecclesiastical historians betray the haphazardness of private enterprise, sporadically supported, even exploited, by Rome (by which we now mean Constantinople), but also sometimes undermined. Since the events depicted were destined to become foundation myths of Christian posterity in the places concerned, and since they all occurred far from the Mediterranean cities where ecclesiastical historians lived and wrote, our narratives tend to be partial and even at times imaginative. The progress achieved in the fourth century was probably less or at least slower than our sources claim, so a longer perspective may be truer to the actual pace of events. But a longer perspective is imposed anyway, simply because the First Byzantine Commonwealth did not find its most distinctive identity or effective means of self-propagation until the compromise language used by the Council of Chalcedon (451) about Christ's two natures inseparably united had generated its reaction among those who affirmed that the one incarnate nature of Christ is divine—in other words, what we call the Monophysite movement.

THE GEOGRAPHICAL FOCUS

If the importance of the Monophysite movement imposes a long time span on our discussion, it is also one of the reasons why the geographical space covered, while generous enough, will not be unlimited.

In the Transcaucasia-Caucasus region and to the north of it, and also along the Black Sea's eastern and northern coasts and on the Danube (in other words on its northern as well as its eastern frontiers), Byzantium sought by propagating Christianity and contracting alliances with local rulers to ensure its own security.[8] Constantine himself had encouraged the spread of Christianity among the Goths and Sarmatians beyond the Danube;[9] John Chrysostom twice provided a bishop for the Crimean Goths, Justinian once.[10] This last was but one of a series of attempts made by Justin and Justinian to bolster the northern frontier. Justinian fought and intrigued constantly both in Lazica, at the southeast corner of the Black Sea, and beyond. The Hunnic Sabiri, a nomadic people who lived north of the Caucasus between the Black Sea and the Caspian, athwart the strategic approaches to the passes into Georgia, seem to have become Christians through the activity of Albanian and Armenian

---

[8] Obolensky, *Byzantine Commonwealth* 60–63; Patoura, Σύμμεικτα 8 (1989).

[9] See above, p. 93.

[10] Wolfram, *History of the Goths* 78–79.

Monophysites. Despite both their remoteness and their heresy, these missionaries received considerable support from Constantinople. At much the same time, the Danubian Heruls became Christians and allies. An unsuccessful attempt was also made to convert the Crimean Huns. Heraclius had better luck in making alliance with and propagating Christianity among the Onogur Huns north of the Caucasus. No reader of, for example, Theophylact Simocatta's *Universal history* would be inclined to underestimate the importance of these peoples of the North for Byzantium's security. Under the broadest definition of the First Byzantine Commonwealth, they must be included.

But the definition proposed here is narrower. It is based on two main propositions: first, that Iran was the prime political, military, economic, and cultural threat, the prestige enemy, and that Byzantium therefore attached special significance to the zone directly interposed between itself and the Sasanians;[11] and second, that the sixth-century spread of Monophysitism eventually gave most of the lands from the Caucasus to Ethiopia—the vast mountain-rimmed arena of southwest Asia described in chapter 1—a sense of cultural coherence that marked them off from the world of the northern frontier as much as from the other parts of the empire in which Chalcedon prevailed.

Contemplating this region, the hinge (or better, perhaps, the revolving door) between the Iranian plateau and the eastern Mediterranean basin, which any aspirant to world empire had to control, did Constantine appreciate that the areas in which lay the extreme northern and southern points of contact between Rome and Iran were both dominated by immense, fortresslike blocks of mountains, to the North the Caucasus and Transcaucasia and to the South Yemen and Ethiopia? Did he also understand, perhaps already from his own experience in the Mesopotamian campaign of 297/8, the recurrent character of the problems that Rome and Iran would face in attempting to split the region that lay, with no adequately defensible natural frontiers, between these two mountain blocks? If Constantine ever came to see the problem in these terms, he almost certainly concluded that his best hope of containing, let alone assaulting, Iran was by cultivating his position in the Caucasus and Transcaucasia and in the mountains of Yemen and Ethiopia. Armenia had long been of great military interest to Rome because of its importance to the control of Asia Minor and Syria, while Artaxata in particular was a major center for commercial exchange between Rome

[11] This is not of course to underestimate the role played in Romano-Iranian relations by the more northerly areas discussed in the previous paragraph: Hannestad, *Byzantion* 25–27 (1955–57).

and Iran.[12] The trade route down the Red Sea to India kept southwest Arabia and Ethiopia in mind too. And merchants were ideal carriers of Christianity, which was the most direct channel for introducing Roman political influence.

The likelihood that Constantine was able to see all these factors as part of a single strategic picture is increased by two considerations. In the first place Augustus (of whom Constantine often reminds us) had already seen the need to strengthen Rome's position simultaneously in Transcaucasia on the one hand and in southern Arabia and Ethiopia on the other—regions that contemporaries regarded as something of a unity, because they called "Caucasus" the whole mountain mass that extended southward from the Black Sea toward "India" or Egypt.[13] Augustus strove mightily to keep Armenia in the Roman sphere of influence and impose rulers of his own choice;[14] he also sent military expeditions into southern Arabia and "Ethiopia" (though no further than Napata, at the fourth cataract).[15] Both these expeditions, together with his first intervention in Armenia, took place within a space of six years, 26–20 B.C. Nero too appreciated the strategic importance of Armenia and the upper Nile Valley.[16] Armenians, Arabs, and Ethiopians (the latter two categories admittedly very vague) figure regularly in the principate's propaganda.[17] One might add that the emperors of the late fifth and early sixth centuries were no less aware that pursuit of diplomatic and military equilibrium with Iran presupposed a position of strength in both these regions.[18] And Heraclius owed part of his stunning success against Iran to clever use of routes through Armenia.[19]

Second, other minds besides Constantine's were moving in the same direction. The king of Armenia, for example, had already adopted Christianity and in so doing aligned his people with Rome a decade

[12] *Codex Justinianus* IV.63.4 (A.D. 408/9). For general background, cf. Manandian, *Trade and cities of Armenia*; Garsoïan, *P'awstos Buzand* 448–49.

[13] Braund, in *Defence of the Roman and Byzantine East* 43–46.

[14] Chaumont, *A.N.R.W.* II.9.1, 73–84.

[15] Jameson, *J.R.S.* 58 (1968). On whether Napata was reached, see Török, in *Studia Meroitica 1984* 79–80, with S. M. Burstein's comment in the same volume, 226–27, and Török's reply, 372. There is a possibility that this southward extension of Rome's frontier was of longer-term significance than had been thought: Frend, *Archaeology and history* XXI, but also Anderson, Parsons, and Nisbet, *J.R.S.* 69 (1979): 127; Török, *Studia meroitica 1984* 81–82; Török, in *Nubian culture past and present* 163–66.

[16] Pliny, *Naturalis historia* VI.15.40, 35.181.

[17] E.g., on the Aphrodisias Sebasteion: Smith, *J.R.S.* 77 (1987): 117–20, and 78 (1988): 55.

[18] Hannestad, *Byzantion* 25–27 (1955–57); Rubin, in *Eastern frontier*.

[19] Kaegi, *Klio* 73 (1991): 591, 593.

before Constantine gained control of the Roman East.[20] And the Christian Church under more or less direct Roman auspices and with greater or lesser success became involved at the highest levels of political power in Iberia, southern Arabia, and Aksum, either during or not long after the period in which Constantine ruled the whole empire (324–37). Some of the ecclesiastical historians make a point of grouping together the conversion narratives of Ethiopia and Iberia;[21] while in both those lands, and in southern Arabia, Roman political interests were not only served but also acknowledged.[22]

In short, alongside the more obvious problems that spring to mind in analyzing the Byzantine Commonwealth, such as relations between the center (Constantinople) and the periphery, or between Byzantium's political and cultural universalisms, we should also pay due attention to the two geographical extremities or poles just described, and to their influence on the varying degrees of political and cultural flux that existed in between. This is not to suggest that the extremities were always stable; but Iberia and Armenia on the one hand, and Ethiopia on the other, do happen to have remained Christian cultures until our own day, unlike every other part of the First Byzantine Commonwealth.

IBERIA AND ARMENIA

What then was the role of the Caucasus and Transcaucasia, and specifically of its two main polities, Iberia (Eastern Georgia) and Armenia, in the Byzantine Commonwealth? The Byzantine Commonwealth was generated by a combination of political and cultural universalism, but these two impulses were of unequal intensity. Similarly, Armenia had hitherto enjoyed strong cultural and social links with Iran, but a much more variable political relationship. Its Arsacid royal house was the best illustration of this variability, the incarnation of Iranianism until the Sasanid revolution, and thereafter a bone of fierce contention. We shall see that, for Byzantium too, cultural penetration of Armenia was if not easier then at least more stable than political penetration. But the product of that cultural penetration, Armenian Christianity, was by no means a doublet of Byzantine Christianity.

When they turned to Christianity, Iberia and Armenia had at the same time turned away from Iran toward Rome.[23] Although third- and in-

---

[20] See above, pp. 78–79.

[21] Rufinus, *H.E.* X.9–11; Theodoret, *H.E.* I.23–24.

[22] See above, p. 93; below, pp. 109–112.

[23] For what follows see the survey accounts by Chaumont, *Enc.Ir.* 2.427–33; Lang, *C.H.Ir.* 3.520–36; Frend, *Monophysite movement* 308–15.

deed early fourth-century Armenian Christianity had apparently been subject to influences from Syria, especially Edessa,[24] Gregory the Illuminator was probably raised in the Greek milieu of Cappadocia, and the head or Catholicos of the Armenian Church continued until the 370s to be consecrated at Caesarea. Fourth-century Armenian Christianity was in general deeply impregnated with Cappadocian Hellenism. Partly for this reason, Christianity was slow to take root.[25] Its liturgical language was Greek, and since Armenian was not a written language, Greek or Syriac had to be used for all documents. So the Armenians did not receive Christianity "with understanding as is fitting, with hope and faith, but only those who were to some degree acquainted with Greek or Syriac learning [were able] to achieve some partial inkling of it".[26]

Not surprisingly, both Armenia and neighboring Georgia remained fields of cultural as well as diplomatic and military competition between the two superpowers. Iranian pressure mounted in direct consequence of the humiliating peace imposed on the Romans after the failure of Julian's campaign.[27] Shapur's policy in Armenia was to ban Greek, and covertly to undermine Christianity.[28] Probably in 387, Armenia was partitioned between Iran and Rome on terms advantageous in a proportion of four to one to the former[29]—and so it remained until the repartition of 591. Likewise eastern Georgia (Iberia), which had good communications with Iranian Armenia, gravitated to the Iranian sphere of influence, western Georgia (Colchis/Lazica) to the Roman.[30]

But this blow to the rather notional cohesiveness of the Armenian people, dwellers in a region that, although mountainous and therefore protected, was also vaguely defined and caught between belligerent neighbors, was more than outweighed by the invention under Vramsapuh, who ruled Iranian Armenia from 392 to 415, of an Armenian alphabet. Now the Scriptures and much else could be translated into Armenian, which contributed materially to the spread of Christianity and Greek culture, especially given the tolerant attitude of the Sasanian monarch Yazdagird I. In 428 the Sasanians abolished the Arsacid dynasty of Armenia, and in the 440s they began systematic efforts to

[24] See above, p. 78; Klein, *Constantius II.* 179.

[25] Hewsen, *J.S.A.S.* 2 (1985–86): 25–28; Russell, *Zoroastrianism in Armenia* 126–29.

[26] "Pawstos Buzand", *Epic histories* (late fifth century) III.13.

[27] Ammianus Marcellinus XXV.7.12, XXVII.12.

[28] Moses Khorenatsi (eighth century), *History of the Armenians* III.36 (tr. Thomson 294–95).

[29] Blockley, *Historia* 36 (1987)—and cf. the excellent map of the partition at the end of Garsoian, *Epic histories.*

[30] Isaac, *Limits of empire* 229–34.

repropagate Mazdaism in Armenia, Iberia, and Albania. Resistance to this assault on faith and identity was intense, bloody, and ultimately successful. Pressure applied by the Hephthalite Huns to the Sasanians' northern frontiers in the 480s also helped. But by that time the theological orientation of Byzantium's eastern provinces had already long been in the melting pot. The reason went deeper than purely Christological disagreements such as the Chalcedonian-Monophysite rift. It had to do with the nature of monotheism itself.

Constantine had perceived monotheism as an appropriate creed for an autocrat who aspired to rule the whole world. But the particular monotheism he espoused, Christianity, was as careless about the unity of God, Whom it defined as a Trinity, as Constantine himself was about that of his empire when he divided it among his three sons and his half-nephew Dalmatius. Eusebius must have been aware of the connection between these two problems when he formulated the idea that Constantine's three sons and actual heirs (Dalmatius having been eliminated) were little more than reflectors of their deceased father's heavenly glory.[31] It was in any case inevitable that, eventually, somebody would invoke Trinitarianism to justify division of the empire between two or more rulers, or even the existence of several Christian states.[32] The former argument—that Trinitarianism requires three emperors—is not unattested[33] (though it can hardly be said to have changed the course of Byzantine political thought). And the growing controversies about the nature of Christ, particularly about the relationship between his divine and human aspects, certainly reflected Christianity's ambiguous position on the unicity of God. The political consequences of these controversies are not so easily dismissed. Not only did they destroy the Church's aspiration to be one and undivided; some feared that they might even undermine the security of the empire in the face of the barbarian threat.[34]

But the root of the Christian empire's problems was not Trinitarian or Christological. Islam too, after all, was to be afflicted by heresies. And Islam too was a monotheism, albeit more austere than Christianity. We should consider the possibility that monotheism itself may, under certain circumstances, have divisive effects. For where polytheism diffuses

[31] Eusebius, *Vita Constantini* I.1.

[32] Such was Peterson's thesis, *Monotheismus* 96: "Die orthodoxe Trinitätslehre bedrohte in der Tat die politische Theologie des Imperium Romanum." But cp. the cogent criticisms in Schindler, *Monotheismus* 45, 49, 55–70.

[33] Theophanes p. 352 (under Constantine IV, 668–85).

[34] Ambrose, *De fide* II.16.139: "ibi primum fides Romano imperio frangeretur, ubi fracta est Deo". Likewise Michael the Syrian, *Chronicle* VIII.11 (tr. Chabot 2.88).

divinity and defuses the consequences, if not always the intensity, of debate about its nature by providing a range of options, monotheism tends to focus divinity and ignite debate by forcing all the faithful, with their potentially infinite varieties of religious thought and behavior, into the same mold, which sooner or later must break. Monotheism often (though not necessarily) follows its own internal logic and addresses itself to the whole world, proclaiming universally the One God who is, by definition, potentially knowable to all mankind. That makes it seem like a suitable ideology for universal empire, monarchy, or both. But the progress of its missions cannot be wholly uncoupled from that of intolerance and heresy. Even before the Roman Empire acquired a Christian ruler, Origen had foreseen that, desirable though it might be for all men to follow the same doctrine, they were more likely to do so in the next world than in this.[35]

The doctrinal rigidification we observe in the Church from (at the latest) the fourth century, the vain search for precise definitions guaranteed to exclude old heresies and preclude new, would even so have been slower to set in had it not been for another of Christianity's supposed advantages over polytheism, namely its professional priesthood. When bishops were not coasting from council to council bickering over dogma, they were staying at home making even more trouble by building the sort of local power base that constantly recycled imperial officials had always been—and continued to be—denied.[36] No bishop would use such power to usurp the imperial throne, but he might well exercise in his own town an authority more apparent and forceful than the emperor's. He might promote doctrinal idiosyncrasy too. Some sees accumulated influence that reached far beyond their immediate environs—most notably, Caesarea of Cappadocia, Antioch, and Alexandria. Their position toward the periphery made them ideal powerhouses of mission, but also challengers to Constantinople and to the emperor's authority in matters of dogma. It was not for nothing that the Patriarch of Alexandria came to call himself "Judge of the Universe". At the Council of Chalcedon in 451 Constantinople secured not only the doctrinal definition it wanted but also, by the famous canon 28, the exclusive right to consecrate "the bishops of the aforementioned dioceses [Pontus, Asia, and Thrace] in barbarian parts".[37] This gave Constantinople control over the "barbarians" on Byzantium's northern frontier and in the Caucasus—but im-

---

[35] Origen, *Contra Celsum* VIII.72.

[36] On episcopal power and the growth of regionalism, see Guillou, *Régionalisme* 236–54.

[37] A.C.O. II.1.3, p. 89: τοὺς ἐν τοῖς βαρβαρικοῖς ἐπισκόπους τῶν προειρημένων διοικήσεων.

plicitly left those of the East and South to Antioch and Alexandria. Canon 28 of Chalcedon was, in effect, the Byzantine Commonwealth's legal germ.

In this way Christian Rome paid at the periphery—but sometimes nearer the metropolis, too—for what it gained at the center. Monotheism, though welcome for the divine legitimation it supposedly afforded secular authority, also fostered theological controversy and, in effect if not of necessity, a secular extension of priestly authority. The physical distance between Constantinople and the eastern frontier was compounded by differences in mentality and eventually in doctrine. Secession from the empire was not an issue, much less "nationalism"; but whereas once the periphery had defined itself in a vague relationship *with* a weak center, through the general compatibility and mutually reinforcing effect of the various polytheisms, and through the specific action of the emperor cult, much of it came under the Christian empire to define itself *against* a strong center, through "heresy" or, rather, varieties of "orthodoxy", a notion that had been superfluous in polytheism. The emergence of Monophysite Armenia is a characteristic example of this process.

Long-standing links with Syriac Christianity, together with ambiguities generated by the combination of political dependence on Iran and religious kinship with Constantinople, initially favored the influence in Armenia of Antiochene diphysite theology and its leading exponent, Nestorius.[38] But Nestorianism's growing success in Iran made it seem less attractive to Armenians. The pro-Byzantine element in the Armenian Church secured recognition of the Council of Ephesus (431), which had condemned Nestorius. But the Armenians played no part at Chalcedon (451)—they were that very year fighting for their lives against Iran, having been refused help from Constantinople. Once forced to accept that Armenia was Christian, the Sasanians continued to favor the Syriac orientation and Antiochene theology that were now dominant among their own Christians. Wanting on principle none of that, and disposed by religious temperament but also by political tensions with Constantinople against Chalcedon's compromise language about Christ's two natures inseparably united, the Armenians were eventually to choose the third way: Cyril of Alexandria's insistence that the one incarnate nature of Christ is divine, "out of two natures" but not "in two natures", the doctrine scholars call Monophysitism.[39] The

[38] Winkler, *R.E.Arm.* 19 (1985).

[39] Frend, *Monophysite movement*, provides the best account of the rise of Monophysitism, summarized in his *Rise of Christianity*, esp. 837–48, 873–77. Note that, in connection with Monophysitism, contemporaries used the vocabulary of dissidence rather than of irreversible doctrinal otherness: Frend, *Monophysite movement* xiii, 144, 187.

chronology of the gradual process by which in the course of the sixth century Armenia officially rejected Chalcedon is murky; but the "Pancaucasian" First Council of Dvin set the tone in 506 by proclaiming the allegiance of the Armenian, Iberian, and Albanian hierarchies to the councils of Nicaea and Constantinople and condemning Nestorianism along, less directly, with Chalcedon, deemed Nestorian.[40]

In late antiquity the Armenians lost their political independence and saw their country split in two by an international frontier. At the same time they gained a new cultural-religious persona that, placing them within the Byzantine world, albeit for the most part beyond the Byzantine frontier, sustained until our own day an Armenian identity proof against the worst that Byzantium, Iran and eventually the world of Islam could do. These parallel developments reflect both the difficulties and the advantages of a particular geographical position—the Armenians were caught between superpowers but protected by their mountains from total external domination. We find a somewhat similar situation in the mountains of southern Arabia and Ethiopia.

SOUTHERN ARABIA AND ETHIOPIA

In marked contrast with their immediate environs, and especially with the arid wastes of northern and central Arabia, southern Arabia and Ethiopia were both fertile, sedentary, and civilized regions, whose peoples had long-standing links and perhaps some sort of common political identity during the third century and possibly intermittently in the fourth and fifth as well.[41] They were also linked with the Mediterranean world of Rome by the Red Sea trade routes, which probably recovered somewhat in the fourth century from the doldrums of the third.[42] The region's interest for Rome lay in its control of the route to India and its strategic proximity to Iran. Shapur II, in particular, resorted to arms to assert his position in Arabia,[43] and so perhaps did Constantine.[44] Such intervention became all the more pressing because shortly before the end of the third century the various kingdoms of southern Arabia united under the leadership of Himyar and began to extend their activities into desert Arabia. What we for convenience call the Himyarite state had become a regional power to be reckoned with.[45]

[40] Zekiyan, R.E.Arm. 16 (1982).

[41] Munro-Hay, Aksum 61–66, 71–79, 81, 85.

[42] Sidebotham, in L'Arabie préislamique 222–23.

[43] Bosworth, C.H.Ir. 3.603; Crone, Meccan trade 46–50 (on Iran in Arabia up to the rise of Islam).

[44] According to Shahîd, B.A.FO.C. 31–72.

[45] Robin, in Arabian studies.

This was the background against which Constantius sent Bishop Theophilus, a native of an island called Dibos, which scholars identify with the Maldives, Socotra, or various places in or near the Persian Gulf, to the Himyarite ruler.[46] The ecclesiastical historian Philostorgius reports that Theophilus was supposed to convert the Himyarites, which would obviously have been a politically useful thing to do; but he probably made little impression, because there is no evidence for the permanent installation of Christianity in southern Arabia at this period. The three churches Theophilus built may therefore have been used only by Roman merchants and a small group of native converts, but they were all sited for maximum political effect: one in Zafar, the capital; one in the strategic port of Aden near the mouth of the Red Sea; and one near the approaches to the Persian Gulf. An imperial constitution dated 356, forbidding ambassadors "to the people [singular] of the Aksumites and the Himyarites" to stop over in Alexandria for more than a year, suggests that diplomatic contacts were not uncommon at that time.[47]

Continuing his journey, Theophilus made his way to "India" (which may conceivably mean eastern Africa), in order to inspect and where necessary correct the beliefs and rites of its Christian communities. Theophilus was not the first distinguished Roman representative to visit "India" for reasons other than commercial. One of his more recent predecessors had been, in the reign of Constantine (presumably after 324) or possibly of Constantius, an apparently Christian "philosopher" from Tyre called Meropius.[48] On the way home Meropius perished on the Ethiopian coast. His two young companions (and, it seems, relatives), Aedesius and Frumentius, found their way to the court of Aksum at the far northern extremity of the Ethiopian plateau. Mani had regarded Aksum as one of the world's four great empires, and it had benefited from the power vacuum created in the Red Sea by Rome's third-century crisis.[49] Aksum was the next greatest power in Africa after Rome, like both Rome and Iran enjoyed a substantial sphere of influence in Arabia, and like Rome, Iran, and Kushan minted gold coins. The court was sophisticated; Greek was in use there; and the country was also host to a Syrian community.[50] For Greeks and

[46] Philostorgius, *H.E.* III.4–6; Klein, *Constantius II.* 217–27; Fiaccadori, *S.C.O.* 33 (1983): 34 (1984); Shahîd, *B.A.FO.C.* 86–106; Dihle, in *L'Arabie préislamique.* The chronology is controversial. For a general survey of Christianity in Himyar, see Müller, *R.L.A.C.* 15.303–31.

[47] *Codex Theodosianus* XII.12.2.

[48] On Meropius, Aedesius, and Frumentius, see Rufinus, *H.E.* X.9–10; Klein, *Constantius II.* 238–50; Thelamon, *Païens et chrétiens* 37–83; also Dombrowski and Dombrowski, *O.C.* 68 (1984), emphasizing the Ethiopic sources' value.

[49] *Kephalaia* 77, and in general, Munro-Hay, *Aksum.*

[50] Shahîd, *B.A.FO.C.* 91.

Romans Ethiopia may have been the edge of the known world, but it does not seem to have been an entirely barbaric land. Frumentius found favor there and acquired influence, which he used on behalf of Christianity, known to Aksumites as the religion of the Roman merchants who passed their way.

The ecclesiastical historian Rufinus, on whom all later accounts depend, does not go so far as to claim that the ruler of Aksum became a Christian, and the earliest Christian Aksumite coins and inscriptions remain hard to date.[51] What does seem increasingly likely, though, is that Ezana, a powerful and epigraphically well-documented king of Aksum at this period, issued gold coins adorned with a cross at a weight used before Constantine's currency reform, while another such issue by Ezana weighs less, apparently to bring it into line with Constantine's solidus.[52] This implies some degree of official, if not necessarily popular, Christianization already in the time of Constantine or soon thereafter. Thanks to a letter addressed to him by Constantius (see below), we know that this Ezana was the ruler with whom Frumentius dealt. Clearly he was sympathetic to Christianity. In his inscriptions we see him moving from polytheism to monotheism, and then (arguably) to explicit Christianity; and he allowed Frumentius to return to the Roman Empire and request a bishop for the Christian community in his kingdom. The tactful next move for a newly converted ruler was to send an official embassy to the Roman emperor, like the one the Iberian king had sent when he converted,[53] asking for priests and, it seems, some form of political alliance. But Aksum was at a safer distance from Rome, and Ezana knew very well how to feign ignorance of what Rome expected.[54]

Frumentius's request for a bishop may in any case have been his own, not the king's, initiative. Wanting no dealings with the Arian Constantius, Frumentius went instead to Athanasius of Alexandria, who consecrated Frumentius himself and no doubt rejoiced exceedingly at this addition to his sphere of influence. When Constantius discovered this he sent Ezana a letter in which he demanded that Frumentius be sent back to Alexandria for reeducation and reconsecration by the Arian Bishop George (356–61). Although Theophilus visited Aksum on his way back from "India" and there too "put things [ecclesiastical][55] in

[51] Thelamon, *Païens et chrétiens* 75–83; Dihle, in *L'Arabie préislamique* 463–68 (against whom see Munro-Hay, *Rassegna di studi etiopici* 32 [1988]: 126–27); Török, *Late antique Nubia* 37–38 (against whom see Munro-Hay, *Aksum* 205–6).

[52] Munro-Hay, *Aksum* 189–90, 205–6.

[53] See above, p. 93; and cp. also Rufinus, *H.E.* XI.6, on the Saracen Queen Mavia's request to Valens for a bishop.

[54] Athanasius, *Apologia ad Constantium Imperatorem* 31.

[55] Such is Philostorgius's implication, since his whole emphasis is on the ecclesiastical character of Theophilus's mission.

order", he can hardly have been the bearer of Constantius's letter. Embassies to the Aksumites were not uncommon, and Constantius's communication was too important and urgent to be delivered via Himyar and "India".

Constantius's letter is of interest to us because it contains a particularly strong statement of Byzantine universalism:

> It is altogether a matter of the greatest care and concern to us, to extend the knowledge of the supreme God; and I think that the whole race of mankind claims from us equal regard in this respect, in order that they may pass their lives in accordance with their hope, being brought to the same knowledge of God, and having no differences with each other in their inquiries about justice and truth. Therefore considering that you are deserving of the same provident care as the Romans, and desiring to show equal regard for your welfare, we bid that the same doctrine be professed in your churches as in theirs.[56]

The relationship between the cultural-religious and the political components of the Byzantine Commonwealth—from the Constantinopolitan point of view—is here perfectly exposed: to accept Christianity is to acknowledge Constantinople's spiritual authority, and such acknowledgment gives the emperor the right of reprimand, even if the other party is safely beyond direct political or military interference. But though Constantius's letter is a fine theoretical statement of Byzantine universalism, it probably undermined the progress of Christianity in Aksum.

Both Aksum and southern Arabia, then, may not have been much Christianized at all before the fifth century. It seems there was a Christian and eventually mainly a Monophysite presence in southern Arabia from the early fifth century,[57] while the general Christianization of Aksum may have been stimulated by Monophysite missionaries from Egypt and Syria, beginning perhaps quite soon after the Council of Chalcedon.[58] In the 520s Aksum imposed a Christian ruler on Himyar.[59] That Monophysitism rather than Chalcedonianism became at this time

---

[56] Quoted by Athanasius, *Apologia ad Constantium Imperatorem* 31 (tr. Stevenson, *Creeds, councils and controversies* 34–35).

[57] Shahîd, *B.A.FI.C.* 149, 360–81.

[58] Frend, *Monophysite movement* 304–8; Engelhardt, *Mission und Politik* 128–47; Rubin, in *Eastern frontier* 394–97; Lepage, *C.R.A.I.* (1990), esp. 822. Jerome, *ep.* CVII.2, remarks that "Ethiopian" monks are a familiar sight in Palestine. Theodoret of Cyrrhus, *Historia religiosa* XXVI.1, asserts that Simeon the Stylite was famous in "Ethiopia".

[59] See below, p. 115.

5. The Nine Saints, Monophysite
missionaries in fifth-century Aksum.
Magic scroll, early nineteenth century,
from the Tigre region of Ethiopia.

the dominant form of Christianity in both Ethiopia and southern Arabia
draws attention to the crucial role played by Monophysitism in the
formation of the Byzantine Commonwealth, but also to the commonwealth's scope for independence or, from Constantinople's viewpoint,
disloyalty.

In the case of Aksum, Monophysitism combined with a strong local
tradition and a geographical position at once strategic and safely remote
from both Byzantium and Iran to provoke a counterclaim to universal
authority. Such at any rate is Irfan Shahîd's attractive interpretation of
Ethiopia's national epic, the *Kebra Nagast* or *Glory of kings*, on the
assumption that its original form goes back to the sixth century and the

reign of the Negus Ella-Asbeha or Kaleb.[60] The *Kebra Nagast* depicts Kaleb as a righteous Christian king, a crusader against the Jews, who travels to Jerusalem to meet the Emperor Justin and agrees with him to partition the *oikoumene* between Ethiopia and Byzantium.[61] But Ethiopia is superior to Byzantium—the Negus is descended from Solomon's firstborn, while the Byzantine emperor can claim only a younger son as ancestor;[62] and Byzantium, having deviated from (Monophysite) orthodoxy, will be destroyed by Iran, while Ethiopia will endure forever.[63] That this prophecy is placed in the mouth of Saint Gregory the Illuminator, the apostle of Armenia, is remarkable testimony to the sense of cultural cohesion and shared tradition that, thanks in large part to the mediating role of Syria,[64] might unite even the remotest extremities of the Byzantine Commonwealth. The implication both of Saint Gregory's appearance and of the division of the world between Byzantium and Ethiopia is that Ethiopia is the protector of the Monophysite world, itself more or less coterminous with the Byzantine Commonwealth.

Kaleb's hour of greatest glory in this international role came, as duly "foreseen" by the prophetic author of the *Kebra Nagast*,[65] when he had to step in to defend the Monophysite Christians of Himyar just across the Red Sea.[66] Christianity was never more than patchily spread in southern Arabia, mainly on the coast and in certain inland areas such as Najran. But the Najrani community contained Arabs from northern Arabia (Hira) and subjects of Rome, Iran, and Aksum, as well as Himyarites.[67] This microcosm of the Byzantine Commonwealth was prominent enough to attract the hostility of the sizable Jewish community; and about the year 518 a Jew called Joseph or Dhu Nuwas became ruler of Himyar. Probably Dhu Nuwas regarded Judaism as a means to

[60] Shahîd, *Byzantium and the Semitic Orient* X, omitting reference to Mani's much earlier assertion that Aksum was one of the world's four great empires: *Kephalaia* 77.

[61] *Kebra Nagast* 19–20, 117.

[62] Ibid., 20, 95.

[63] Ibid., 93, 113, 116.

[64] Syrian influence on Armenia: see above, pp. 78, 104–5. Syrian influence on Ethiopia: Ullendorff, *Ethiopia and the Bible* 55–62; Kaplan, *Monastic holy man* 16–17; Cowley, *Ethiopian Biblical interpretation* 375–76; Lepage, C.R.A.I. (1990). On the role of both Syria and Ethiopia in the formation of the Armenian alphabet, see Olderogge, *IV cong.int.st.etiop.* Iberians, Armenians, and Himyarites at Simeon the Stylite's pillar: Theodoret of Cyrrhus, *Historia religiosa* XXVI.11.

[65] *Kebra Nagast* 116–17.

[66] On sixth- and seventh-century southern Arabia, see Pigulewskaja, *Byzanz auf den Wegen nach Indien* 175–271; Shahîd, *Martyrs of Najrân*; Rubin, in *Eastern frontier*; and, on the chronology, de Blois, *Arabian archaeology and epigraphy* 1 (1990), and Shitomi, *Orient* 26 (1990).

[67] *Book of the Himyarites* p. 14b.

mark political distance from Byzantium, for he was resolved to terminate the constant interference in Himyarite affairs of what we must admit, despite the *Kebra Nagast*, to have been Byzantium's satellite, Ethiopia. "This was an unprecedented confrontation between Judaism and Christianity as two state religions, a confrontation unique in the history of the Near East."[68] Hoping that not only the pro-Sasanian Lakhmid Arab ruler of Hira, but also perhaps Iran itself, would come to his assistance, Dhu Nuwas began a persecution of his Christian subjects that culminated in notorious massacres at Najran in 523. But Dhu Nuwas's diplomatic initiatives came to nothing, while the Himyarites appealed to Aksum and Byzantium too, doctrinal differences being subordinate to an issue of life or death. The Emperor Justin, though a Chalcedonian, was no less a realist, and well aware of the Byzantine Commonwealth's potential usefulness on the strictly political level. Together with the (Monophysite) bishop of Alexandria, Justin encouraged Kaleb to invade—and the *Kebra Nagast* to take (eventually) its high view of Ethiopia's role in the world. Dhu Nuwas was defeated and killed in the first encounter with the Aksumites, as they were landing from their ships (ca. 525–27).

Kaleb's victory ensured that for the next half-century southern Arabia would remain either more or less an Aksumite protectorate,[69] but in any case with a Christian ruler. It was wide open now to further Christianization, initially under Monophysite but subsequently perhaps also Chalcedonian auspices: Arethas and the other martyrs of Najran were adopted as saints of the Chalcedonian Church.[70] Himyar became an additional though weak and usually quite unhelpful ally in Byzantium's power play with Arabs and Iranians within the great Mountain Arena that defined the Byzantine Commonwealth. In an inscription dated 542, King Abraha boasts of having received ambassadors from Aksum, Byzantium, Iran, and the Arab rulers of the Lakhmids and Ghassanids.[71]

The *Life of S. Gregentius*, parts at least of which go back to the sixth century, asserts that a not otherwise known Chalcedonian bishop of that name drew up a law code for Himyar, the *Laws of the Himyarites* (*Leges Homeritarum*). Though there is much that is suspect in this *Life*, and no external evidence that Gregentius's laws were ever used, the code's exaltation of the Byzantine-appointed bishop's authority over that of the

---

[68] Shahîd, *Byzantium and the Semitic Orient* X.148.

[69] Abel, *IV cong.int.st.etiop.*

[70] Engelhardt, *Mission und Politik* 171–73; Shahîd, *Byzantium and the Semitic Orient* IX; Shahîd, *Martyrs of Najrân* 206–7.

[71] *C.I.S.* 4.541.

king, together with the mixture of Byzantine and local elements in the legislation it contains, perhaps indicates what sort of society Himyarites who looked to Byzantium aspired to create.[72] It is interesting also to note that the city of Sana was adorned with a fine church said to have been built by artisans and with mosaic and marble sent from Constantinople, and apparently related in design to the Aksumite churches of the period.[73] But not long after 570, Khusrau I contrived to expel the Aksumites and bring southern Arabia once more into the Sasanian sphere of influence, where it stayed until the rise of Islam. Like other peripheral areas of the Byzantine Commonwealth such as Armenia, Himyar could quite easily float from one political bloc to the other. But its Christian communities were still there when the Muslims arrived and transformed both the political and the cultural landscape—indeed, they survived at least until the tenth century.[74]

NUBIA

Aksum's newly acquired but self-confident Christian identity was projected not only eastward into Himyar but also northward into Nubia, a land that, though probably to some extent familiar with Christianity, was not yet Christian.[75] We know that missionaries were sent into Nubia from Aksum; but they were in competition with others, Chalcedonian as well as Monophysite, sent at the initiative of Justinian and Theodora respectively. These latter missions resulted in the conversion of Nubia to the Egyptian brand of Monophysitism, as distinct from the Syrian-influenced doctrines that prevailed in Ethiopia. John of Ephesus's account of the conversion underlines the Monophysites' proclamation that "the true God is one and there is no other god but he".[76] This made a deep impression on people who, as John of Ephesus has the Nubian king remark, did not wish to abandon their old gods merely to fall into a similar error. That the Chalcedonian missionaries got so unsympathetic a reception was probably due in part to the difficulty of explaining how they differed from the Monophysites. Diphysite theol-

[72] Pigulewskaja, *Byzanz auf den Wegen nach Indien* 201–10; Patlagean, *Structure sociale* XIII.593 n. 43, and "Addenda" p. 3; Shahîd, *Byzantium and the Semitic Orient* IX.33–35; Papastathis, *Graeco-Arabica* 4(1991).
[73] Serjeant and Lewcock, *Ṣanʿāʾ* 44–48.
[74] Ibid., 45, 47.
[75] On Nubian Christianity, see Frend, *Monophysite movement* 297–303; Shinnie, in *Cambridge history of Africa* 2; Vantini, *Christianity in the Sudan*; Krause, in *Nubian culture past and present*; Scholz, A.W. Sondernummer (1987): 131–45; Török, *Late antique Nubia* 69–73.
[76] John of Ephesus, *H.E.* III.4.7.

ogy was much less straightforward than the Monophysites' proclamation that Christ is God. Obviously there were political considerations as well; the choice between two different imperially sponsored deputations cannot have been easy. But the beautiful simplicity of monotheism, a crucial advantage in the mission situation, perhaps weighed in favor of the Monophysites.

The evangelization of Nubia was part of an extraordinary Monophysite missionary effort that transformed the ecclesiastical map of the Byzantine East between the 520s and the 570s. The Council of Chalcedon defined for all time the theological stance of the Byzantine center, despite such early hesitations as the attempt of Zeno (474–75, 476–91) to impose a compromise formula, or Anastasius's open support of Monophysitism, at least at the end of his reign (491–518). But the theological definition Chalcedon offered was heavily influenced by Constantinople's wish to keep in step with Rome, which always followed a two-nature Christology. The price of this tribute to the West, to the old Roman ideal of a single Mediterranean world, was the alienation of the East—and so of any prospect of world empire. By excluding them, Chalcedon gave impetus and sharper profile to the two doctrines, Monophysitism and Nestorianism, that did so much to focus the Byzantine Commonwealth's self-awareness.

Growing Chalcedonian harassment of Monophysites under Justin and Justinian met with a striking response: expansion. There are parallels here with Manichaeism, which must have derived some of its missionary impetus from the adversity of persecution. There is the same fallout from the tensions of the Fertile Crescent onto neighboring regions. Once again, the cultural and linguistic diversity of the Fertile Crescent helped its products project themselves. Monophysitism was not just Syriac or Coptic but Greek too, and therefore international.[77] The full story of the Monophysite missions of John of Ephesus and Jacob Baradaeus in Asia Minor, and of their sequel, has yet to be told.[78] John was supported by Justinian himself, even though the emperor usually backed the Chalcedonians; but such ambiguities could not last forever. The Monophysite communities of Asia Minor largely disappear from view after the 580s; clearly they were absorbed by the official Chalcedo-

[77] John of Ephesus, *Lives of the Eastern Saints* XLIX, p. 493; and X, p. 155, on the linguistic skills of the Monophysite bishop Simeon of Beth-Arsham, whose career encapsulates the whole historical conjuncture here described: cf. Shahîd, *Martyrs of Najrân* 159–79. The parallels between Simeon and Mani, both ardent emulators of Paul, are striking.

[78] See, e.g., Engelhardt, *Mission und Politik* 12–22a; Roueché, *Aphrodisias in late antiquity* 144–46; Haldon, *Byzantium* 338–40.

nian Church after the first generation or two. But further from Constantinople the Monophysite missions were more durable.

In the case of Nubia it was not, as in Asia Minor, Syria, and Egypt, just a matter of superimposing a Monophysite hierarchy on a map the imperial Church had already Christianized. Nubia was almost virgin soil so far as the Gospel was concerned—and fertile soil too, since Nubian Christianity was not finally extinguished by Islam until the fifteenth or sixteenth century. Given the difficulty of communicating with Constantinople through Muslim Egypt, Christian Nubia retained a striking cultural Byzantinism.[79] Greek remained in use at the court and, as late as the thirteenth century, for at least parts of the liturgy. Official titles followed Byzantine models; so did ecclesiastical art, though naturally there were influences from Coptic Egypt too. A certain conservatism that has been observed in some of the medieval Greek texts found at Qasr Ibrim is just what one would expect in a culture cut off from its paradigm; but there is also evidence that points the other way, toward direct and possibly quite frequent contact, perhaps also with non-metropolitan centers of Hellenism such as Sinai or Jerusalem. Indeed, since Greek also continued to be used well into the Islamic period by the Monophysite Church of Egypt,[80] we should perhaps regard late Nubian Hellenism as a function of Greek culture's role as common denominator within the Byzantine Commonwealth rather than as proof of direct contact with the metropolis.

Whatever the final resolution of these ambiguities, the recent excavations at Faras and Qasr Ibrim have shown with unparalleled vividness what the First Byzantine Commonwealth could mean, even once the attention of the Byzantines themselves had shifted to the emergent Christian lands of Eastern Europe, the Second Byzantine Commonwealth. The Arab invaders of Egypt failed fully to subdue Nubia, and instead made a treaty with it, giving it an anomalous position stranded between the Dar al-Islam (House of Islam) and the Dar al-Harb (House of War). Nonetheless, Nubia's isolation from the Christian world outside the Islamic Empire, and its lack of the protection afforded by still more remote Ethiopia's distinctive relief, made its eventual Islamization inevitable. The mountains of Ethiopia and Transcaucasia certainly gave the Byzantine Commonwealth its best hope of longevity. Nubia, strung out compactly but less defensibly along the Nile, may be said to have

---

[79] Frend, *Archaeology and history* XVI.359–60, XIX–XX; Donadoni, in *Nubische Studien*; Zaborski, *Nubische Studien* 407–8; Frend and Dragas, *Jb.A.C.* 30 (1987); Frend, *Jb.A.C.* 32 (1989); Innemée, *Jb.A.C.* 32 (1989).

[80] MacCoull, *D.O.P.* 44 (1990): 39–40.

reached middle age; so too may the peoples of the Fertile Crescent, whose Christianity, more or (as time went by) less Byzantine, survived long but unconvincingly, and still hangs on in the mountains of Lebanon and in the cities, which after the mountains have always been the best place for minorities to hide. But beyond the Fertile Crescent lay the Syro-Arabian desert and its Arab tribes, cousins of the Fertile Crescent's Semitic populations. These Arabs were the Byzantine Commonwealth's case of infant mortality—or rather, they were the uncontrollable child who destroyed the parent.

THE ARABS

Like the Iberians and Armenians, the Arabs were caught up in the terrible tensions of the superpowers; unlike the mountain-dwellers, they enjoyed little natural isolation or protection.[81] Indeed, unlike all the other elements in the Byzantine Commonwealth, they were of no fixed address. The desert was theirs in the winter, and no Roman or Iranian dared venture into it. The summer desert, though, was intolerable, even to the Arabs, who were forced out into symbiosis with the Fertile Crescent. And to the extent that desert and sown generated different life-styles, there emerged in Syria-Mesopotamia a two-speed Byzantine Commonwealth, the tribes of the desert more independent than the mixed Semitic and Greek peoples of the Fertile Crescent, who drifted with greater gradualness away from the Byzantine center. Yet the enforced interaction of desert and sown underlines how relative was the freedom of the desert tribes. The Fertile Crescent as a whole was incapable of autonomous action. Admittedly local powers within the region, such as Palmyra, might in extremis act on their own. And nothing was more common in late antiquity than for an Arab potentate dissatisfied with Iran to treat with or even transfer his allegiance to Rome, or vice versa.[82] This could on rare but gratifying occasions lead to spectacles such as that offered by the conference at Ramla (near Hira) in 524, when ambassadors from the Byzantine emperor, the King of Kings, the Monophysites of Iran, the Chalcedonians of Iran, the Nestorians, the Jewish ruler of Himyar Dhu Nuwas, and a Christian south Arabian ruler too (possibly an Ethiopian) all begged the Lakhmid Arab ruler, Mundhir

---

[81] On the Arabs in late antiquity see Sartre, *Trois études*; Shahîd, *B.A.FO.C.*; Shahîd, *B.A.FI.C.*; Shahîd, *Enc.Is.²* 2.1020–21, 5.632–34; also Matthews, *Ammianus* 342–55; Peters, *Annales archéologiques arabes syriennes* 27–28 (1977–78); Trimingham, *Christianity among the Arabs* (to be used with caution).

[82] Malchus fr.1 (Müller; Blockley); Letsios, in *L'Arabie préislamique*.

ibn Numan, to intervene on their side in the crisis created by Dhu Nuwas's massacre of the Najrani Christians.[83] Writing of the Byzantine-Iranian conflict under Anastasius, Joshua the Stylite remarked that "to the Arabs on both sides this war was a source of much profit, and they wrought their will upon both kingdoms".[84] From as early as the third century the various tribes of the Syro-Arabian desert were beginning to form confederations and in this way strengthen their bargaining position vis-à-vis their neighbors. This is part of the remoter background of the Islamic conquests in the seventh century. But in the intervening centuries the Arabs were more often just buffers between the super-powers, their rulers serving or surviving only at their patron's pleasure.

This tension between autonomy (or the desire for it) and influence exercised from outside the region also underlies the history of Christianity among the Arabs. When in the reign of Valens Queen Mavia brought what was probably a confederation of Syrian Arabs into conflict with the Romans, she used the military advantage she gained in order to force the emperor to give her a particular bishop she wanted, a non-Arian by the name of Moses who refused to accept consecration from the officially approved hierarchy. This is our earliest substantial evidence of Christianity among the Arab tribes.[85] Yet this display of independence only underlined how spiritually dependent the Arabs were on Constantinople. The spiritual dependence was used to intensify their political dependence too,[86] and turn them against Iran.[87]

From the first half of the fifth century, Nestorian Christianity began to spread among the Lakhmid Arabs on the lower Euphrates (though Monophysitism too made some headway among them). From the 540s the Ghassanid Arabs of the western areas adopted Monophysitism. Both tendencies marked a kind of independence vis-à-vis Constantinople. In the vast area under Ghassanid control, for example, Monophysites were relatively safe from imperial persecution. But the Arabs were not all "independent" in the same way, and this only made it easier, in the long run, for the great powers to exploit them strategically. The Monophysites—at least those who lived within the Roman sphere—confirmed once more the commonwealth's political usefulness by remaining loyal to Constantinople. The Nestorians cooperated with Iran, though Iran also courted its own Monophysite Arabs by encouraging,

---

[83] Shahîd, *Byzantium and the Semitic Orient* VI; Shahîd, *Martyrs of Najrân* 120 n. 3.

[84] Joshua the Stylite, *Chronicle* 79 (Wright), p. 302 (Chabot).

[85] Rufinus, *H.E.* XI.6; Sozomen, *H.E.* VI.38.1–9; Matthews, *Ammianus* 350–51. On bishops of the Arabs before Moses, see Shahîd, *B.A.FO.C.* 330–40.

[86] Sozomen, *H.E.* VI.38.9 (καὶ διαλλάξας αὐτοὺς Ῥωμαίοις).

[87] Ibid., VI.38.16.

for example, the construction at Qasr Sarij, just east of Jabal Sinjar, of a martyrium for the Arabs' favorite saint, Sergius.[88] This was supposed to rival the Sergius cult at Sergiopolis-Rusafa on Roman territory, though Khusrau II became a patron of that sanctuary too, dedicating there various gifts including sacred vessels and "a gem-studded cross made of gold", as thank-offerings for Sergius's assistance in both love and war.[89] In ways such as these the superpowers either poached each other's allies or enjoyed the luxury of war by proxy, especially in the long reigns of those two inveterate enemies, Harith ibn Jabala the Ghassanid (529–69) and Mundhir ibn Numan the Lakhmid (503–54). But as soon as Emperors Maurice and Khusrau II decided they could do without the Ghassanids and Lakhmids, great-power treachery brought these tribal federations down.

The history of the next half-century showed that neither Iran nor Rome was capable of filling the vacuum alone. Once they had exhausted each other in the attempt, the Arabs themselves came up with a solution nobody had thought of before. If the center, the desert enclosed by the Fertile Crescent, could not be controlled from its peripheries, how about controlling the peripheries from the center? What actually happened was not in fact quite such a neat inversion. Mecca and Medina themselves belonged to the urbanized, mercantile periphery; but the manpower they drew on was that of the desert. Not so much by inverting the traditional domination of desert by sown as by coordinating what had hitherto seemed, at least to the "civilized", barely compatible ways of life, and by simultaneously exchanging their superficial Christianity for a new faith born in their midst, the Arabs realized, for the first time since Cyrus, the dream of world empire.

CHRISTIANS OF IRAN AND BEYOND

Beyond the international frontier and yet, as far as their Mesopotamian heartland was concerned, still within the great Mountain Arena of southwest Asia, lay the Christians of Iran. Iranian Christianity was part of the Byzantine Commonwealth's context—it was even, in a sense, its "might have been".[90]

Automatically suspect because of its presumed and indeed demonstrable links with the rival empire, the Christians of Iran earned the

---

[88] Oates, *Northern Iraq* 106–17.

[89] Theophylact Simocatta, *Historia universalis* V.1.7–8, V.13–14.

[90] On Christianity under the later Sasanians, see, e.g., Spuler, in *Handbuch der Orientalistik* I.8.2; Asmussen, *C.H.Ir.* 3.942–48; Morony, *Iraq* 332–83, 620–32 (bibliography).

Mazdean state's toleration by self-consciously marking themselves off from Rome. In the decades after Chalcedon, Nestorianism was being progressively excluded from its west Syrian heartland. In 489 the Nestorian School of Edessa, the Antiochene theology's powerhouse, was finally liquidated and removed to Nisibis on Sasanian territory.[91] The Synods of Beth Lapat in 484 and Seleucia-Ctesiphon in 486 became, at least in the eyes of posterity, a milestone in the Nestorianization of the Church in Iran[92]—and allegiance to Nestorius allowed Iranian Christians to proclaim themselves un-Roman with a clear conscience.[93] Indeed, Timothy I, Catholicos of the Nestorian Church from 780 to 823, was to go so far as to assert the see of Ctesiphon's primacy over the patriarchates of Rome, Alexandria, Antioch, and Constantinople. He offered five reasons that perfectly illustrate how such universalist claims grew out of the conviction of those who lived in the Fertile Crescent that their land was the world's center. These reasons were: the East had been honored above all other lands; the Garden of Eden, which was the terrestrial reflection of the Kingdom of Heaven, had been situated there; Nimrod had been the first man to wear a crown; Christ's ancestors according to the flesh, notably Abraham, had come from there; and the East in the shape of the Magi had embraced Christianity before the rest of the world.[94] By Timothy's day, the Nestorian Church's extraordinary expansion into Asia had fulfilled some of Constantine's wildest dreams, but at the cost of the Constantinian vision of an indissoluble Church-state alliance. Unencumbered by Rome, Nestorianism had spread fast; but unsupported by Rome, or by any other Christian state, it enjoyed a relatively brief history as a world religion.

The leaders of the Nestorian Church, well aware of the interdependence of culture and politics, cultivated good relations with the King of Kings, calling him a new Cyrus and praying for the extension of his empire across the whole world.[95] Their community acquired official status; many of its members obtained honor and even power. But they did not supplant Mazdaism as the religion of state. They had to compete with a growing and vigorous Monophysite community. And the coming of Islam gradually reduced the relative security and steady stream of

[91] Vööbus, *School of Nisibis* 30–56.

[92] Fiey, *L'Eglise en Iraq* 113–20; Gero, *Barṣauma* 94–95.

[93] Michael the Syrian VIII.14, XI.9 (tr. Chabot 2.123–24, 437–38); John of Ephesus, *Lives of the Eastern Saints* X, p. 142. There remained a few "Orthodox", especially prisoners of war and their descendants, who depended on the Patriarch of Antioch: Dauvillier, *Eglises orientales* XVI; Nasrallah, *Proche-Orient Chrétien* 25 (1975), 26 (1976). And the Monophysites soon began to make some headway: Morony, loc. cit.

[94] Catholicos Timothy I, *ep.* 26.

[95] Chabot, *Synodicon orientale* 69–70, 131, 563.

converts the Nestorian Church had benefited from under the later Sasanians.

The Nestorians' famous Asiatic missions were some compensation for these obstacles and losses.[96] Beginning in the fifth century, they had extended their diocesan organization eastward from their Mesopotamian heartland, as far as Afghanistan and India. They are first attested at the Chinese court in 635, and built up a considerable presence in China that lasted until the ninth century, and revived again under Mongol patronage in the thirteenth and fourteenth centuries. Christianity never attracted many of the Chinese themselves, and it remained a religion of foreigners; but the Nestorian *Drang nach Osten* was undeniably the most successful attempt ever made to evolve an indigenous Church in Central Asia. Compared to Mazdaism, a national rather than universalist and proselytizing religion, Christianity must also have seemed well suited to Sasanian imperial pretensions. Khusrau II, already sympathetic to Christianity, recognized this in a most remarkable way. He conquered so much of the Byzantine East that he came nearer than any other Sasanian ruler to reestablishing Cyrus's world empire. Yet when he took Edessa, for example, and wished to weaken its citizens' allegiance to Constantinople, the religion he offered them was non-Chalcedonian Christianity—either Nestorianism or Monophysitism.[97] Mazdaism was not even an option. Once the Sasanian state collapsed under the assault of Islam, it gradually became apparent that the Iranian gods had little staying power even among the Iranians themselves. Now, with southwest and parts of central Asia united under Arab rule, there were Nestorian churches from the Yemen and Syria to China.[98]

Yet Iranian Christianity too failed in the long run, and again for a political reason—because it never found a patron to replace Rome.[99] Cultural universalism, carried in the minds of men, could spread more easily than political universalism, but bore within itself a fatal weakness, once it was divorced from political power. Nestorianism acquired considerable influence in the Mongol elite, to the point that Hulagu the conqueror of Baghdad (1258) and his wife Doquz Khatum could be greeted by some Oriental Christians as the new Constantine and

---

[96] Spuler, in *Handbuch der Orientalistik* I.8.2; Enoki, in *L'Oriente cristiano*; Dauvillier, *Eglises orientales*; Klimkeit, *Begegnung* 11–20.

[97] Agapius of Manbij, *Historia universalis* pp. 198–200.

[98] Tisserant, *Dictionnaire de théologie Catholique* 11.192; Fiey, *Assyrie chrétienne* 3.230; Schick, *Christians in Palestine* 291–93.

[99] The Chinese Nestorians' habit of calling themselves "Ta-ch'in" (East Romans) was clearly a device to distinguish themselves from competitors, not an assertion of political identity: cf. Enoki, in *L'Oriente cristiano*, 71–77; Lieu, *Manichaeism* 232–33.

Helena.[100] But Hulagu, unlike his wife, was not a Christian, nor did the Mongols ever officially adopt Christianity. On the contrary, they were very soon, at the end of the thirteenth century, to become Muslims. The Nestorian empire of Prester John was a mirage, a twelfth-century European fantasy.[101] Prester John was the mythical incarnation of precisely that universal Christian empire that had been Constantine's ideal, toward whose realization the Nestorians so energetically strove, and to whose unity and, ultimately, survival Christian schism, Mazdean Iran, Buddhism, and Islam posed successive obstacles.

THE POLITICO-CULTURAL ENTITY

From Iberia to Ethiopia, "in the lands of the Romans, the Persians, the Indians, the Kushites, the Himyarites and the Armenians" (as Michael the Syrian puts it in describing the spread of the Julianist version of Monophysitism),[102] the First Byzantine Commonwealth's constituent parts can now be seen to have shared certain historical experiences. These bear some recapitulation, in the course of which we will more clearly perceive how this common past evolved into a shared cultural and even political identity.

What we know about early Edessene and Armenian Christianity indicates that the Byzantine Commonwealth was already emerging before the explosion of energy unleashed by Constantine when he not only became a Christian himself but dared also to dream of a Christian world empire. Indeed, remoteness from the capital and dangerous proximity to Iran had always imposed a degree of self-reliance on Rome's eastern provinces, even when they had ceased being client kingdoms. Palmyra had shown herself ready in the third century to assume Rome's mantle in the wider region.[103] Edessa, whose last native prince is attested as late as 240,[104] gained wide cultural influence by its early espousal of Christianity, as is already apparent from Eusebius on the Abgar letter. And once the imperial center subjected itself to a faith it had neither created nor

---

[100] Stephen Orbelian, *History of Siounia* pp. 234–35, quoted by Runciman, *History of the Crusades* 3.304. Fiey's notion (*Muséon* 88 [1975]: 59–64) that Constantine and Helena are represented in a thirteenth-century North Mesopotamian Gospel book (Vat. syr. 559, fol. 223 v.: photograph in Nasrallah, *Proche-Orient Chrétien* 26 (1976), facing p. 24) with the facial features of Hulagu and Doquz Khatum ignores a wider tendency in this area and period to use a "Seljuk" style for royal figures: Nassar, in *Syria and the Jazīra* 85–88.

[101] Beckingham, *Between Islam and Christendom* I, II.

[102] Michael the Syrian IX.30 (tr. Chabot 2.251).

[103] Potter, *Prophecy and history* 152–53.

[104] Teixidor, *C.R.A.I.* (1990).

assimilated, loyalty to Rome's god began to count for as much as loyalty to Rome itself. What if Rome should diverge from the path of "true belief"? The capital's transfer from the Tiber to the Bosphorus already demonstrated that Romes might be multiplied, according (among other factors) to the shifting geography of faith and, naturally, of local self-interest. The Byzantine Commonwealth was no less the product of provincials' mimicry of the center and awareness of their personal, vertical relationship with God, than of imperial impetus and missionary monotheism, universalism's horizontal plane. And all this was of course still truer of those Christians who lived beyond Rome's frontiers. But rather than pursuing provincial viewpoints in all their particularity, in the present chapter I have preferred to ease exposition by concentrating on common denominators and on identities, such as Ethiopia's, that were widely projected.[105]

By the death of Valens in 378, the First Byzantine Commonwealth had been sketched along the empire's eastern and southeastern frontiers from Iberia and Armenia in the North via incipient alliances with the tribes of the Syro-Arabian desert down to the kingdom of the Himyarites and Aksum. Sometimes the empire supported these missions, though it perhaps did not need to: subsidies are more easily withdrawn than is monotheism.[106] In any case, Rome seems quite quickly to have lost sight of Constantine's vision of mission as part of a coherent political design. The ecclesiastical historians were aware of their interrelatedness,[107] but more within the context of the Gospel's spread than that of Rome. It is striking, for example, how often the ecclesiastical histories represent captives, especially captive women, as responsible for the Christianization of peripheral regions, not only before Constantine's reign,[108] but during and after it too.[109] This is a topos the degree of whose historical accuracy or romantic inventiveness is less interesting than the proof it offers that the missionary process

---

[105] Further investigation of the sociopolitical structure of and competing power centers within kingdoms such as Aksum or Armenia would reveal the distinctiveness in local situations that complemented the structural similarities highlighted in this essay. This is material for future studies, passed over here for the sake of brevity and clarity.

[106] I owe the formulation to Peter Brown.

[107] E.g., Rufinus, *H.E.* X.9–11; Sozomen, *H.E.* II.6–8; Theodoret, *H.E.* I.23–24.

[108] Sozomen, *H.E.* II.6.2.

[109] Rufinus, *H.E.* X.9–10 (Aksum), 11 (Iberia); John of Nikiu, *Chronicle* LXXVII. 106–8 (Yemen, "India"); Theophanes p. 64 (Arabs). See also, on the role of the Hripsimian maidens in the conversion of Armenia, Hewsen, *J.S.A.S.* 2 (1985–86): 19, 21–22, 24; also al-Tabari, *Tarikh* I.919–22 (tr. Nöldeke 177–82) on Najran. Theophilus was sent to Himyar by Constantius, but he had converted to Christianity when a hostage at the Roman court: Philostorgius, *H.E.* III.4.

could be seen in a humble and evangelical as well as an aggressive and imperial context. The development even of this modest and informal substitute for world empire was impeded not only by the inner tensions of Christianity, as in the case of Frumentius, but also by the growing disunity and eventual division of the empire: Greek East and Latin West began to go their separate ways. The long and unhappy divorce was not reversed even by Justinian's attempt to regain the West, which was itself delayed by the need to square accounts with Iran first. The eastern empire could not operate effectively on both fronts at once. Nonetheless, merely being Christian implied, in the East, a political orientation toward Constantinople. In this respect the First Byzantine Commonwealth was a notable innovation in international relations. Shared culture or religion, provided its identity was strong and clear enough, as Christianity's certainly was, now created a presumption of common political interest even in the case of populations far beyond the borders of the Roman Empire. That had never been true of Hellenism, for example. The Christians of Iran discovered by bitter experience how difficult it was to counter such a presumption, once it was established.

With the reaction to Chalcedon and the spread of Monophysitism not only in fringe areas such as Georgia, Armenia, the Syro-Arabian desert, southern Arabia, Ethiopia, and Nubia, but also in the core regions of the Byzantine world, Egypt, Syria, and even, if only for a few decades, Asia Minor and Constantinople,[110] the Byzantine Commonwealth assumed a clearer identity. In particular, the two-speed Byzantine Commonwealth of the western Fertile Crescent on the one hand and the Syro-Arabian desert on the other, the former traditionally much more closely tied to Byzantium than the latter, acquired through Monophysitism a greater sense of homogeneity and common interest. Nonetheless, the reaction to Chalcedon's overzealous attempt to define Christianity for all the peoples of the empire crystallized slowly. If from the 530s the emergence of a parallel Monophysite hierarchy made schism virtually irreversible, that was in response to the fierce repression unleashed by Justin and Justinian, as well as in order to ensure that the growing mass of the faithful in Asia Minor, Syria, and Egypt could receive the sacraments from the hands of bishops and priests who believed as they did. The attempt to find compromise formulas to reconcile Chalcedonians and Monophysites remained one of Byzantium's highest political priorities up to the Arab conquests. Even Justinian contrived, through his wife Theodora's patronage of their movement, to prevent the Monophysites from feeling excluded from the empire. As late as the reign of Heraclius

---

[110] On the role of Constantinople, see Frend, *Monophysite movement* 288–93.

6. Solidus of Heraclius, Heraclius Constantine, and Heraclonas, 632–38.

there was still room to maneuver. The Monophysites, although most of them were by then irreconcilable to Chalcedon, no more wished to leave the empire than Constantinople dreamed of expelling them. After all, it was the Monophysites who preached one-nature Christology, which meshed much better than Chalcedon's apparent dualism with Constantine's belief in one god, one empire, and one emperor.[111] It was not only the Monophysites who were to blame for undermining the universalist dream.

The Byzantine Commonwealth's identity was twofold, political and cultural, Roman and Christian. But as it came gradually under the influence of Monophysitism, the commonwealth substituted a more specifically Constantinian and Nicaean persona for generalized identification with Rome and the Church.[112] In practice this meant that the Byzantine Commonwealth, or at least the part of it that lay within the Byzantine frontier, stayed loyal to the throne, however bitter the condemnation of some of its occupants: "Some [Egyptians] said: 'The death of Heraclius is due to his stamping the gold coinage with the figures of

[111] Michael the Syrian, *Chronicle* VIII.14 (tr. Chabot 2.122), abuses Marcian for dividing the empire in just the same way as he did the faith, at Chalcedon.

[112] See, e.g., Severus of Antioch, *Hymni* 200–203 (in praise of four special emperors: Constantine, Gratian, Theodosius, and Honorius). On Ethiopia's reverence for Constantine see *Kebra Nagast* 93; Budge, *History of Ethiopia* 1.261, and cf. Shahîd, *Byzantium and the Semitic Orient* IX.64 (the Negus Ella-Asbeha/Kaleb also called Constantine and David); Nikolaos, Metropolitan of Aksum, Διάσκεψις 32, 56, 95 (the Emperor Haile Selassie hailed as the Constantine of the Monophysite world at the conference of Monophysite hierarchs he himself summoned to Addis Ababa in 1965). See also *History of the Patriarchs of Alexandria* p. 394, on the early eighth-century Nubian king Mercurius, "who was called the New Constantine". On Nicaea: see above, p. 109; "Sebeos, *History of Heraclius*" 46 (tr. Macler 116); *Letter of Pisentius* p. 320; Frend, *Monophysite movement* 20, 138; Nikolaos, Metropolitan of Aksum, Διάσκεψις 32, 56, 90.

the three emperors—that is, his own and of his two sons on the right hand and on the left—and so no room was found for inscribing the name of the Roman Empire.'"[113] Likewise the Councils of Constantinople (381) and Ephesus (431) remained acceptable, even when Chalcedon was excoriated.

This situation is reflected, naturally enough, in the Monophysite and Nestorian collections of Church canons.[114] Closely associated with this literature,[115] we also find the so-called Syro-Roman law book, the *Laws of Constantine, Theodosius, and Leo*. Originally compiled in Greek in the fifth century, the *Laws* present themselves as Christian Roman law, and allude in text as well as title to Constantine, Theodosius (I or II?), and Leo, though they draw on pre-Constantinian legislation too,[116] and at one point refer by name to Diocletian.[117] At some point before the end of the seventh century,[118] the *Laws* were translated into Syriac, and eventually also into Armenian, Georgian, and Arabic.[119] Their wide dissemination in both the Monophysite and the Nestorian spheres provided a body of practical law,[120] and a powerful symbol not only of the Byzantine Commonwealth's shared culture but also of its prestigious relationship to the Byzantine center. Yet the legal tradition the *Laws* reflected was that which existed before the hated Justinian's reforms. The *Laws* were conspicuously not the *Justinianic Code*.[121]

If they wished to resolve their disagreement with Constantinople while maintaining the alliance of throne and altar, which was as crucial for them as for the Chalcedonians, the Monophysites had only two options. Either, as had seemed increasingly possible under Anastasius,

[113] John of Nikiu, *Chronicle* CXVI.3 (tr. Charles). Cf. Hahn, *Moneta Imperii Byzantini* 3.85–88 and pl. 2–3.39–53; and plate 6.

[114] Selb, *Orientalisches Kirchenrecht*. The canons of Chalcedon were sometimes included for the sake of their disciplinary content (2.103–4).

[115] Ibid., 1.63, 2.129–30.

[116] Selb, *Bedeutung* 220.

[117] *Leges Constantini Theodosii Leonis* R II, §151 = Sachau pp. 134–35; L, §121 = Bruns and Sachau pp. 33 (text), 37 (tr.). These allusions are important because they prove that the Syro-Roman law book was *known* to be Roman, unlike the closely related *Sententiae syriacae*, whose sources are Roman but never named: cf. Selb's edition, 87.

[118] Kaufhold, in *Akten des 26. Deutschen Rechtshistorikertages* 511–18.

[119] See the *Bibliography*.

[120] Crone, *Roman, provincial and Islamic law* 12 and 119 n. 121, arbitrarily asserts that the *Leges* were never applied, but designed only "to refute Arab accusations to the effect that Christianity had no law". Their wide dissemination argues against this, as do the Armenian and Georgian translations.

[121] The translator's preservation of the *Leges*' attribution to Leo (457–74), who was no paradigm of orthodoxy for non-Chalcedonians, may indicate a later date, when memory of this emperor's exact identity had faded; but it is also compatible with a date in the first half of the sixth century, more credit being assigned Leo for having lived before Justinian than discredit for postdating Chalcedon.

the imperial Church and consequently the emperor too would accept Monophysite theology, thus transforming the establishment from within, or there would have to be a new Monophysite empire on at least some of the territory traditionally ruled from Constantinople. The *Kebra Nagast* propounds the latter solution; but such radicalism came more easily to Ethiopians who had never been part of the Byzantine Empire than to people who, whatever their theological differences, had always been Rome's loyal subjects. All they could do was pray

> for the prosperous life of the kings, that they may reach a great age; and for the devout Caesar, that God would continue to preserve him; and that every barbarian nation, unto the ends of the earth, may be in subjection under their hands; and that the whole world may become one body; we begging God the Christ that He will speak unto his [altered from "their"] heart for the peace and concord of the holy apostolic Church, that we may pass a quiet and still life and be found in all piety and holiness, by the grace and loving kindness and mercy of the great God, Our Savior Jesus Christ Our Lord.

The words are those of Damianus, Monophysite Patriarch of Alexandria (578–607), in the synodical letter by which he announced his election.[122] Similar formulas were used by Chalcedonian bishops.[123] The universalist dream was the same, even if the theology was different.

In the absence of a Monophysite empire, only Monophysite dogma was left as a common denominator. When John of Ephesus speaks of the Monophysite world as "the *politeia* of the party of the believers",[124] he means more than just a Church but less than an empire, though the context concerns the Empress Theodora's patronage of Monophysitism. "Commonwealth" seems to be the translation that best conveys the mix of cultural-religious and political connotations. Another leading Monophysite missionary, Simeon of Beth-Arsham, was in the habit of extracting statements of belief from the Monophysite communities he visited and keeping them together on "great linen cloths" specially treated to preserve them; "and above the belief he affixed the seals of the king of that people and of the bishops of the same and of their chief men in lead upon these cloths, and thus confirmed it", lest anyone try to bring in alterations.[125] Simeon's collection of cloth creeds was reas-

---

[122] Crum and Evelyn White, *Monastery of Epiphanius* 2.148–52 (text), 332–37 (tr.). Peter Brown kindly supplied this reference. On Damianus, see Müller, O.C. 70 (1986).

[123] E.g., Sophronius of Jerusalem, *Epistola synodica ad Sergium Patriarcham Constantinopolitanum* 3197–3200.

[124] John of Ephesus, *Lives of the Eastern Saints* XLIX, p. 490.

[125] Ibid., X, p. 156 (tr. Brooks).

suringly tangible proof that the Monophysite world was indeed one; but there will certainly have been far more episcopal seals than royal ones, and none of them prevented doctrinal disputes, such as those that nourished the thirty-year schism between the Syrian and Egyptian hierarchies in the late sixth and early seventh centuries, with Patriarch Damianus as one of the protagonists.[126] The coexistence in the Monophysite world of two patriarchates of equal rank, Alexandria and Antioch, was always an obstacle to ecclesiastical unity.

Only beyond the Byzantine frontier could Monophysites aspire to mold distinctive political entities under Monophysite princes. In this direction the First Byzantine Commonwealth did acquire independent political as well as cultural identity; but in describing it we must show sensitivity to its many modalities.[127]

Granted the obscurity of Himyar's brief mid-sixth-century history as a Christian state, and our ignorance of events in Nubia between its conversion to Christianity and the arrival of the Arabs at its borders, we must turn to the Ghassanid Arabs and Aksum if we are to glimpse something of what it meant to be a Monophysite polity. When, for example, the King of Kings imprisoned a number of leading Monophysite clerics at Nisibis in the 520s, it was the king of Aksum, probably Kaleb himself, who secured their release through ambassadors he sent to the Iranian court.[128] One of the prisoners was Simeon of Beth-Arsham, who had written to Kaleb about doctrinal matters and considered this document significant enough to merit circulation among his episcopal colleagues.[129] From the 540s onward the Ghassanid ruler Harith ibn Jabala also became personally committed to Monophysitism and actively protected its representatives, who in turn publicly recognized Harith's political suzerainty and used him as a mediator in their internal disputes.[130] The distribution of Monophysite monasteries suggests that they tended to be built near the residences of the Ghassanid princes.[131] But these princes were neither strong enough nor sufficiently independent of Rome to develop a distinctively Monophysite foreign policy. Such a stance is, though, attributed to sixth-century Aksum in the Ethiopian national epic, the *Kebra Nagast*.

---

[126] Meyendorff, *Imperial unity* 254–58, 268–70, 274–76; Müller, O.C. 70 (1986).

[127] Cp. Obolensky's comments on the difficulty of defining the Second Byzantine Commonwealth: *Byzantine Commonwealth* 1–2.

[128] John of Ephesus, *Lives of the Eastern Saints* X, pp. 152–53; Shahîd, *Martyrs of Najrân* 162.

[129] Simeon of Beth-Arsham, *Letter G* IXB.

[130] Chabot, *Documenta* 143–44, 197–98, 199, 202, 205–6.

[131] Sartre, *Trois études* 183–86.

In the form in which we have it, the *Kebra Nagast* is a much later composition. But the idea that Aksum as a strong Christian state could become a foundation or at least a buttress of Christian world empire is clearly implicit in Justin's incitement of Kaleb to invade Himyar.[132] All the *Kebra Nagast* does is present that basic idea from an explicitly Monophysite point of view. That this point of view, together with the reaction it inevitably evoked in Chalcedonian circles, was already there in the sixth century, one can easily see by comparing the Monophysite and Chalcedonian accounts of the martyrdoms of Najran. While the Syriac *Book of the Himyarites*, for example, presents Kaleb as the protector and liberator of his fellow Monophysites, the Greek *Martyrdom of Arethas* reduces Kaleb's role in the suppression of Dhu Nuwas and magnifies that of Byzantium.[133] In the seventh century, power in Ethiopia passed from Aksum to other centers farther south. But whether or not the Ethiopians themselves still had the resources for a decisive Monophysite-oriented foreign policy at this period, the Syriac *Apocalypse of Pseudo-Methodius* indicates that elsewhere the idea continued to be conjured with, and opposed.

The *Apocalypse of Pseudo-Methodius* was written in northern Mesopotamia between the Arab conquest and the end of the seventh century.[134] The writer interprets Psalm LXVIII.31 ("Kush will hand over the hand [i.e., dominion] to God", in Ps.-Methodius's version) explicitly in order to exclude an exegesis favored by certain (clerical?) opponents to the effect that "the blessed David spoke his word concerning the kingdom of the Kushites",[135] that is, the Monophysite kingdom of Ethiopia, and perhaps that of Nubia too.[136] (Just at this time, in the 680s, the Monophysite Patriarch of Alexandria, Isaac, was mediating between Nubia and Ethiopia.)[137] Ps.-Methodius explains that "Byzas King of the Greeks . . . took Kusheth, daughter of King Pil of the Kushites. And there was born to him from her a daughter, and he named her Byzantia because of the name of the city that he built. . . . And the offspring of Queen Kusheth, daughter of Pil king of the Kushites, possessed the kingdom of the Macedonians and Romans and Greeks."[138]

[132] See above, p. 115.
[133] Shahîd, *Martyrs of Najrân* 203–5.
[134] Alexander, *Byzantine apocalyptic tradition* 13–33; Suermann, *Reaktion* 159–61; Reinink, in *Byzantine and early Islamic Near East*. I am grateful to Gerrit Reinink for providing an advance copy of his article.
[135] *Apocalypse of Ps.-Methodius* 126ʳ (tr. Alexander 42).
[136] The LXX has Αἰθιωπία. "Kush" might mean either what we call Nubia or what we call Ethiopia, especially since the Greeks called Nubia Ethiopia.
[137] *History of the Patriarchs of Alexandria* p. 278.
[138] *Apocalypse of Ps.-Methodius* 125ʳ-126ʳ (tr. Alexander 41–42).

Accordingly, "the kingdom of the Greeks, which is from the seed of the Kushites, will hand over the hand [i.e., dominion] to God at the end of times."[139] This is the second prong of Ps.-Methodius's thesis, a firm rebuttal of any notion that Ethiopia-Nubia and the Byzantine Commonwealth will take the lead in destroying the empire of the Ishmaelites. That honor is reserved for Orthodox Byzantium, whose rule will embrace all Christian peoples, including the Monophysites. Ps.-Methodius himself may therefore have been either a Chalcedonian, a Nestorian, or a realistic Monophysite.[140]

What is most significant in the present context, though, is that Monophysite political pretensions were still thought worth refuting in Ps.-Methodius's milieu. Our author has the king of the Greeks "go forth against them [sc., the Arabs] from the sea of the Kushites".[141] After his victory there will be peace and prosperity. Then will come fearsome invaders from the North; and when the king of the Greeks has disposed of them too, he will go to Jerusalem and place his crown on the Holy Cross at Golgotha and hand over his kingship to God the Father in fulfillment of "the saying of the blessed David which he prophesied concerning the end of times".[142] We are reminded of how, in the *Kebra Nagast*, Kaleb and the Emperor Justin travel to Jerusalem and there divide the world between them.[143] The *Kebra Nagast* likewise, as one would expect, has much to say about Psalm LXVIII.31, and a considerably more literal interpretation than that of Ps.-Methodius. In short, it seems highly likely that Ps.-Methodius wrote his *Apocalypse* in response to some early version or at least antecedent of the Ethiopian national epic.[144] Muslim writers confirm Ethiopia's hold on the imagination at this time. They make much of a letter in which the Negus Abraha gave the impression of being disposed to accept Islam at Muhammad's per-

[139] Ibid., 126ʳ (tr. Alexander 19).
[140] On "Melkites" in Iran before and after the Arab conquest, see above, p. 122 n.93.
[141] *Apocalypse of Ps.-Methodius* 133ʳ (tr. Alexander 48). Martinez, in *IV symposium syriacum* 348, suggests that this reference to the "sea of the Kushites" betrays a desire for a Byzantine-Ethiopian alliance.
[142] *Apocalypse of Ps.-Methodius* 135ᵛ (tr. Alexander 50).
[143] See above, pp. 113–14.
[144] This point was noted briefly by Shahîd, *Byzantium and the Semitic Orient* X.174–76, and Alexander, *Religious and political history and thought* XI. Reinink, in *Byzantine and early Islamic Near East* (and cf. Reinink, *B.Z.* 83 [1990]: 44 n. 96), dismisses Ethiopia's pretensions as "obscure" and denies that Ps.-Methodius responds to them, but has no explanation for early Islamic preoccupation with Ethiopia (see next note). Reinink rightly emphasizes Ps.-Methodius's conciliatory, ecumenical aspect, imposed by the new threat from Islam, but he did not need to deny the element of polemic against those more extreme Monophysites who opposed political alliance with Constantinople. The one does not exclude the other, and both intentions seem to me to be present. The Monophysite community was far from monolithic.

sonal invitation,[145] a sort of Islamic Abgar-legend reflecting a sense that the birth of religions is better adorned by somewhat noncommittal kings than by no kings at all.

Within the Christian empire's frontiers it was much more difficult for Monophysites to bring themselves into sufficient political focus to deserve full membership in the Byzantine Commonwealth. Political separatism, Syrian or Coptic "nationalism", cannot convincingly be shown to have formed part of their agenda.[146] And in the more peripheral areas a desire for greater political freedom might even dictate loyalty to Byzantium, for the sake of protection against overbearing neighbors. The effectiveness of this policy depended on Byzantium's ability or, preferably, inability to supervise one's daily doings as well as defend one's frontiers. Nowhere is it more difficult to sort out motives or judge the effectiveness of policies than in the Caucasus and Transcaucasia. In the aftermath of Maurice's favorable settlement with Iran in the treaty of 591,[147] it was not surprising that the Church in those parts of Armenia regained from Iran should briefly revert to Chalcedon; its bishops had little choice.[148] But when in the first decade of the seventh century the Iberian Church too parts company with Armenian Monophysitism and affirms allegiance to Chalcedon, we may reasonably suspect that this is a response to Byzantium's once more *waning* military strength—a desire, in other words, for breathing space more likely to be had in alliance with the Church of distant Constantinople than with that of adjacent Armenia.

The problem for those caught between the two superpowers, Rome and Iran, was how to maximize choice. Probably this was what lay behind the loyalty of the Church in Iranian Armenia to the non-Christian Sasanians,[149] but also the omission of the rulers of the Lakhmid Arabs, allies of Iran, to follow their people and become Christian, until the end of the sixth century.[150] The greater the number of apparent contradictions one introduced into one's position, the wider the choice of exits from the tight corners in which one was bound to find oneself. As Immanuel Wallerstein has observed: "Universalism is a 'gift' of the powerful to the weak which confronts the latter with a double bind: to refuse the gift is to lose; to accept the gift is to lose. The only

---

[145] Raven, *J.S.S.* 33 (1988).

[146] Moorhead, *Byzantion* 51 (1981), presents some of the arguments against Monophysite nationalism. But alienation there was, at least in the seventh century; see below, p. 135.

[147] Zekiyan, *R.E.Arm.* 16 (1982); "Sebeos, *History of Heraclius*" 3 (tr. Macler 27).

[148] Garsoian, *Armenia* IX.223–28.

[149] Ibid., VIII, IX—brilliant studies of the Byzantine Commonwealth at its most complex.

[150] Morony, *Iraq* 375–76.

plausible reaction of the weak is neither to refuse nor to accept, or both to refuse and to accept—in short, the path of the seemingly irrational zigzags (both cultural and political) of the weak that has characterized most of nineteenth and especially twentieth-century history."[151] One of the themes of the Byzantine Commonwealth's history is precisely this interplay between the search for cultural identity and the longing for political allies or protectors. It is striking, for example, how Armenian writers loved to draw parallels between their people's struggles and those of the Jews, especially the Maccabees; while at one stage the Himyarites, caught between Byzantium and Iran, actively espoused Judaism.[152] Monophysite Christianity compensated up to a point for this sense of isolation, giving the Armenians a context, a reassuring sense of not being alone in the world, that the Jews lacked. The Byzantine Commonwealth helped too—though its development was spread out over a longer period of time, and more ambiguous, than that of Monophysitism, which was enshrined in formulas, incarnated in preachers, and sheltered in church buildings.

We should not search, then, for any neat definition of the Byzantine Commonwealth. We may take our cue from what I have already described as the Byzantine Commonwealth's legal germ, Chalcedon's canon 28, which gave Constantinople the right to consecrate bishops "in barbarian parts" of the dioceses of Pontus, Asia, and Thrace.[153] What this meant has been endlessly debated—areas conquered by the barbarians, or ecclesiastical jurisdictions established beyond the frontiers? The ambiguity was no doubt intended, and reflected the Byzantine center's awareness of how difficult it was to circumscribe the periphery. So we had better define the First Byzantine Commonwealth loosely and negatively—as those parts of the Byzantine Empire and of other lands inhabited by Eastern Christians whose population was *not* (as in Palestine) mainly composed of Chalcedonians loyal to the Byzantine emperor. These populations may in turn be divided into four main categories. First, there was a leavening of Chalcedonians.[154] Second, there were non-Chalcedonians—not only Monophysites but Nestorians too, until their removal to Iran—who dwelt on indisputably Byzantine territory, wanting nothing to do with Chalcedon but loyal nonetheless to the emperor. Third, there were non-Chalcedonians dwelling in disputed or vaguely allocated lands such as Armenia or the Syro-Mesopotamian desert, who as Christians felt some theoretical preference for Rome but

[151] Wallerstein, *Geopolitics and geoculture* 217.
[152] Thomson, in his edition of Elishe, *History of Vardan and the Armenian War*, 9–16; Shahîd, *Byzantium and the Semitic Orient* VI; Rubin, in *Eastern frontier* 401–3.
[153] Quoted above, p. 107; cf. Dagron, *Naissance* 483–84.
[154] Moorhead, *Byzantion* 51 (1981): 580–82.

understood that they were more likely to preserve their version of Christianity inviolate either as more or less independent allies of Constantinople (the Ghassanid Arabs) or under Iranian rule (Armenia). Fourth, there were non-Chalcedonians who lived indisputably beyond the Byzantine frontier, were loyal subjects of the King of Kings or whatever other prince had jurisdiction over them, and invoked the Byzantine connection only if it suited and did not threaten them. To assert that any one of groups two to four was more typical of or pivotal to the Byzantine Commonwealth than the others would imply a formality or clarity of self-definition that the Commonwealth never possessed. It was a wide and varied spectrum. But non-Chalcedonianism, especially Monophysitism, was a common denominator—Chalcedonians leavened the mix, were even in a sense its raison d'être, but were also very much "the other".

The Byzantine Commonwealth's political aspect was diverse and fluctuating. But the early seventh century saw a gradual change in the political attitudes of many of Byzantium's Oriental subjects. They began to acquire a clearer sense of the limits of Byzantine power, but also a greater sensitivity to its encroachments and abuses. The campaigns of Khusrau II and Heraclius reopened in spectacular fashion the whole question of frontiers and allegiances. For a time the Sasanians absorbed most of the Byzantine East. A generation grew up that had known only their rule. Then Heraclius struck back, right into the Sasanian heartlands. The old lines of political demarcation could already be seen to be crumbling, before the Arab armies appeared. It was only natural that the Byzantine Commonwealth *intra fines* should at such a juncture come into clearer focus as a political as well as a cultural entity, especially when Constantinople began to repress the newly reconquered populations. "The hostility of the people to the Emperor Heraclius, because of the persecution wherewith he had visited all the land of Egypt in regard to the orthodox faith",[155] made the Muslim conqueror seem, at least to some, a tolerable alternative.[156]

So it fell to the Muslim conqueror to realize fully the Byzantine Commonwealth's political potential—but not as a Byzantine Commonwealth. To the extent that Monophysite political ambitions still lingered after the rise of Islam, they did so beyond the Muslim frontiers. If they impinged on the Islamic Empire, it was only briefly or symbolically. A mid-eighth-century king of the powerful and civilized kingdom of Nubia undertook a campaign in Egypt to protect the Copts against their

---

[155] John of Nikiu, *Chronicle* CXV.9 (tr. Charles); cf. LXXI.2.

[156] Frend, *Archaeology and history* XVI, XVIII. Note especially, for Syria, Michael the Syrian's bitter comment, *Chronicle* XI.3 (tr. Chabot 2.413).

rulers,[157] while in 835–36 King George of Nubia visited Baghdad in order to regulate a dispute about the treaty between the Islamic Empire and Nubia.[158] During the long and arduous journey, George and his retinue were received with royal honors and greeted with emotion by their coreligionists, who had never in their lives set eyes on a Christian monarch, much less a black Christian monarch. King George rode a camel and was sheltered by a richly decorated dome-shaped parasol surmounted by a golden cross. In one hand he held a scepter, in the other a cross. Before him rode a bishop; beside him marched young Nubians, all carrying crosses of gold. At Baghdad he was received with unusual ceremony. Wearing a crown surmounted by a cross, he approached the Caliph al-Mutasim, who was seated on a throne of exceptional magnificence, and a lavish exchange of gifts underlined the mutual esteem of the two states, Muslim and Christian. Mar Dionysius of Tell Mahre, the Patriarch of Antioch, journeyed to Baghdad specially to meet the Nubian king and celebrate the liturgy. One could scarcely imagine a more vivid yet fleeting symbolic evocation of the Byzantine Commonwealth—two centuries exactly after the armies of Islam had entered the Fertile Crescent.

Even less is known of Ethiopia than of Nubia in this period, but we have seen that the Monophysite Patriarch of Alexandria, Isaac (686–89), mediated between their kings, with what hopes (beyond aggrandizement of his see) we can only guess; while the *Apocalypse of Pseudo-Methodius*, and the *Kebra Nagast*'s steady accretion over the centuries, illuminate Ethiopia's ambitions even if achievement lagged far behind. In similar vein, Coptic Christians hymned the Nubian king as crowned from heaven and lord of everything as far as the earth's southern extremities, including Ethiopia (unless by that term is meant southern Nubia).[159] Some even envisaged the emperor of Rome's conversion to Monophysitism by the Ethiopian monarch.[160]

Cultural and primarily religious links between the Monophysite communities—such as those between Alexandria and Ethiopia or Alexandria and Antioch[161]—proved more durable. Still wider links are sug-

[157] *History of the Patriarchs of Alexandria* pp. 398–99 (using, as is clear from this passage, a contemporary albeit excitable source, identifiable as John the Deacon's *Life* of Patriarch Michael I: Den Heijer, *Mawhūb* 145–46).

[158] *History of the Patriarchs of Alexandria* pp. 617–21; Michael the Syrian, *Chronicle* XII.19; Vantini, in *Kunst und Geschichte Nubiens*.

[159] *History of the Patriarchs of Alexandria* pp. 399–400.

[160] *Letter of Pisentius* (an at latest tenth-century Arabic translation of a lost Coptic original: Abdel Sayed, *Pesyntheus* 10, 295–98) pp. 320–21. For more recent expressions of the unity of the Monophysite world, see Shahîd, *Byzantium and the Semitic Orient* X.157 n. 56.

[161] *History of the Patriarchs of Alexandria* pp. 621–22.

gested by the cultural Hellenism of medieval Nubia. A shadow of this world still lingers today. It has somewhat the aspect of the Marib dam, which once nourished the Monophysite kingdom of Himyar until—in the time of Muhammad, appropriately enough—the waters swept it away, leaving a wide and empty wadi. Of the dam itself there survived only the two great bastions on the rocky heights to the North and South, just as today Transcaucasia and unhappy Ethiopia, in their mountain fastnesses, are (along with the Copts) the only substantial remnants of the Oriental Christian world of which they were once but the extremities. As recently as 1965, the Ethiopian Emperor Haile Selassie summoned and, as "Defender of the Faith", presided over a gathering at Addis Ababa of the heads of all the Monophysite Churches, which he intended as a first step toward the reunion of the Chalcedonian and non-Chalcedonian communions.[162] The Byzantine Commonwealth is more interesting, though, as precursor than as survivor. If through dialogue with Hellenism the Oriental polytheisms had acquired greater self-awareness and a common frame of reference,[163] Oriental Christianity had in a much more profound, formative way found its true self in dialogue with Greek Christianity. From Georgia and Armenia to southern Arabia and Ethiopia, Monophysitism had become a fertile shared spiritual ground and a community, the Byzantine Commonwealth. Within that community one is struck by the growing importance of southerly regions such as Arabia and Ethiopia.[164] Then Khusrau II demonstrated that the political reunification of the eastern Mediterranean and Iranian spheres was once more a practical option. To an extraordinary extent, both culturally and politically, Islam and its empire was already implicit in late antiquity.[165] It is the obverse of the remark by the scholar Qatada b. Diama, who died in 117 of the Muslim era, that before Islam the Arabs were "confined on top of a rock between (the two lions) Faris and Rum".[166]

[162] Nikolaos, Metropolitan of Aksum, Διάσκεψις.

[163] See above, pp. 58–59.

[164] Emphasized by Shahîd, *Martyrs of Najrân* 172 n. 2. Southern Arabia in particular is largely ignored in Frend's *Monophysite movement*.

[165] Becker, *Islamstudien* 1.17–18. Crone and Cook, *Hagarism*, have little to say about Monophysitism as a unifying factor, but perceive that "from the point of view of the Arabs, the provincial character of the culture they encountered rendered it less overpowering—it was in this respect wise to conquer Syria without Byzantium, much as it was prudent to take Spain without Rome" (80).

[166] Quoted by Kister, *Jāhiliyya* III.143. Hence P. Crone's conclusion to her *Meccan trade*: "it is . . . the impact of Byzantium and Persia on Arabia that ought to be at the forefront of research on the rise of the new religion, not Meccan trade" (250), the study of which tends to presuppose the exteriority of Mecca and Arabia generally to the Byzantine-Iranian sphere.

6

ISLAM: WORLD EMPIRE, THEN COMMONWEALTH

THE BUILDING OF WORLD EMPIRE

The Islamic Empire was implicit in late antiquity, but nothing quite like it had ever been seen before.[1] Cyrus's coming to power was the product of internecine strife within an empire that already existed; Alexander's was an off-the-rack empire, ready-made when he conquered it. But by early 628 Heraclius had reversed Khusrau II's conquests and restored the status quo between Rome and Iran. Muhammad and his successors had to conquer not just one but two empires, if they were to reunite the Iranian plateau and the eastern Mediterranean basin for the first time since the demise of the Achaemenid-Macedonian state. And the Islamic achievement did not stop there. Besides a new secular order Muhammad also proclaimed a fresh revelation from the One God, and in doing so created (whether or not this was fully understood at the time) a new religion, as well as giving impetus to the emergence of a new culture. Cyrus had not done that. He had preferred to be all things to all men. Even the Jews had seen in him "the Lord's anointed".[2] Alexander had been content with an Egyptian oracle's declaration that he was the son of Zeus-Ammon; and the culture he took in his baggage train was a mature formation.

What Alexander did share with Muhammad and his successors was an origin, in a vigorous and wealthy but culturally ambiguous society at

---

[1] For this chapter's historical background, consult Kennedy, *The Prophet and the Age of the Caliphates*. I have benefited from the attempts of Patricia Crone and others to get behind the fully formed Islamic tradition to a clearer view of its relationship to the world it inherited, especially to Judaism and Rome. (See esp. Crone and Cook, *Hagarism*; Crone, *Roman, provincial and Islamic law*; Crone, *Meccan trade*; and the last two notes of the previous chapter.) These attempts have tended, though, to emphasize Islam's vulnerability or its absorptive action at the expense of its regenerative effect and, a fortiori, of pre-Islamic Arabia's contribution. See now the important corrective offered by Décobert, *Le mendiant et le combattant*, esp. 30–54, who prefers, "dans la voie d'un I. Goldziher ou d'un J. Schacht, à suivre les traces de l'élaboration islamique à partir d'un substrat arabe primitif, de superstrats (romains, chrétiens, judaïques . . .) et d'adstrats (hellénistiques, rabbiniques . . .) étrangers" (47).

[2] *Isaiah* XLV.1.

the edge of the civilized world. They were outsiders in relation to what they conquered, near enough to appreciate and covet the prize, remote enough to dispose of military potential their victims had not already tapped—the tough infantry of Macedonia and neighboring regions, the nomad warriors of Arabia. An insider could not have disposed of such advantages, nor perhaps would he have dared dream such dreams.

Constantine too had dreamed, and his god had spoken to him in visions. Admittedly he was an insider, the ruler and symbol of the empire he in part inherited, in part conquered, and simultaneously converted to faith in Christ. Even so, Constantine is a more interesting parallel with Muhammad than is either Cyrus or Alexander, because though not a prophet sent directly by God he did see himself as the equal of Christ's apostles. His commitment to the propagation of monotheism was intense, and the faith itself was still young and full of missionary zeal. Constantine grasped and pursued the unprecedented opportunity of world empire, of an infinite extension of the dominions he had inherited and conquered, offered by the union of imperial impetus and missionary monotheism, Christianity and Rome. But the odds were stacked overwhelmingly against him. Iran was not to be overthrown by Rome. Even the marriage of Church and Empire took much longer to consummate than to proclaim; and the empire's subsequent division, together with the proliferation of heresy, sapped or diverted energies through which the Constantinian ideal might have been realized. From the perspective of northern Mesopotamia in the late seventh century, it was clear that the empire in which "each year they made a new creed" had been punished by God through the Arabs.[3]

For Constantine, then, the conjunction of historical circumstances had been opportune yet insufficient. Muhammad shared Constantine's ability to perceive the historical moment, but was both more radical and luckier. On the political level he was able to set in motion a sequence of conquests that resulted in world empire. And on the cultural level he did not merely choose one religion rather than another and then rewrite history accordingly. Instead he gave history new impetus by proclaiming a new revelation and a new religion, while cleverly drawing on the momentum built up by earlier monotheist prophets. Muhammad's career was the product of a conjunction of opportunities, but also of his personal ability to recognize that conjuncture and communicate it to others. Within a decade of the Prophet's death in 632 his followers had invented a brand-new system of numbering years, counting from his flight (*hijra*) from Mecca to Medina—this at a time when the Christian

---

[3] John Bar Penkaye, *Ris Melle* II.15, p. 144* (= pp. 172*–73* of Mingana's tr.).

world had still after over six centuries not got used to counting from the birth of Christ.[4] As for the problem of dissent, it took Christ's followers three centuries to come to see heresy as an object of attention for political authority, for the simple reason that previously they had little access to political power.[5] For Muslims, heresy was a political problem almost from the beginning; but that was because Islam was from the beginning in a position of dominance, not subjection.

Muhammad's first two successors, Abu Bakr (632–34) and Umar (634–44), conquered Mesopotamia, Syria, Palestine, and Egypt. Two aspects of these conquests deserve special emphasis. In the first place, the abolition of the frontier that had split the Fertile Crescent down the middle turned the region's natural unity into political unity for the first time since the Seleucids. Second, control of this long stretch of Mediterranean coastline brought control also of the cabotage along it and therefore by definition of most maritime traffic in those regions. Even the major sea battle (and Byzantine defeat) at Lycian Phoenix in 655 occurred just offshore—and was fought mainly with grappling irons and swords, as if on land and not at sea.[6] The Mediterranean's great open spaces, "aussi vides que le Sahara",[7] were of almost as little interest to dwellers around the inland sea as were those distant unproductive tracts, *ta eschata*, which played so small a part in their definition of the "whole world", the *orbis terrarum* or *oikoumene*. And once the Arabs had, in addition to control of the Syro-Egyptian coast, achieved a sufficient level of strategic terrorism of certain major islands such as Rhodes and Cyprus, they launched a sequence of assaults on Constantinople itself (668–718).[8]

This degree of maritime supremacy meant that the Fertile Crescent was henceforth and with only occasional significant lapses, such as the raids on the Palestinian coast (ca. 684–85),[9] secure against Byzantine counterattack from the sea. So while the mature Islamic Empire and the commonwealth that succeeded it were different from Rome in that their sympathies and center of gravity lay away from the Mediterranean and

[4] Herrin, *Formation* 4–6.

[5] For example, Aurelian's involvement with the Paul of Samosata affair in 272 concerned Church property, not doctrine.

[6] Canard, *Byzance et les musulmans* II.63–67.

[7] Braudel, *Méditerranée* 1.94.

[8] Rhodes: Theophanes p. 345. Cyprus: S.E.G. 35 (1985) [1988]: 1471. In general, see Canard, *Byzance et les musulmans* I; Ahrweiler, *Byzance et la mer* 17–35, underlining (25) how Byzantium's creation in response to this challenge of the special fleet of the *karabisianoi* showed that it had lost the naval initiative in the eastern Mediterranean; Kaegi, *Byzantium and the early Islamic conquests* 246–48.

[9] Rotter, *Umayyaden* 171, 172, 180; Bashear, *J.R.A.S.* 1 (1991): 202–4.

their maritime focus, increasingly, in the Indian Ocean, it took the Mediterranean some time to become merely a "backwater", "numbed extremity", or "distant fringe area",[10] at least if by such expressions we are to understand a zone of no strategic significance. Throughout the first Muslim century it was firmly believed that the last times were imminent and that they would be marked by the conquest of Constantinople. Before that happy ending, it was assumed that the Byzantines would launch fierce attacks on the coasts of Syria and Palestine. The eastern Mediterranean was central not only to strategy but also to eschatological expectation.[11]

From a West European viewpoint it may seem that "the political unity of the Mediterranean world was irrevocably lost at that time",[12] but the situation looks less negative when viewed from the Caliphate's perspective. In fact, the triumph of Islam brought greater unity to the Mediterranean world, for its eastern, southern, and (for a time) western shores now came under what in ancient terms, allowing for the problems caused by local dissent and poor communications, was recognizably a single and indeed distinctly dynamic political authority. Even when Spain detached itself from the Abbasids in 757, three of the Mediterranean's four shores still remained under Islamic political control—and Islamic in culture. If anything it was the northern shores, from southern France to Cilicia, that were in disarray. They had already, long before the Muslim conquests, been divided among various Frankish, Lombard, and Byzantine rulers, while the Balkan sector had been under growing pressure since Justinian's time. Now, their conquest by the armies of Islam was imminent and eagerly awaited.

By the death of Muhammad's third successor, Uthman (644–56), Muslim control had also been extended from Mesopotamia across the Iranian plateau. This meant that the geopolitical preconditions of world empire had now been met. Byzantium had not been destroyed—it might still threaten the Fertile Crescent from the North, and some of the caliph's Christian subjects ("Pseudo-Methodius," for example) clearly prayed it would. But the Christian Empire had been effectively crippled. Already in the reign of al-Walid I (705–15), the Islamic Empire reached its greatest extent, embracing all the lands from the Pyrenees through Spain and North Africa to the Indus Valley in the East. Not since the emergence of the Seleucid and Ptolemaic states in the aftermath of Alexander had there existed in this region an empire that had no serious

[10] Brown, *World of late antiquity* 21, 202; *Society and the holy* 69. For a more nuanced formulation, see Miquel, *Géographie humaine* 2.532.

[11] Bashear, *J.R.A.S.* 1 (1991).

[12] Herrin, *Formation* 6, invoking the Belgian historian Henri Pirenne.

competitor to fear. Some hold that "the advent of Islam in the Mediterranean sealed the end of Late Antiquity";[13] but the Muslims themselves took the view that they had consummated all that was most essential in the late antique world.[14] They proclaimed this belief in the 240-meter-long inscription that was placed around the drum of the Dome of the Rock in Jerusalem and bears the date A.H. 72 (A.D. 691–92).[15] Before the installation of electric light the inscription was decipherable from below only when the sun's rays fell on it, so it was never at any one time legible in its entirety. And presumably few non-Muslims saw it. But its position confirms its centrality to the intentions of those who erected the building. Containing some of the earliest surviving versions of any texts known to us from the Quran, the inscription includes the following exhortation "unique for its emphasis on the relations between Islam and Christianity":[16]

> O ye People of the Book, overstep not bounds in your religion; and of God speak only truth. The Messiah, Jesus, son of Mary, is only an apostle of God, and His Word which he conveyed into Mary, and a Spirit proceeding from Him. Believe therefore in God and His apostles, and say not 'Three'. It will be better for you. God is only one God. Far be it from His glory that He should have a son. His is whatever is in the heavens, and whatever is on the earth. . . . God witnesses that there is no God but He: and the angels, and men endowed with knowledge, established in righteousness, proclaim there is no God but He, the Mighty, the Wise. The true religion with God is Islam.

On the north gate we read:

> He it is who has sent His messenger with the guidance and the religion of truth, so that he may cause it to prevail over all religion, however much the idolaters may hate it.[17]

Just as its inscriptions proclaim that Islam has triumphed over polytheism and purged the error of Christianity, so too the Dome of the

[13] Herrin, *Formation* 134, again invoking Pirenne.

[14] Becker, *Islamstudien* 1.201: "Der Islam . . . ist die Weiterbildung und Konservierung des christlich-antiken Hellenismus. . . . Es wird eine Zeit kommen, in der man rückwärtsschauend aus der islamischen Tradition heraus den späten Hellenismus wird verstehen lernen."

[15] Van Berchem, *Matériaux* no. 215; Kessler, *J.R.A.S.* (1970). For further discussion, see Grabar, *Studies* II; Grabar, *Formation* 46–64; Grabar, in *Medieval Mediterranean*; Busse, in *Jerusalemer Heiligtumstraditionen*.

[16] Grabar, *Studies* II.54 n. 117.

[17] Van Berchem, *Matériaux* no. 217.

Rock, by its very siting, where once the Temple had stood, and by certain aspects of its decoration,[18] underlines that Judaism too has at last found its truest expression,[19] while Christ's prophecy of the Temple's destruction is now made null and void. Islam has come not to destroy universal human history but to fulfill it—except in the case of the rulers of the old, partial empires, who must throw down their crowns before the Commander of the Faithful. The regalia of Iran and Byzantium are duly depicted, according to Oleg Grabar, in the mosaic decoration on the inner face of the octagonal colonnade, facing the rock itself.[20] Still, the Dome of the Rock's site and inscription alone sufficiently underline that although Islam had brought new wine, the universality of Muhammad's message ensured that this fresh vintage could be poured even into wineskins as old as Jerusalem, and rejuvenate them.

Although we have little unfiltered evidence of any sort from the first century after the *hijra*, we can at least study Islam's appropriation and fulfillment of the Old World through the unique buildings constructed in this early period. Islam was as yet far from having achieved a mature style, and these transitional, experimental buildings left no posterity—they were not copied. But in themselves they speak volumes about the *process* of the first Muslim century. The Dome of the Rock is the best-known example; but east of the Jordan the painted Umayyad residence and bathhouse at Qusayr Amra has remained relatively neglected.[21] Its iconography makes a somewhat less aggressive statement of Islamic universalism, emphasizing the strength and prestige to be derived from Islam's appropriation of earlier traditions. This is important in the present context, since we shall see that part of the Islamic Empire's success lay in its willingness to coexist even with internal dissenters.

Of Qusayr Amra's frescoes the most famous, in the right aisle of the "throne-room", shows six standing kings labeled in both Arabic and Greek: "Caesar" and "Khusrau", the emperors of Byzantium and Iran;

---

18 Soucek, in *Temple of Solomon* 94–98.

19 On the political as well as religious aspect of this Jewish orientation, toward the example of kingly rule set by David and Solomon and praised in the Quran, see Rabbat, *Muqarnas* 6 (1989).

20 For qualified support of this view (originally published in 1959) see Stern, *C.Arch.* 22 (1972): 216–17. Rosen-Ayalon, *Al-Ḥaram al-Sharīf* 46–69, calls for a less partial interpretation of the decorative scheme, perhaps as a representation of Paradise. M. Gautier-van Berchem, in Creswell, *Early Muslim architecture* 1.280–81, prefers a purely aesthetic interpretation.

21 Creswell, *Early Muslim architecture* 1.390–415; Almagro and others, *Qusayr 'Amra*; Ettinghausen and Grabar, *Art and architecture of Islam* 52–67. I have benefited enormously from discussing Qusayr Amra with Glen Bowersock, Oleg Grabar, Ann Kuttner, and Irfan Shahîd.

7. The "Six kings", Qusayr Amra. Fresco, first half of eighth century.

Roderic the Visigoth, king of Spain, whom the Muslims defeated in 711 (our building's earliest possible date); the Negus of Ethiopia; and two whose labels are lost, perhaps the emperor of China and the Khazar khagan.[22] The whole panel is unique, but King Roderic in particular betrays an artist not afraid of unconventional allusion.

Much of the rest of Qusayr Amra's decoration consists of scantily clothed or naked women, or episodes of hunting and merrymaking. Greek labels identify allegorical figures of Poetry, History, and Philosophy brooding over the riotous scene. If the artists were not themselves of Greek culture,[23] they could at least make clumsy copies of Greek models. Probably they were Christians, working for a late Umayyad prince: a caliph would have found better artists, and an Abbasid would

---

[22] Grabar, *Ars orientalis* 1 (1954); Grabar, *Formation* 43–46; plate 7. On Roderic in Arabic literary tradition, see Miquel, *Géographie humaine* 2.61–62, 350.

[23] As argued by Becker, *Islamstudien* 1.293–94.

have preferred Mesopotamia. Al-Walid II (743–44) liked Greek women, Greek letters, wine, and poetry;[24] Yazid III (744) was given to boasting

> I am the son of Khusrau; my father is Marwan.
> One grandfather is a Caesar; the other a khagan.[25]

Naturally enough, the historian lingers in front of the "Six kings", and they gesture with outstretched hands, in an attitude of respect, toward the painting adjacent and at a right angle to the kings on this aisle's end wall.[26] There we see a woman reclining on a richly decorated couch under a tent, flanked on the left by a young female attendant holding, probably, a fan, and on the right by a mature man with a staff and wearing a decorated version of the "low *qalansuwa*", a rounded hat affected by high Sasanian and Umayyad officials.[27] Two childen sit between her and the man; one wears a plain low *qalansuwa*, the other a scarf rather than a full veil.[28] A label identifies our panel as ÇAPA NIKH—"The victory of Sarah" or "Victory to Sarah".[29] At first glance one might take the reclining woman to be the owner's wife—he himself

[24] Hillenbrand, *Art history* 5 (1982): 17–20. Note especially Abu'l-Faraj al-Isfahani, *Kitab al-aghani* VI.103 (tr. Derenk, *al-Walīd ibn Yazīd* 80–81).

[25] Al-Tabari, *Tarikh* II.1874.

[26] Illustrations in Musil and others, *Ḳuṣejr ʿAmra* 2, pl. XXV; Almagro and others, *Qusayr ʿAmra* pl. XIV; Grabar, *Revue des études islamiques* 54 (1986); this photograph is plate 8 here. For a similar scene united into a single composition on a single surface, see, e.g., Jerphanion, *Eglises rupestres*, album 3, pl. 156.2 (Cappadocian fresco of the Presentation of the Virgin).

[27] Ettinghausen, *From Byzantium to Sasanian Iran* 28–34 and figs. 49, 68; see below, n. 38; plate 9c.

[28] For a conventionally veiled woman at Qusayr Amra, see Almagro and others, *Qusayr ʿAmra* pl. IXb. The reclining woman wears nothing comparable. So I doubt the suggestion (ibid., 56) that the second child is a girl. The headgear in the "Six kings" panel is likewise problematic, and unbearded males at Qusayr Amra tend to look effeminate. (When first discovered, some of the six kings were taken for queens.) If the scarf is a Beduin headdress (*kaffiya*), note that some of the Caliph Abd al-Malik's coins may show him thus attired—or simply with long hair: Miles, *Museum notes (American Numismatic Society)* 13 (1967): 212, 216, and pl. XLVI–XLVII; plate 9d.

[29] Almagro and others, *Qusayr ʿAmra* 56, read ΘAPA. Of the first letter, the most I can detect on the excellent photographs kindly provided by Oleg Grabar is a vague lunate shadow. The letters of ÇAPA are sloppier than those of NIKH—the second "A", in particular, looks like a Latin "R". The arguably Greekless artist (Creswell, *Early Muslim architecture* 1.409) is probably less to blame than the Spanish restoration completed in 1973. Whereas originally all the labels were painted in white (Mielich, in Musil, *Ḳuṣejr ʿAmra* 1.196, 199), and some are still, ÇAPA NIKH has been repainted in black. As for whether ÇAPA is genitive or dative, the Septuagint and the papyri suggest that the genitive ought to be ÇAPAC, though the artists' (probably) Semitic linguistic instinct would have favoured the indeclinable form (no article needed: cf., e.g., P. Amherst 150.11). But one can always fall back on a dative, as at *Gen.* XII.11.

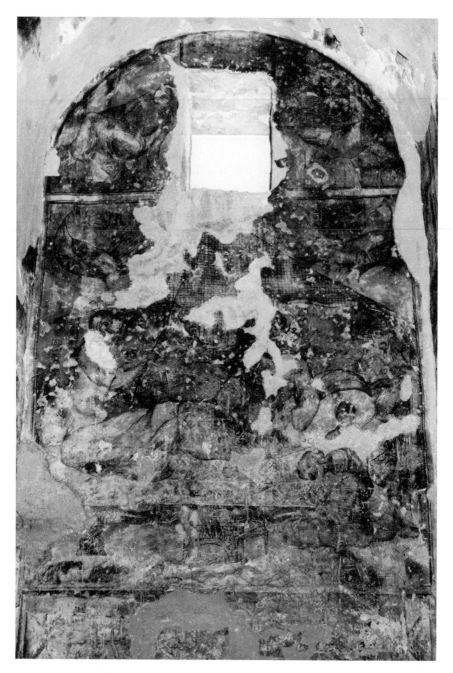

8. "The victory of Sarah" or "Victory to Sarah", Qusayr Amra.
Fresco, first half of eighth century.

is depicted, enthroned and similarly fanned, on the corresponding end
wall of the central aisle. And an acclamatory text of this sort is a normal
way of marking places of honor in an Arab prince's reception hall: we
find something similar in the apse of the Ghassanid "praetorium" at
Rusafa-Sergiopolis.[30] But the allusion to Sarah suggests there is more to
the Qusayr Amra fresco. The closest parallel to this composition is
offered by the Ashburnham Pentateuch, a seventh-century Latin manuscript often suspected of having benefited from some Eastern inspiration. Here, "Sarah's complaint" (*Gen.* XXI.10) has (from left to right)
standing figures of the slave-woman Hagar and Sarah, the diminutive
forms of Sarah's son Isaac and Hagar's son Ishmael, and a commanding,
seated Abraham, whom Sarah begs to disinherit Ishmael.[31]

Qusayr Amra appears to present an Arab Muslim reinterpretation of
exactly this scene, which was presumably not invented by the Ashburnham Pentateuch's artist. Qusayr Amra deliberately shifts the emphasis from complaint to victory, from Abraham to Sarah, who is the
only sure source of ethnic legitimacy, Hagar being a slave (though not
without honor in early Islam)[32] and Abraham having slept around.
Christian writers had long maintained that the Arabs were called "Sar-
acens" because they were ashamed of their ancestor Ishmael's real
mother, Hagar, and adopted Sarah instead.[33] In fact, most pre-Islamic
Arab polytheists seem to have been unaware of any such biblical ancestry; but Muhammad saw in Abraham the first monotheist, and from that
point onward Abraham's women and progeny had to be taken more
seriously.[34] If the Qusayr Amra artists were indeed of Christian background, part of their usefulness to their patron will have been precisely
their knowledge of Old Testament stories and iconography. An Arabic

[30] NIKA H TYXH AΛAMOYNΔAPOY: Sarre and Herzfeld, *Archäologische Reise*
2.41, fig. 156; Sauvaget, *Byzantion* 14 (1939): 115–30. The reference is to al-Mundhir
(569–81). Elizabeth Key Fowden drew my attention to this inscription.

[31] Von Gebhardt, *Ashburnham Pentateuch* pl. VI (= fol.18ʳ), and description at p. 14.
See also Rickert, in *XIᵉ Congrès International d'Archéologie Chrétienne*. Note that Jewish
tradition had often placed Sarah in a tent: Goodenough, *Jewish symbols* 9.72–73 (though
his detection of Sarah in the Dura Europus synagogue is not widely accepted: St. Clair,
Jb.A.C. 29 [1986]; Kessler, in Weitzmann and Kessler, *Dura synagogue* 157 n. 14). For
Sarah depicted at San Vitale, Ravenna, in a house under a pointed gable-end that recalls
the shape of the Qusayr Amra tent, see Goodenough, *Jewish symbols* 11, pl. 100.

[32] Ibn Ishaq, *Sirat an-Nabi* 5 (tr. Guillaume 4), with Ibn Hisham's note (tr. Guillaume
691).

[33] Jerome, *In Hiezechielem* VIII.25.1–7, p. 335; Sozomen, *H.E.* VI.38.10; Cyril of
Scythopolis, *Vita Euthymii* 10, p. 21.

[34] Dagorn, *Geste d'Ismaël* (slightly modified by Shahîd, *B.A.FI.C.* 345–49, 382–83);
Firestone, *Journeys*.

text they painted on the end wall of the left aisle says "O God, bless the emir as you blessed David and Abraham".[35]

Just as Ishmael became the Arabs' ancestor in this new Muslim world-view, Isaac became the ancestor of the Iranians. A poem by al-Jarir, an Umayyad court poet who died circa 728/29,[36] vaunts the descent of all Muslims from Abraham, takes credit for Jacob, Moses, Solomon, and Jesus too, and boasts of the Islamic "empire without end". Al-Jarir takes special pride in the Arabs' kinship with the Iranians, "the nobles, the children of Sarah, . . . the sons of Isaac. . . . If they [the Iranians] want to boast, they have but to number in their ranks al-Sabahbad, Khusrau, the family of the Hormizds and Caesar." The inclusion of Caesar as an Iranian, and apparently of Khusrau II's horse al-Shabhdez, reveals no profound grasp of history. But an allusion to the Muslim Berber prince al-Waddah parallels the appearance of Roderic and the Negus in the "Six kings" fresco, and underlines the propagation of Islam in space as well as backward in time that preoccupied al-Jarir no less than it did the Qusayr Amra artists.[37]

In the light of this parallel, it may be suggested that the Sarah fresco simultaneously legitimates the Arabs ethnically by deriving them, through Ishmael, from Abraham's lawful wife, underlines the Arabs' kinship with Isaac's descendants, the Iranians, and proclaims Sarah's (that is, the Arabs')[38] victory over the six kings who stand before her. That victory is more than just a military triumph—it is the key to

[35] Sauvaget, *J.A.* 231 (1939): 14.

[36] Al-Jarir, *Naqaid* CIV.27–40, composed in the 720s; tr. and comment in Dagorn, *Geste d'Ismaël* 205–11.

[37] Compare John Bar Penkaye, *Ris Melle* (a universal history written in northern Mesopotamia, probably in the late 680s) XIV.142* (tr. Brock 58): "Who can relate the carnage they [the Arabs] effected in Greek territory, in Kush, in Spain and in other distant regions. . . ?" At this date "Kush" and "Spain" can only mean "the far South/West"; but at Qusayr Amra the metaphor has become reality, at least in the case of Spain; hence the pride implied by the unusually precise reference to Roderic. Kush (Nubia), though, was never conquered. For further seventh-century literary parallels to my interpretation of the Qusayr Amra frescoes, see Kaegi, *Byzantium and the early Islamic conquests* 214–16.

[38] This identification of Sarah with the Arabs will have been underlined if the Qusayr Amra patron's wife sat in front of the fresco on formal occasions. The princely portrait on the central aisle's end wall likewise combines contemporary and biblical reference, this time to Adam seated in royal majesty in paradise: cp. the mosaic in the Hama Museum, illustrated and discussed by Donceel-Voûte, *Pavements* 1.113. Abraham's "low *qalan-suwa*" is perhaps another such iconographical "bridge". It is tempting to add that some of the "standing caliph" figures on early Umayyad coins resemble the Qusayr Amra Abraham (long, flowing garments; staff; a vestigial Byzantine crown that looks like a flattened version of the "low *qalansuwa*") as well as being a deliberately Arabized version of imperial portraits on Byzantine coins. When juxtaposed (e.g., plates 6 and 9b), these Islamic coins and their Byzantine prototypes produce the same effect as the juxtaposition of Abraham and the six kings at Qusayr Amra.

political legitimation and cultural appropriation. Having defeated them, the Arabs can now feel worthy to exercise the political power symbolized by the six kings.[39] As for the process of cultural appropriation, that starts with the image itself, for Sarah had already enjoyed a brilliant career as the symbol of Christian victory. In Rome's Santa Maria Maggiore we see her in the fifth-century mosaics on the "triumphal arch" at the east end, amid images rich in imperial reminiscence, presenting the Christ child in a vision to the newly wed Joseph and Mary, while Abraham, upstaged here as at Qusayr Amra, does obeisance. Elsewhere Sarah is throned beside Christ as the Magi pay him homage.[40] "She will become nations: kings of peoples will issue from her."[41] In the Syrian world that produced the Qusayr Amra artists, the Church had been known to some as the "House of Sarah", who stood for freedom rather than the enslavement represented by Hagar.[42] And throughout early Christian literature can be traced the idea of Sarah as antetype of the Mother of God, Byzantium's protectress. In something comparable to this role of liberator and protectress, no less than as the first monotheist's wife, Sarah needed to be made Islam's own—not least because Byzantium, unlike the Sasanian Empire, still existed. So did the Christian kingdom of Ethiopia. The fresco of the six kings and indeed the whole decorative scheme at Qusayr Amra carries the same message—that Islam has triumphed but cannot yet entirely dismiss what went before as *jahiliyya*, or "ignorance". Islam has inherited a world whose variety it is compelled to accept and called to exploit.

But it was only when the Umayyad dynasty fell in 750 and the Abbasids replaced Damascus, one of the world's oldest inhabited places, with a completely new capital called Baghdad, that this process of domination but also acceptance and transformation of the Old World by Islam attained its most forcible expression. Construction of "the City of Peace" (*madinat as-salam*) began in 145/762.[43]

Though it was a new foundation, Baghdad stood in proximity to

---

[39] See above, p. 143; Donner, *J.A.O.S.* 106 (1986): 289–90, esp. n. 32; and Bates, *S.N.R.* 65 (1986), on use of Byzantine and Sasanian royal imagery in Umayyad political propaganda.

[40] I am grateful to Archer St. Clair for drawing my attention to Suzanne Spain's article in *Art Bulletin* 61 (1979), esp. 535–40.

[41] *Gen.* XVII.16.

[42] Ephraem the Syrian, *Hymns on the Nativity* 20 (anticipating Qusayr Amra's play on the idea of the complaining/victorious Sarah, but emphasizing the uniqueness of Abraham's "blessed seed" [i.e., Isaac as antetype of Christ], whereas Qusayr Amra admits the equality of Ishmael, who for Ephraem is "accursed"); and cf. Cyril of Scythopolis, *Vita Euthymii* 10, p. 21.

[43] For general accounts see Grabar, *Formation* 64–68, 156–69; Ettinghausen and Grabar, *Art and architecture of Islam* 75–79.

Babylon, which Alexander had apparently intended to make the capital of his empire, as well as to two later metropolises, Seleucia and Ctesiphon. There were sound geographical reasons why this area had been so central to successive empires, for its position by the Tigris and near the Euphrates put it athwart one of the ancient world's great trade routes between the Persian Gulf and the Mediterranean, while the way to the Iranian plateau was also close at hand. This latter consideration was crucial for the Abbasids, whose power base lay in Khurasan. Conjoined with the new dynasty's loss of effective control over Spain, this factor determined the transference of the Islamic Empire's capital from the western to the eastern sector of the Fertile Crescent. Baghdad was, objectively speaking, the center of the world, at least of the Abbasid world.

Baghdad was built on a strictly circular plan, like various Sasanian cities before it, and within high walls pierced by only four gateways. These, though located not at but midway between the cardinal directions, were nonetheless so arranged that lines linking them would have divided the city into quadrants and intersected at the center of the circle where stood, amid a vast open space, the caliph's palace and a mosque. Of the city's gates, one was associated with Solomon, another with a pharaoh or some other ancient ruler.[44] Within the walls were arranged in concentric rings the living and working quarters of the city's inhabitants, that is, of the caliphal bureaucracy together with the traders and other workers necessary to the functioning of this large establishment, though there were markets, military camps, and residential areas outside the city walls as well. At the circular city's center, then, in solitary majesty but surrounded by at least the more trustworthy of his subjects, lived the caliph in his palace with its famous green dome of obvious celestial symbolism, amid wealth so fabulous that even Byzantium's envoys were struck dumb with astonishment.

Scholars have detected in the plan and structures of this remarkable city all sorts of cosmic symbolism and allusions to empires of the past. Baghdad is held to have stood for the universality, self-sufficiency, and completeness of the Islamic Empire. Our sources are inexplicit about these hidden significances.[45] But the Arabic geographers, especially Yaqubi, do underline the centrality of Iraq to their scheme of the world,

[44] Wendell, *International Journal of Middle East Studies* 2 (1971): 113–17.

[45] Lassner, *Shaping of 'Abbāsid rule* 163–241. Illawi, *Cités musulmanes* 81–87, emphasizes Baghdad's astrological symbolism, but lacks clinching evidence that it was read in a universalist sense. I am grateful to Oleg Grabar for sight of this unpublished work. Note the striking resemblance between Baghdad and Ecbatana as described by Herodotus II.98–101, emphasizing the city plan's deliberate monarchical symbolism.

and of Baghdad, in turn, to Iraq. To its population, all the peoples of the world have contributed; the city contains a quarter for each of them. Likewise, its markets display produce from all over the world. Baghdad is, in short, "the crossroads of the universe".[46] And a prophesy attributed to Muhammad about the catastrophic downfall of "a city built between the rivers Dijla and Dujayl and Qatrabull and as-Sarat in which the treasures of the earth will be amassed and in which the kings and tyrants of the earth will assemble"[47] underlines clearly enough how Baghdad was not only objectively at the world's center, but also played on that fact sufficiently to acquire numerous detractors. If these detractors invoked Muhammad in their attacks on the city, it is unlikely that the Baghdadis were content with any lesser authority in support of their city's claims.

Perhaps, indeed, it is to the Baghdadis themselves, rather than to the stones of their city, that we should turn for the clearest evidence of the Abbasid view of Islam as history's culmination. The scholar Ibn Ishaq, for example, though a Medinan by origin, made his way like many others to al-Mansur's new capital, where until his death (ca. 767) he found eager students and patronage for his book on the life of the Prophet, the *Sirat an-Nabi*.[48] Ibn Ishaq saw Muhammad's career as the culminating moment in the history of God's dealings with first the Jews and then the Christians; to the story of these dealings he devoted much space and energy. This long perspective on history was necessary if the central importance of Muhammad and the completeness of the revelation he received was to be made apparent. And the *Sirat an-Nabi* remains today our best source for Muhammad's life. What we now read is but an epitome—many who came after Ibn Ishaq doubted that Muhammad needed this sort of historical introduction. Fortunately, though, Ibn Ishaq's account of history before Muhammad can be recovered from those, like the historian al-Tabari, who plundered it for their own narratives. Al-Tabari too worked at Baghdad, where he died in 923. The glory of the Abbasid Caliphate was by then indisputably past; but the influence of al-Tabari's monumental account of history from the Creation to the Abbasids remained. And thanks not least to the impetus he gave the endlessly plastic Alexander legend, Muslim Iran gained a model of the prophet-king destined to play a central role in its literature and art.[49]

[46] Yaqubi, *Kitab al-buldan* 233–34, 237; cf. Miquel, *Géographie humaine* 2.61, 68–70, 527–30.

[47] Juynboll, *Muslim tradition* 208, 212–13.

[48] Newby, *Last prophet.*

[49] Abel, in *La persia.*

Through the scholars of Baghdad, the Greek as well as the Judeo-Christian past was absorbed into the fabric of Islam.

EMPIRE AND RELIGION

By the time Baghdad was built, the primitive Islamic community had already for a century been maturing into antiquity's one and only true world empire. Its initial military successes, from the 630s, had been spectacular. By the early 690s it had recovered from a period of severe dissension caused by problems of political legitimacy. For more than a century after that[50]—in other words, for roughly a half-century on either side of the foundation of Baghdad—the Islamic Empire was both prosperous and unchallenged from without and maintained a quite extraordinary coherence within, given its enormous size. What was the secret of its dominance and stability?

There are many possible answers to this question.[51] Unlike Byzantines and Sasanians caught in ancient and hardened systems of thinking and doing in which much was comprehensible only to a small elite, the Arabs came fresh and without rigid division of labor to the job of building society and government. At the same time, they were far from being a people without an identity or self-image. The Germans, for example, had brought an unsophisticated language and culture into the monolithically Latin world of the Roman West, so that, as Theodoric the Ostrogoth remarked, rich Goths longed to play the Roman, but only poor Romans played the Goth.[52] The Arabs, by contrast, brought a much more self-confident culture and flexible language into a region that had been dominated by two polyglot and culturally diverse empires. Above all, they brought a holy book written in a language largely unencumbered by the dead weight of past association that had so afflicted Christians when they tried to bend Greek to their new ways of thought.[53] Not only, then, did the Arab not need to assimilate in order to retain self-respect; he was actually in a strong position to impose his own language and eventually culture too as normative. The initial predominance of Greek and Iranian in the administration was already giving way to that of Arabic in the 690s. At that time too the coinage ceased to mimic Byzantine and Sasanian models and became authen-

---

[50] This is a deliberately conservative figure. Clover and Humphreys, in *Tradition and innovation*, 13, claim "two hundred years by any reasonable calculation", from Muawiya's seizure of power in 660 to al-Mutawakkil's assassination in 861.

[51] I owe some of them to Kennedy, *The Prophet and the Age of the Caliphates* 117–23.

[52] *Anonymus Valesianus* 61.

[53] I owe this point to Elizabeth Key Fowden.

tically Arabic, adorned with a firm declaration of Muslim belief.[54] And it is with precisely what the coins symbolize, namely the strength the Islamic Empire derived from the mutually reinforcing but at the same time (as we shall see) flexible relationship between religion and empire, that we are chiefly here concerned.[55]

We may begin with the mutual reinforcement of religion and empire. Membership in the Muslim community, the *umma*,[56] rested on acceptance of Muhammad as the One God's last and most authoritative prophet, and therefore also as ultimate authority in all aspects of life, private and public. In its earliest origins, soon after Muhammad's flight from Mecca to Medina, the *umma* was the community of those who had joined the Prophet and abandoned their traditional clan affiliation in Mecca. They were without corporate identity or protection in a society in which both were indispensable. By forming the *umma* they regained the identity and protection they had lost, and invited others from the polytheist and Jewish population of Medina to join them. But because in joining it one accepted not only Muhammad's political authority but also his status as Prophet of the One God, the *umma* was more than just another tribe. Once one had joined the *umma*, it was clearly not merely undesirable but a terrible sin to leave it. And one was now accountable for one's misdeeds not just to one's kin and their ancestral gods but to the One God of all mankind. The *umma* had considerable leverage over its members.

Muhammad's successors, including all the Umayyads and the Abbasids, were proclaimed *khalifat Allah*, "Deputy of God" or "Caliph", as we say, and *amir al-muminin*, "Commander of the Faithful". These two titles reflect the interdependent religious and politico-military authority exercised by the rulers of the Islamic Empire—and the unique prestige that accrued to the *single* successor of a prophet of the One God rather than the many.[57] Since it has traditionally been held that the

---

[54] Bates, *S.N.R.* 65 (1986); plates 9a–e.

[55] For a different view of religion's role in the formation of late antique empires see Herrin, *Formation* 8: "the Christian and the Muslim inheritors of the Roman Empire . . . came to define their world solely in religious terms. As the ancient world collapsed, faith rather than imperial rule became the feature that identified the universe. . . . Religion had fused the political, social and cultural into self-contained systems, separated by their differences of faith." Also see 38–39, claiming that acceptance of Christ was as big a threat as Iran to Roman imperial authority. I have tried to stay as close as possible to late antique ways of seeing this relationship.

[56] On the *umma*, see the remarks of Donner, *Conquests* 55–62.

[57] Donner, *J.A.O.S.* 106 (1986): 290–93, 295; Crone and Hinds, *God's Caliph*. (For reservations about the use of literary evidence in this book, see N. Calder's review, *J.S.S.* 32 [1987].) Only Muhammad's first successor, Abu Bakr, seems not to have been called "Caliph".

9a. Solidus/dinar of Abd al-Malik (685–705), imitating the Byzantine issue shown in plate 6 but removing or modifying crosses. No date.

9b. Solidus/dinar of Abd al-Malik, Arabized version of 9a. On the reverse margin, the earliest use on a coin of the Muslim confession of faith: "In the name of God: there is no god but God alone; Muhammad is the messenger of God." No date.

9c. Dirham of Abd al-Malik, with Sasanian-style royal portrait. No date.

9d. Solidus/dinar of Abd al-Malik, with Muslim confession of faith on reverse, dated 75 A.H.

9e. Dinar of Abd al-Malik, dated 77 A.H. The first issue to abandon the imitation of Byzantine and Sasanian models and use only religious texts.

caliph exercised a purely political authority, it is worth emphasizing here that this was not the way the office was understood in the first Islamic centuries. In those days, caliphs were put on the same level as prophets, of whom Muhammad had been the last. The calpih's authority came straight from God, therefore, just as Muhammad's had. The caliph maintained and defended the *umma*, which could not exist without its leader. He also preserved the community from doctrinal error, and was the source of Islamic law and indeed of salvation. Caliphal verdicts counted as sacred law alongside those of the prophets and great scholars with whom this corpus of opinions, examples, and decisions (the *sunna*) is usually associated.

The combination of religious and political authority in a single individual was not wholly original. "[Constantine] openly declared and confessed himself the servant and minister of the supreme King. And God forthwith rewarded him, by making him ruler and sovereign." The pages that followed this quotation from Eusebius at its first appearance have already emphasized how Constantine too had integrated political and religious authority.[58] Several of his successors—one thinks especially of Zeno, Justinian, and Heraclius—took an equally active and at times considerably more assertive part in efforts to resolve the Church's cancerous Christological debates. But to these three emperors and to many more, the Christological problem was in fact a fatal stumbling block. Monotheism tends to be inherently divisive because of precisely this tension it sets up between orthodoxy and heresy. Although universalist by inner logic, it ends up generating pluralism. The factors that enabled the early Islamic Empire to deal more successfully with the problem of dissent are the same as some of the basic reasons for the ease of its initial expansion: in other words, the simultaneous conception of religion and empire by a single person, Muhammad; the synchronization of imperial impetus with the advance of a monotheism that was, at least potentially, a missionary monotheism;[59] a much more thoroughgoing combination of moral and political authority in the person of the caliph than had been achieved by the rulers of either Rome or Iran;[60] and the caliphs' propagation of Islam with sufficient personal authority and at the same time regard for consensus (*ijma*) in the question of

[58] See above, pp. 88–90.

[59] For a similar view of the political consequences of early Islamic monotheism, articulated against those who discount the religious factor, see Donner, *Conquests* 255–56, 269–70; Décobert, *Le mendiant et le combattant* 52, 65: "la guerre . . . était . . . un *instrument* politique, instrument d'affirmation d'une forme spécifique de monothéisme".

[60] Crone and Hinds, *God's Caliph* 114–15.

"orthodoxy" to postpone heresy's development into a structural problem of empire.[61] In all these respects the Islamic Empire consummated rather than contradicted the themes of late Roman history. For a time, it succeeded where Rome had failed.

The flexibility in the mutually reinforcing relationship of early Islamic religion and empire was not confined to the Muslims' own internal business—the definition of orthodoxy against heresy. It was extended to other religions too; for whereas subjection to the calpih's secular authority was the attribute of all, Islam long remained the faith of the relatively few. One of Oleg Grabar's brilliant observations about the arts of Islam may be adduced at this point as a parallel.[62] In early courtly art, Grabar observes, "there was almost nothing that could not have been accepted and understood by non-Muslims", to the point that it is often difficult to distinguish what was Umayyad or Abbasid from what was Byzantine or had been Sasanian, or a Muslim silver or ivory object, for example, from a Christian one. "The art of princes in the early Middle Ages . . . was not tied to any single culture but belonged to a fraternity of princes and transcended cultural barriers, at least in the vast world from the Atlantic to India and the Pamirs which owed so much to Hellenistic civilization." Indeed, the range and variety of the influences that Muslim princes displayed in their arts and buildings was testimony to the universality of their dominions. In contrast to this princely mode, "the art of the mosque was far more conservative and tended much more consistently to use local architectural and even decorative forms. . . . Its impact was limited because its functions were exclusive and culturally restricted."

This distinction between the Islamic Empire's political universality and Islam's initial confinement, despite its doctrinal universality, to certain milieus in no way contradicts what has already been said about the mutual reinforcement of religion and empire within the caliphate. In fact, the distinction arises from the nature of the religion itself.

Of the five fundamental principles of Islam, four concern practice and only one concerns belief: in God and his prophet Muhammad. To distinguish Islam from other monotheist traditions, we naturally emphasize the second part of this confession, Muhammad rather than God. But in doing so we disguise the fact that Judaism, Christianity, and Islam

[61] Ibid., 48–54; Mottahedeh, *Loyalty and leadership* 19–22; Bello, *Medieval Islamic controversy* 17–28. That the private beliefs or behavior of individual caliphs might be flagrantly unorthodox (e.g., Hillenbrand, *Art history* 5 [1982]: 16–17) is immaterial in the present context, but a salutary reminder of the level of generalization and even, to some extent, formality on which we are moving.
[62] Grabar, *Formation* 167–69.

were united by more than what divided them. All three confessed the One God; they differed principally over the identity of his last and most authoritative prophet.

Confession of faith in the One God automatically excludes coexistence with polytheists. This principle had become axiomatic in Christian Rome, and Muhammad's was (at least in this respect) a no less missionary monotheism. He and his successors proscribed polytheism in Arabia and everywhere else that came under Muslim rule. We have already seen a perfect example of this in al-Mamun's treatment of the polytheists of Harran, who had to start calling themselves Sabians in order to pass for People of the Book and thus earn Islam's protection.[63]

But as the last, not the first, of the prophets, Muhammad had to have a view not just about polytheism but also about the validity of the revealed religions. After the conquest of Mecca he cleansed the sacred center, the Kaba, of its idols. By teaching that the Kaba had been founded by Abraham and his son Ishmael,[64] he made it clear that Islam was the restoration, not the invention, of true religion,[65] that there could be no other gods besides God, but also, logically, that those whose ancestors had already confessed God should not be seriously molested. God was the God of Jew and Christian as well as Muslim, and Muhammad acknowledged the authority of Abraham and Jesus, and taught his followers to pray facing Jerusalem before he had them turn to Mecca.[66] The Quran contains various and inconsistent pronouncements on the "People of the Book".[67] Sometimes they are denounced, but elsewhere it is allowed that they too can achieve salvation. Jews, Christians, and Sabians are specifically mentioned, and Mazdeans came by convention to be included, despite their mixture of henotheist and polytheist beliefs.[68] There is a partial parallel here with Constantine, who had treated Jews much more favorably than he had polytheists.[69] But Islam's monotheist predecessors loomed much larger over Muhammad than Christianity's had over Constantine. In practice, then, the People of the Book were allowed to keep their faith, and no strenuous effort was made to convert them. The value of their otherness was even reinforced by a special tax (*jizya*) imposed on them but not on Muslims. This may have

[63] See above, pp. 62–5, and below.
[64] Paret, *Enc.Is.*[2] 3.980–81; Wensinck, [Joumier], *Enc.Is.*[2] 4.317–22; Firestone, *Journeys* 80–103.
[65] See, on this theme, the reflections of Décobert, *Studia Islamica* 72 (1990).
[66] Wensinck, *Enc.Is.*[2] 5.82.
[67] Vajda, *Enc.Is.*[2] 1.264–66.
[68] Morony, *Iraq* 286–91, 300–302; Morony, *Enc.Is.*[2] 5.1110, 1117.
[69] See above, p. 87.

become an incentive for them to convert, but it was a disincentive for the state to encourage them to convert. In short, the Islamic Empire's policy was to enforce universal monotheism.[70] Islam itself, a monotheism so pure that it did not allow itself to say of God, as the Christians did, that He is "three",[71] was open to all who chose it, and was regarded as the only sure passport to the Heavenly City. But it was first enjoyed by the Arabs; and although the Arabs knew well that they were but messengers to the rest of mankind,[72] they always cherished a special relationship with the faith proclaimed in the Quran, which was not translated into other tongues. They were perfectly happy to allow other monotheists to continue to adhere to their own partial revelations, if they insisted on doing so.

This readiness to accept that the Earthly City could not wholly antici-pate the Heavenly City's austerely Muslim character[73] provides a strik-ing parallel between the thought-worlds of Augustinian Christianity and Islam, common ground that was not shared by the Greeks, with their mystical sense of the perfectibility of man here on earth. The Latins and the Muslims had a puritanical awareness of the Fall and the deep discontinuity it had introduced betwen man and God. The Greeks kept their Platonist belief in the continuity of the "ecclesiastical" and the "celestial" hierarchies. In the laws against heresy and the acts of one Church council after another, but also in the early accounts of Justi-nian's Haghia Sophia church, one has a strong sense of the Greeks' belief in the possibility of building heaven on earth. In few places in the Mus-lim or Latin world can one find as arresting a symbol of the unity of the *kosmos*, human and divine, as is offered by even the humblest village church in Greece, with its Pantokrator presiding in the dome over a carefully zoned hierarchy of angels, evangelists, apostles, hierarchs, saints, and martyrs. Incapable of the realism that allowed Muslims to tolerate the People of the Book and Latins to carve out fiefdoms in Syria under pretext of saving the Holy Places, the Byzantines succumbed to both.[74]

70 This is an emphasis central to Cook's *Muhammad*.

71 *Quran* V.74; and see above, p. 142.

72 *Quran* III.111, XXXIV.29.

73 This is the element of historical reality missing from Chelhod's otherwise excellent discussion, *Sociologie de l'Islam* 149–63, of the contrast between Islam's doctrinal uni-versalism and its "application politique"—in theory, that is—"l'exclusivisme" (155).

74 See, along similar lines, Canard's comparison of Islamic, Latin, and Byzantine attitudes to "holy war": *Byzance et les musulmans* VIII. The Greek tradition attains its most complete expression in Gregory Palamas's controversy with Barlaam: "Entre le dualisme platonicien et le monisme biblique, le docteur hésychaste fait un choix résolu: l'homme n'est pas un esprit emprisonné dans la matière et aspirant à sa libération, mais un

In short, what made the Islamic Empire, however briefly, into a successful world empire was the combination of imperial impetus with a universalist monotheism that was inflexible with regard to doctrinal essentials and full of missionary zeal toward polytheists but flexible, or at least prepared to exercise economy, in its dealings with other monotheisms. The Islamic Empire was actually and aggressively universal, Islam only potentially—and the empire consented to tolerate a degree of cultural-religious pluralism. Had the Islamic Empire been prepared to tolerate only Islam, it would have had to impose the inhuman uniformity for whose sake Constantinople had vainly struggled through more than three centuries of Christological debate. It would have dissipated its energies in internal strife, and "might well have shrunk back to the wastes of Arabia from which it had sprung".[75] Alternatively, Islam would have become the very diverse religion it eventually became anyway, but without the memory of the Golden Age of Abbasid Baghdad—one god, one empire, one emperor—to sustain it. It is to the origins of that diversity—to the evolution, in other words, of world empire into Islamic Commonwealth—that we must now turn.

THE ISLAMIC COMMONWEALTH

The enthusiasm and impetus generated by Muhammad's revelation, together with the need to consolidate the *umma*'s Arabian power base and to direct outward, to the *umma*'s profit, energies traditionally expended in intertribal raiding, impelled Muhammad's followers from the peripheries into the heartlands of Byzantium and Iran. The merchant-milieu in which Muhammad is said to have grown up undoubtedly possessed excellent intelligence on its neighbors' condition after two decades of merciless war. Muhammad himself may have initiated the conquest of Syria. Abu Bakr and Umar seem to have thought primarily in terms of spreading Islam to the kindred Arab peoples of Syria-Mesopotamia. Umar did not desire the conquest of Egypt, whose population was not Arab; but in the end he approved it, and in so doing removed, whether or not he understood it, any likelihood there had ever been that Islam would remain a purely Arab religion. Egypt stayed largely Christian for several centuries, but in time Islam became the religion of the majority. The conquest of Iran had the same long-term implication.

être qui, par son caractère composite même, est appelé à établir sur la matière et l'esprit, dans leur indéfectible union, le Règne de Dieu" (Meyendorff, *Palamas* 326).
[75] Mottahedeh, *Loyalty and leadership* 20.

At the end of the nine decades during which the Umayyads possessed the caliphate (661–750), the non-Arab subject populations seem still to have been relatively little Islamized. Some administrative assistance was initially accepted from former Byzantine and Iranian officials, but Arab Muslims had a monopoly on the levers of power from the beginning. "Arab" and "Muslim" remained substantially synonymous terms under the Umayyads. But the stigma attached to non-Arab converts (*mawali*) gradually attenuated.[76] We can also observe the beginnings of the process whereby the caliphal armies ceased to be simply a projection of the free Arabian tribes and took on first an identity and eventually a non-Arab servile personnel of their own.[77] The Arabs settled and enjoyed the fruits of their exertions, and the *mawali* fought on their behalf, especially in the remote frontier areas. Umayyad armies struck westward through North Africa and Spain into southern France, and eastward as far as Sind. Spain in fact became the Umayyads' refuge when they were overthrown by the Abbasids in 750. And the Abbasids themselves owed their power base to Khurasan at the empire's opposite extremity. In their different ways, these facts illustrate the multiplying options presented by the vastly expanded caliphate. It was now big enough that its extremities could provide both safe refuge for a fallen dynasty[78] and a viable power base for its supplanter. But the center could not forever be preserved from the corrosive effects of such interdynastic rivalries, or of such diversity.

Early Abbasid government was highly centralized at Baghdad, whose appearance of being the axis on which the world turned was no mere conceit—it had to carry conviction too. For a time it did; but that time was brief enough. What is cause for surprise is that so stupendous an empire lasted even as long as the period of rather more than a century that it can (conservatively) be credited with, from the firm establishment of Umayyad power against all dissenters by Abd al-Malik (684–705) until the death of Harun al-Rashid (786–809), the last caliph who contrived to rule over all the Islamic lands from Africa to Sind. Harun al-Rashid's reign was followed by a tremendous civil war (809–33), and the Abbasid Empire began to fall slowly apart, at first socially more than territorially.

While much of the Abbasid elite had continued to be purely Arab, the men of Khurasan were of varied origin. Often the leaders were of Arab

---

[76] Décobert, *Le mendiant et le combattant* 83–95.

[77] Crone, *Slaves on horses*, esp. 37–40, 74–81; Pipes, *Slave soldiers* 107–39, 167–74.

[78] Though only until 757, when the Umayyads ceased to recognize the Abbasids and seceded: Collins, *Arab conquest of Spain* 126–34. Note also the foundation of an independent Alid dynasty in Morocco in 789.

descent, but many of their followers were Iranians who spoke their own language. The Khurasanis multiplied influence in both the army and the administration; one has only to think of the great bureaucratic dynasty of the Barmakids. The army, once drawn from the Arab heartlands, became a separate caste dominated by ethnic minorities: Turks, for example, Armenians, and Berbers. The removal of the capital during the half-century from 836 to 883 to Samarra, some one hundred kilometers north of Baghdad, likewise reflected the emergence of a new elite dominated by Turkic soldiers, and its desire for a space of its own, away from the vested interests of Baghdad. The ninth-century caliphs often exercised extremely effective control at least over the central parts of their empire: this was still easily the most powerful state in the European and West Asian world. But there was a growing distinction between areas really and nominally under Abbasid control, while the centralization of power, impressive at first glance, led to the widespread anarchy of the early tenth century. Stability was too dependent on the behavior of a tiny elite and the military cliques, often of servile origin, that depended directly on it. By the 920s effective power in the capital was passing once and for all into the hands of these soldiers, while even the central parts of the empire, including Iraq itself, were cutting loose from Baghdad, and fragmenting into a kaleidoscope of successor states. In an anguished but illuminating passage the contemporary writer Masudi (d. ca. 956–57) bemoans the Islamic Empire's sorry state, the Byzantine threat, the decline of the pilgrimage to Mecca, the expiry of holy war against the infidel, the danger of the roads, and the self-isolation and independence of the military leaders, each in his own region—all this, Masudi claims, came to a head under the Caliph al-Muttaqi (940–44).[79]

Meanwhile, the pace of conversion to Islam was gathering. Evidence is extremely thin, but a recent estimate places the Muslim population of early ninth-century Iran at about 40 percent, growing to over 90 percent by the mid-tenth century.[80] Iraq, Syria, Egypt, and North Africa lagged behind this very rapid conversion rate from the mid-eighth to the late-tenth century, but the result was the same—an almost entirely Muslim population by the eleventh century. An increasing diversity of people, further and further from the Arab heartlands, came to feel they had a stake in the fortunes of what was now a decidedly Islamic rather than Arab empire, a politico-culturally universalist empire in which conversion, though not imposed by mission, had nonetheless come to seem expedient.

[79] Masudi, *Kitab muruj al-dhahab* §504.
[80] Bulliet, *Conversion*, especially the graphs on pp. 82, 97, 109, and the summary at pp. 128–38.

Richard Bulliet has argued that once the growing rate of conversion made the Islamic religion's hold seem no longer in peril, it became legitimate to reassert local identities long submerged. Anything that might have looked like revolution against Islam had been inconceivable; but revolution within Islam became less and less objectionable as the strong center came to be seen as an exploitative obstacle to provincial development, which could be handled much better by local dynasties. This interpretation is quite speculative and certainly not above criticism.[81] There continues to be dispute about the speed and chronology of conversion. It was certainly also true that Islam's political hold on the empire's provinces was an essential factor in encouraging further conversion and giving the process critical impetus. Nor should we assume that the only way Islam could become impregnable was by absorbing a "democratic" majority of the population. Some converts were more influential than others. But it remains likely that the conversion process did, along with other developments such as the growth of agricultural wealth thanks to diversification of crops and improvement of farming techniques,[82] gradually create an atmosphere in which the political disintegration of the Abbasid Empire seemed less unthinkable.

The probability that there was such a connection appears most clearly when we consider the relationship between the upswing in conversions and the multiplication of heresy[83]—or perhaps it would be better to say the subdivision of "orthodoxy", since Islam's doctrinal center was to begin with relatively ill defined, a considerable variety of teachings being allowed to pass for orthodox. Here the causative role of conversion is less in dispute. Admittedly it takes only two to make an argument—the possibility of doctrinal discord was present in Islam as in all other religions from the moment the founder acquired his first follower. And the chronological priority of orthodoxy over heresy or vice versa is a notorious conundrum, in Islam as in Christianity. But here, as in our discussion of the First Byzantine Commonwealth, we are concerned with heresy's acquisition of stable, nonclandestine structures and hence of political potential or actual power; and that can hardly come about until heresy has at least some mass together with unmistakable momentum, while "orthodoxy" has lost full control of the situation, even within the wide parameters Islam permitted. Despite the considerable disruption caused by such early dissenting movements as Kharidjism,[84]

[81] E.g., Morony, in *Conversion and continuity*.

[82] Watson, *Agricultural innovation*.

[83] Mottahedeh, *Loyalty and leadership*, 20–25, is excellent on the subject matter of this paragraph.

[84] Levi della Vida, *Enc.Is.*[2] 4.1074–77.

this did not happen until the Abbasid period. Richard Bulliet has argued that the different schools of law and theology came into being at different points on the "conversion curve" and reflected needs and attitudes characteristic of those who were converting at that time.[85] Although Islam had no clergy, it did have its local learned elites. The cohesiveness of the *ulama* as a group is easily overestimated—it was closer to that of modern "intellectuals" than to that of the medieval European Church.[86] Even so, particularist feelings slowly congealed around them, somewhat as local loyalties had focused on late antique bishops. Once teachings became movements and acquired regional roots they could hardly be ignored; and official attention, especially if heavy-handed, naturally led them—and the center as well—to sharpen their ideological profile.

This was certainly the case with the Sunni-Shiite divide, which had started as a difference over the role of Ali in Muhammad's succession but came to acquire extremely specific associations with the various parties contending for power amid the ruins of the Abbasid state. By the tenth century Sunnis and Shiites were generating not only religious but also social milieus, often in separate quarters of the same city, but of very different emotional textures: the Shiites peripheral (in the universal if not always in the local perspective), speculative, and esoteric, the Sunnis insistent on the codification and preservation of tradition and precedent (*sunna*), especially the gathering and interpretation of Muhammad's "sayings" (*hadith*). For the rewriting of history did not leave even the Prophet unscathed. His sayings became a battleground for rival aspirants to legitimacy.[87] This was scarcely a problem under the Umayyads; but toward the end of their period there are signs that the *ulama* were developing a *sunna* supposedly derived directly from the Prophet and his *hadith*, without caliphal intermediaries and indeed often conceived in opposition to caliphal claims. This was the beginning of the process that was complete by the mid-ninth century, whereby the caliphate was reinterpreted as a largely political institution without substantial religious authority and obliged therefore to follow those who did have religious authority, the *ulama*.[88] The consequences of this reinterpretation are still with us, not least in the difference between on the one hand the Sunnis' willingness to make do with the Prophet's example and the scholarly tradition, and on the other hand the Shiite assumption that, at least in an ideal world, religious and secular authority are united in the person of the Imam. The caliphate was still further undermined, and

---

[85] Bulliet, *Conversion* 59–63.
[86] Mottahedeh, *Loyalty and leadership* 136–38.
[87] A good example is quoted above, p. 151.
[88] Crone and Hinds, *God's Caliph* 58–99.

such symbolic unity as the *umma* had retained was shattered, when in the course of the tenth century rival dynasts—the Umayyads in Spain, and the Ismaili Shiite dynasty that ruled Egypt, the Fatimids[89]— adopted the title "Caliph" for themselves.

Ultimately, then, and to some it may seem paradoxically, the quickening pace of conversion in the ninth to tenth centuries—the reduction, in other words, of the distance and flexibility that had once existed between the empire that was for all and the religion of the Arab few— helped bring about the fragmentation of the Islamic world empire, whose birth and growth had owed so much to the power of religion. Gradually the Islamic Empire ceased to be the dominant player on the stage of world affairs. What remained was the Islamic Commonwealth or the Muslim world, at first alongside a decaying remnant of world empire, then just nourishing a memory of a Golden Age associated particularly with Baghdad.[90] At times that memory was more effective and creative than at others—as, for example, under at least the earlier of the Mamluks who ruled in Cairo from 1250 to 1517, stood up to the Mongols, and reinvigorated the Islamic faith they had adopted as slaves.[91] Eventually the Ottoman sultans reassembled most of the Islamic Empire west of the Zagros, added Anatolia, long-desired Constantinople, and the Balkans, and adopted the title "Caliph". In this guise the Islamic Empire, ruled once more by a caliph, survived until Kemal Atatürk abolished it in 1924.

But the Islamic Commonwealth was not exactly like either the First or the Second Byzantine Commonwealth. Although important parts of the First Byzantine Commonwealth lay outside the Byzantine Empire, much of it occupied soil universally acknowledged to be under Byzantium's rule. The Second Byzantine Commonwealth, the mainly Slavic world of Eastern Europe, consisted entirely of autonomous states; but unlike most of the First Byzantine Commonwealth, these states were Orthodox in Constantinople's eyes, so the tensions between center and periphery

[89] For these and other later examples see Crone and Hinds, *God's Caliph* 17–19, 100 n.18.

[90] It is of the transitional moment between empire and commonwealth that Miquel's four volumes of *Géographie humaine* provide so wonderful and exhaustive a description. But because Miquel is concerned with the Arabs' understanding of events rather than with the events themselves, his fully fledged Islamic Empire, the *mamlakat al-Islam* of the mind, emerges only in the ninth and tenth centuries (2.525–28, 3.X–XI), when the politico-military strength of the Abbasid Caliphate was already, objectively speaking, on the ebb. For Miquel's geographical sources, the memory of empire is extremely powerful, and the reality of commonwealth sinks in only later, in the likes of Ibn Battuta (early fourteenth century): 1.IX, 337–38.

[91] Little, *Mamlūks*, X.

were mainly political rather than ideological, and therefore reasonably soluble. In other words, both Byzantine commonwealths not only reproduced the character of their living and vigorous parents—the diversity of the vast East Roman Empire before the Arab invasions, and the more focused Orthodoxy of the reduced Byzantine Empire in the aftermath of Islam and Iconoclasm—but also enjoyed a dynamic relationship with them. One could even say, in the case of the earlier of the two commonwealths, that the relationship was more like that between an older and a younger sibling. The Second Byzantine Commonwealth did in fact outlive its parent, and Moscow succeeded Constantinople as the Third Rome when the latter fell to the Turks; but by that time the commonwealth seemed as mature as the empire itself.

The Islamic Commonwealth was different. Whereas Christianity had far outstripped Rome's imperial impetus, the Islamic Empire had never left the religion of Islam to fend for itself. The sword had everywhere been at the service of the Quran, even if it had more often been wielded to defend than to impose the new faith. But perhaps in the process of expansion the empire had exhausted itself; certainly dissolution rather than consolidation was its response to the mounting curve of conversion to Islam. Far from being built in a mission-field that the imperial armies and bureaucracy were still striving to reach, the Islamic Commonwealth arose on the ruins of the empire that had generated it. When the first political cracks appeared in the Abbasid edifice, the caliphs of Baghdad still on the whole continued to recognize the rulers of the successor states, whom they called "kings". In this way, the Islamic Empire's notional unity was maintained. But when, after the fall of Baghdad to the Turks in 1055, the power of the Abbasids dwindled to insignificance, the Islamic Commonwealth was left with no single point of political reference, no secular equivalent of Mecca where the *hajj* remains to this day a spectacular statement of the ultimate oneness of Islam, both Sunnite and Shiite. The caliph's title continued to bestow a certain political legitimacy on the power that possessed it, but the legitimacy and the power were as likely to be shadow as substance. The commonwealth, whose common denominator was cultural and religious much more than political, related better to its senescent or dead parent, Baghdad, than to more vigorous siblings such as Fatimid or Mamluk Cairo or Ottoman Istanbul, except insofar as the commonwealth was identical with the possessions of Cairo or Istanbul.[92] Inevitably, the Islamic Commonwealth was even less coherent than either of the Byzantine commonwealths.

[92] Even here one has to allow for such factors as the differences in outlook between, say, Arabs and Turks within the Ottoman Empire.

وَكَادَيْزَعُ الجَمَالَ الشِّرَّ وَانْشَدَ

مَا الْحَجُّ سِيَرَكَ تَأْوِيَاوَادَلاجَا وَلَا الْعِيشَامَ الْجَمَالَا رَاجَدَلاً

10. Pilgrim caravan on the way to Mecca, painted by Yahya ibn Mahmud al-Wasiti
in a manuscript of al-Hariri's *Maqamat*, dated 634 A.H./A.D. 1237.

Nonetheless, the Islamic Commonwealth's emergence was far from
being the negative experience described by those historians who concentrate on the central political structures of the Abbasid state. Despite
its political and to some extent doctrinal multipolarity, the commonwealth was founded on a faith confessed by peoples more numerous and
in lands more extensive than could be claimed by any other religion.[93]
And at least to begin with—which is all that seriously concerns us
here—it was founded on the Arabic language and a shared bureaucratic
culture that allowed top administrators to move from one Muslim court

[93] Brice, *Atlas of Islam* 8.

---

to another; on recognition that only the caliph could confer political legitimacy; and on freedom of travel and trade between the commonwealth's constituent parts. Not a few of the commonwealth's parts were at times prosperous and well governed—a condition for which strong central government is far from being a sine qua non.[94] And the availability of a number of different and competing patronage centers encouraged a remarkable cultural efflorescence in the tenth century, the "classical" moment of a mature Islamic style, which in turn strengthened the Islamic Commonwealth and confirms its importance for us. It was above all this cultural strength of the Islamic Commonwealth that allowed it to absorb and convert the Turkish invaders who arrived in such force during the eleventh century, and captured Baghdad in 1055. That the energy of the Turks was turned to Islam's account was one of the decisive events in history. It ensured that the Byzantine Empire would eventually be eliminated and that the Umayyads' goal of taking Constantinople for Islam would one day be achieved, with, among other results, the deepening of the profound influence Islam had already exercised over the development of Eastern Christianity.

Islam's role in the evolution of Western Christendom was no less fundamental, molding it by forcing it to recoil, then retaliate, and once more, under Ottoman leadership, threatening its integrity as recently as the seventeenth century. Still today the Islamic Commonwealth provides a powerful bond between Asia and Africa and, in the opinion of many of its intellectual and political leaders, a potential base for less fragmented and unstable political structures than those in place at the moment. At the same time the religion of the Quran goes on expanding beyond its own territories. Islam today provides, along with but often more self-confidently than Christianity, clear proof that the difficult late antique marriage of political and religious universalism, the Emperor Constantine's greatest vision and legacy, still endures.

---

[94] Note Kennedy's intelligent remarks in this connection, *The Prophet and the Age of the Caliphates* 249, 266; and in general his chapter "The structure of politics in the Muslim Commonwealth", esp. 201, 204–5.

Epilogue

> Again, the devil taketh him up into an exceedingly
> high mountain, and sheweth him all the kingdoms of
> the world, and the glory of them; and saith unto him,
> All these things will I give thee, if thou wilt fall down
> and worship me. Then saith Jesus unto him, Get thee
> hence, Satan: for it is written, Thou shalt worship the
> Lord thy God, and him only shalt thou serve. Then the
> devil leaveth him, and, behold, angels came and minis-
> tered unto him.
>
> —*Matt.* 4.8–11

LATE ANTIQUITY'S legacy of commonwealths is not exhausted by the
two on which this book has concentrated. Even as the Islamic Empire
stood at the apogee of its fortunes in the last decades of the eighth
century, Byzantium began its recovery from the humiliations and confu-
sions of the Dark Age. This recovery soon led to the re-Christianization
of the Balkans and the inauguration of the Second Byzantine Commonwealth in Eastern Europe. The emergence of the Carolingian Empire
and the growing power and claims of the Papacy gave similar impetus
and focus to Western Christendom, which despite the language and
occasional reality of empire was always essentially a commonwealth.
The medieval European and west Asian world was dominated, then, by
three commonwealths born in or descended from late antiquity—the
Islamic, the Second Byzantine, and the Latin—together with one
anomalous survivor from among the antique empires, Byzantium. But
it is the three commonwealths that constitute late antiquity's distinctive
sociopolitical legacy, for empires antiquity had produced abundantly in
all the phases of its history. The memory or reality of Rome, Constantinople, and Baghdad kept at least the idea of empire alive in everyone's
mind; but it was commonwealths that provided most people with a
practical frame of reference wider than the state to which they were
immediately subject.

Nonetheless, there could be no commonwealth without a preceding
empire; even Western Christendom derived from Rome, despite the
intervening upheavals of the Dark Age. Nor could just any empire generate commonwealth; imperial impetus had first to be conjoined with a
universalist (not ethnic) monotheism in an aspiring or realized world
empire. This was late antiquity's other permanent legacy—not mono-

theism *entre nous*, as the Jews had practiced it, but monotheism as the legitimator and even motor of multiethnic politico-cultural federations.

In short, late antiquity's contribution to the technique of empire was the discovery of a nonmilitary and only partially political basis for self-perpetuation. The invention of commonwealth was an unintended result of Constantine's adoption of monotheism as a suitable creed for empire, and Muhammad's association of the two from the outset. In practice this ideal association proved only briefly realizable, partly because monotheism could not maintain its own unity, and partly because empires cannot either, for reasons neglected in this book because others have discussed them endlessly. But commonwealth allowed Rome and Baghdad to survive symbolically in a way that Nineveh, Babylon, and even Ctesiphon had not. What the symbols stand for is Christendom or Europe and the Muslim or Arab world. The terminological slippage in both cases is significant, for these commonwealths depend on political and real or supposed ethnic links as well as on a shared religion, or at least culture. And implicit in commonwealth is always the possibility of political revival. Today, Christian Europe is reconstituting itself politically. There is no rush to allow Turkey to join the emerging union; but now there are comparable stirrings in the Muslim world too, and not only in the part of it that can or does claim to be "Arab". Clearly the relationship between religions and large-scale political structures (if not exactly empires) remains a living issue.

But between late antiquity and now, things have become much more complicated. In the medieval and modern worlds monotheism continued to fertilize the discourse of cultural and political conquest and colonialism.[1] Those who worshipped the only God saw themselves as by definition the only people who knew how to live fully human lives. This assumption was second nature to Muslims and to Eastern Christians just as much as to Western Christians; but it was Western Christendom that conquered the world, including much of Eastern Christendom and Islam. And Western discourse of conquest and colonialism evolved directly from the universalist ideas prevalent in late antiquity. It reached its most totalitarian form in the medieval Papacy's claim to authority over all mankind, whether actually or as yet only potentially Christian, and irrespective even of whether they were non-Christian monotheists. Jews and Muslims were now on the same footing as polytheists. "Pagans" were admitted to have natural-law rights to lordship and property, but were deemed to forfeit these if they did not behave according to

---

[1] See recently Williams, *American Indian in Western legal thought*; Pagden, *Spanish imperialism*, esp. ch. 1–2.

"rational" European norms, and particularly if they resisted evangelization. The Protestant cultures of northern Europe took over the same ideas, which served as death warrant no less for the North American Indians than for their Central and South American counterparts under Spanish rule. With their Catholic faith and their vast possessions in both Europe and the New World, the Spaniards thought themselves uniquely suited to universal monarchy. Their apologists proclaimed them the heirs of Cyrus himself.

But by the time the Spanish Empire went into decline, the post–Era of Discovery world had apparently grown too large and complex for old-style political universalism ever again to be a practical possibility. Instead there was now emerging a "world economy" that surpassed even Europe's boundaries and was big enough to embrace a variety of empires.[2] The "Age of Imperialism" saw an unprecedented projection of European power; but the European bases of the power projected—small nation-states such as Portugal and Holland or even England and France—were minute and remote when plotted on the expanding world map. And the process of secularization initiated by the Renaissance was no less fatal to old-style universalism than the Era of Discovery. Eventually, in a world made small again by the population explosion as well as by the communications revolution, humanity's irrepressible diversity asserted itself and came back to haunt the West. As the colonial empires crumbled it was gradually accepted, at least in theory, that peoples have the right to determine their own destiny without external interference. Pluralism based on tolerance of or indifference to difference appeared to be the best solution in a world that still seemed large enough for "self-determination" to be based on genuine choice.

At the same time, though, the local cultural identities and homogeneities that were the sine qua non of this "strong" pluralism were being attenuated, outside the West because of the West's own all-pervasiveness, and within the West thanks to colonial immigration into Europe, and first European, then international, immigration into the New World. Attenuation of local identities in the "global village" is now generating a new, "weak" pluralism based not on tolerance of difference but on positive (or at least affected) esteem for and even adoption of "the other". Strong pluralism has begun to evolve syncretistically into "multiculturalism". Social groups inevitably privilege their own beliefs, but are cross-fertilized by those of other groups, and feel threatened only by those that assert the exclusive validity of a universal credo.

"Multiculturalism" is an understandable response to the problems of

---

[2] Wallerstein, *World system* i, ch. i.

intimate cohabitation in the global village, and it is not completely without late antique precedent. But even the overlay and interpenetration of Buddhism, Nestorianism, and Manichaeism along the Silk Route[3] almost certainly had its competitive aspects: some cultures absorb better than others, and neither Nestorianism nor Manichaeism survived the experience. Esteem for one's own language and beliefs and desire for a distinctive identity are deeply rooted in human nature, but the ideals multiculturalism offers are lowest common denominators— peace, prosperity, and a "variety" sufficiently neutered to be shared. Instead of propagating this new but anodyne and demoralizing universalism and regarding political structures as sacrosanct, we would do better to design political structures loose enough to contain cultures whose differences sometimes overshadow their common ground. Since economic world domination is already with us, the battles over "multiculturalism" now being fought within such economic power centers as the United States and Europe are of long-term significance for everyone. There is a real danger that the world economy will evolve into the biggest world empire yet, and there will be those on the winning side who will hail it, as Origen did the Roman Empire, for the peace it will bring and the limitless prospects for propagating their particular ideologies.[4] But in our world of many cultures we need a more flexible model than that, one that will suppress the strife of nation-states but also nourish our religions, languages, and customs.[5]

"A language is a much more ancient and inevitable thing than a state."[6] And although the same language may express several religions, concurrently or successively, religion is the language we use with God as well as with our fellow humans. As such, it is even less capable than our social language of being wholly accommodated to political structures. Partial accommodation there may, of course, be; this book has discussed

[3] See above, pp. 72–73, 76, 123.

[4] Origen, *Contra Celsum* II.30: "It would have hindered Jesus's teaching from being spread through the whole world if there had been many kingdoms . . . because men everywhere would have been compelled to do military service and to fight in defence of their own land. . . . How could this teaching, which preaches peace . . . have had any success unless the international situation had everywhere been changed and a milder spirit prevailed at the advent of Jesus?" (trans. H. Chadwick).

[5] See the remarks of a more enlightened apologist of empire than Origen, the Ottoman mutassarif of Amasya, to an audience of Armenians in 1893: "You pay little tax; you are free from military service; you keep your religion, your language and your customs. Would the Power coming in our place give you the same liberties?" (Quoted by Kedourie, in his admirable essay "Minorities", *Chatham House Version* 297.)

[6] Joseph Brodsky, in a letter to Leonid Brezhnev (1972), quoted by Remnick, *New York Review of Books* (14 May 1992): 44.

one phase in its history. We have even seen much that was positive in the
workings of the monotheist empires and commonwealths of late antiquity. They gave shape and direction to history and helped crystallize and
preserve elements that were and are thought to be of value from the past.
On the level of the spiritual life too, it was more often than not the case
that to pursue the Christian way was easier under Christian princes, and
likewise for Muslims under Muslim princes. Even heretics rarely felt so
harassed that the jurisdiction of an "infidel" ruler seemed preferable. To
live in a polity that professes and advances one's own faith was and
remains the ideal. But the ideal is easier to depict than to realize. The
enlightened ruler, who conquers the world that others may renounce it,
is a powerful paradigm precisely because he is so rare. And the ruler
himself cannot so easily renounce the world. Even Ashoka gave up wars
of conquest only once they were no longer necessary, following a model
already contained in the early Buddhist literature.[7] Eusebius painted
Constantine as more of a saint than he was. Muhammad established his
earthly authority at sword-point. Understandably, some philosophers
and theologians hold that knowledge of God should not be used in order
to realize or sanction social and political ends. The historian too may
legitimately ask to what extent it is inevitable that belief in one god,
monotheism, will be turned to the sort of political ends we have been
investigating.

A first step toward answering this question would be to rejoin Leo and
Gobazes at the foot of Daniel's pillar. Writing from a point of view
familiar by now to the reader of this essay, the author of the *Life of S.
Daniel the Stylite* depicts the ascetic as a decisive influence in the Byzantine capital's power play. The one emperor is linked to the One God
through a holy intermediary. We may wonder, though, what priority
Daniel himself assigned to this aspect of his life. A possible answer is
provided by a recent representative of the same tradition:

> The usual way to acquire knowledge, the one we all know, consists
> in the directing of the intellectual faculty outwards where it meets
> with phenomena, sights, forms, in innumerable variety—a differ-
> entiation *ad infinitum* of all that happens. This means that the
> knowledge thus acquired is never complete and has no real unity.
> Insistently seeking unity, the mind is forced to take refuge in syn-
> thesis, which cannot help being artificial. The unity arrived at in
> this way does not really and objectively exist. It is merely a form of
> abstract thinking natural to the mind.
>
> The other way to acquire knowledge of being is to turn the spirit

[7] Tambiah, *World conqueror* 41–42, 45, 55–56.

in and towards itself and then to God. Here the process is the exact reverse. The mind turns away from the endless plurality and fragmentariness of the world's phenomena, and with all its strength addresses itself to God in prayer, and through prayer is directly incorporated in the very act of Divine Life, and begins to see both itself and the whole world.

To obtain knowledge after the first manner is natural to man in his fallen state. The second is the way of the Son of man.

Now the beginning of the second manner of obtaining knowledge is pure prayer and the gift of performing miracles. Inserting themselves in the current of the will of the Father, the Saints, like the Son of God, performed miracles, and thus became partakers and laborers together with God in the Act of the creation of the world. Within the confines of earthly life experience of this kind of knowledge is always incomplete, but after they have left this world those who are growing to God become associates in divine omniscience and omnipotence.[8]

Political authority, perceiving the relevance to its own aspirations of this turning away from plurality and of the powerful (albeit incomplete) experience of union, omniscience, and omnipotence, attempts to harness the sage's God in order to extend itself throughout the *oikoumene*. Inevitably, political authority overextends itself, the *oikoumene*'s sum of humanity and human knowledge being too large and diverse to be ruled as a single unit.[9] But in any case knowledge of God in the truest sense has to do with creation, not politics.[10] What allows us to overlook this fact, to ignore the uncompromising sage while annexing his belief in the One God, his monotheism, is that basic flaw in our human nature so memorably depicted and incarnated by Dostoevsky's Grand Inquisitor. "The need of universal unity", the Inquisitor declares in his famous monologue,

> is the third and last torment of men. Mankind as a whole has always striven to organize itself into a world state. There have been many great nations with great histories, but the more highly devel-

[8] Archimandrite Sophrony, *Monk of Mount Athos* 60.

[9] Cf. Theophylact Simocatta, *Historia universalis* IV.13.7–8, quoted above, pp. 98–9.

[10] See above, p. 159 n. 74. For patristic antidotes to Eusebius, see Beck, *Ideen und Realitaeten* IV.651–52, on (universalist) empire as the work of the Antichrist. But these are voices in the wilderness, to whom those who accepted secular authority, if they listened at all, replied that it is not the use but the abuse of power that is bad (Ambrose, *Expositio Evangeli secundum Lucam* IV.29)—"God has made many good men kings" (Jerome, *In Matheum* I.4.9).

oped they were, the more unhappy they were, for they were more acutely conscious of the need for the worldwide union of men. The great conquerors, the Timurs and Genghis Khans, swept like a whirlwind over the earth, striving to conquer the world, but, though unconsciously, they expressed the same great need of mankind for a universal and world-wide union.

Angered by Jesus's refusal, long ago in the wilderness, of Satan's suggestion that he harness the power implicit in this universal need, the aged cardinal admonishes his silent visitor in these words:

> By accepting the world and Caesar's purple, you would have founded the world state and given universal peace. For who is to wield dominion over men if not those who have taken possession of their consciences and in whose hands is their bread?[11]

The ambition to reproduce on earth God's heavenly monarchy—whether in the guise of theocracy or of a more secular autocracy—has always proved an illusion. Even where partially realized, the ideal has been subject to the corruption of power. Not only in his dialogue with Satan in the wilderness, Christ rejected both earthly power and its accompanying illusions and corruptions. Instead he addressed himself to the innumerable individuals who make up mankind, and within them to the immortal soul that is our only truly universal and indivisible attribute.

[11] *The brothers Karamazov* II.5.5 (tr. D. Magarshack).

Bibliography

ANCIENT SOURCES

Most texts available in the Budé, Loeb, Oxford, *Sources chrétiennes*, or Teubner series have been excluded. Translations of sources in languages other than Greek or Latin have been listed where extant.

Abu'l-Faraj al-Isfahani, *Kitab al-aghani* (Beirut, 1969–82).
Aelius Aristides, *orationes*, ed. (1) B. Keil (Berlin, 1898; *or.* XVII–LIII only); (2) F. W. Lenz and C. A. Behr (Leiden, 1976–).
Agapius of Manbij, *Historia universalis*, ed. and tr. A. Vasiliev, *P.O.* 5(4), 7(4), 8(3), 11(1).
Agathias, ed. R. Keydell (Berlin, 1967).
Ambrose, *De fide ad Gratianum Augustum*, ed. *P.L.* 16.549–726.
———, *Expositio Evangeli secundum Lucam*, ed. G. Tissot, *S.C.* 45 bis, 52.
Anonymus Valesianus, ed. J. Moreau and V. Velkov, *Excerpta Valesiana* (Leipzig, 1968²).
Aphrahat, *Demonstrations*, ed. and tr. J. Parisot, *Patrologia syriaca* 1 (Paris, 1894–1907); tr. M.-J. Pierre, *S.C.* 349, 359.
Apocalypse of Ps.-Methodius (Syriac text), ed. and tr. (1) F. J. Martinez, *Eastern Christian apocalyptic in the early Muslim period: Pseudo-Methodius and Pseudo-Athanasius* (diss., Catholic University of America, Washington D.C., 1985), 58–201; (2) H. Suermann, *Die geschichtstheologische Reaktion auf die einfallenden Muslime in der edessenischen Apokalyptik des 7. Jahrhunderts* (Frankfurt am Main, 1985), 34–85; (3) G. J. Reinink (*C.S.C.O.*, forthcoming). Tr. P. J. Alexander (ed. D. deF. Abrahamse), *The Byzantine apocalyptic tradition* (Berkeley, 1985), 36–51.
Arnobius, *Adversus nationes*, ed. (1) C. Marchesi (Turin, 1953²); (2) H. Le Bonniec (Paris, 1982–).
Asclepius, ed. A. D. Nock and A. J. Festugière, *Corpus Hermeticum* (Paris, 1946–54), 2.257–401.
Ashoka, Rock edicts, ed. and tr. U. Schneider, *Die grossen Felsen-Edikte Aśokas* (Wiesbaden, 1978).
Athanasius, *Apologia ad Constantium Imperatorem*, ed. J. M. Szymusiak, *S.C.* 56 bis. 86–174.
———, *Apologia contra Arianos*, ed. H.-G. Opitz, *Athanasius Werke* 2(1) (Berlin, 1935–41), 87–168.
Augustine, *De vera religione*, ed. K.-D. Daur, *C.C.S.L.* 32.169–260.
———, *Sermones de Vetere Testamento*, ed. C. Lambot, *C.C.S.L.* 41.
Bar Hebraeus, *Chronicon syriacum*, ed. P. Bedjan (Paris, 1890); tr. E.A.W. Budge, *The Chronography of Gregory Abû'l Faraj* (London, 1932).
al-Biruni, *Kitab al-athar al-baqiya*, ed. C. E. Sachau (Leipzig, 1878); tr. Sachau, *The chronology of ancient nations* (London, 1879).

Book of deeds of Ardashir son of Papak (Karnamak i Ardasir i Papakan), ed. and tr. D. P. Sanjana (Bombay, 1896).

Book of the Himyarites, ed. and tr. A. Moberg (Lund, 1924).

Chronicle of Seert, ed. and tr. A. Scher and others, *P.O.* 4(3), 5(2), 7(2), 13(4).

Chronicon anonymum ("Khuzistan chronicle"), ed. I. Guidi, *C.S.C.O.* 1, *Syr.* 1.15–39; tr. Guidi, *C.S.C.O.* 2, *Syr.* 2.13–32.

Chronicon Paschale, ed. L. Dindorf (Bonn, 1832).

Codex Justinianus, ed. P. Krueger (Berlin, 1877).

Codex Theodosianus, ed. P. Krueger and T. Mommsen (Berlin, 1905).

Cologne Mani Codex, ed. L.Koenen and C.Römer, *Der Kölner Mani-Kodex: Über das Werden seines Leibes* (Opladen, 1988).

Cyril of Scythopolis, *Vita Euthymii*, ed. E. Schwartz, *Kyrillos von Skythopolis* (Leipzig, 1939), 3–85.

Damascius, *Vita Isidori*, ed. C. Zintzen (Hildesheim, 1967).

Denkard, ed. D. M. Madan, *The complete text of the Pahlavi Dinkard* (Bombay, 1911).

Digesta (Iustiniani Augusti), ed. T. Mommsen (Berlin, 1870).

Elishe, *History of Vardan and the Armenian war*, ed. E. Ter-Minasean (Erevan, 1957); tr. R. W. Thomson (Cambridge, Mass., 1982).

Ephraem the Syrian, *Hymns on the Nativity*, ed. and tr. E. Beck, *C.S.C.O.* 186–87, *Syr.* 82–83; tr. K. E. McVey, *Ephrem the Syrian, Hymns* (New York, 1989), 61–217.

Epiphanius, *Panarion*, ed. K. Holl (Leipzig, 1915–33).

Eunapius, *Vitae philosophorum et sophistarum*, ed. J. Giangrande (Rome, 1956).

Eusebius of Caesarea, *De laudibus Constantini*, ed. I. Heikel, *Eusebius Werke* 1 (Leipzig, 1902), 193–259.

———, *De martyribus Palestinae*, ed. G. Bardy, *S.C.* 55.121–74.

———, *Praeparatio evangelica*, ed. K. Mras (Berlin 1954–56; 1², 1982).

———, *Vita Constantini*, ed. F. Winkelmann (Berlin, 1975).

Eusebius—Jerome, *Chronicon*, ed. R. Helm (Leipzig, 1913–26).

Expositio totius mundi et gentium, ed. J. Rougé, *S.C.* 124.

Festus, *Breviarium*, ed. J. W. Eadie (London, 1967).

Gelasius I, *Adversum Andromachum (Collectio Avellana, ep. 100)*, ed. G. Pomarès, *S.C.* 65.

Gelasius of Cyzicus, *H.E.*, ed. G. Loeschke and M. Heinemann (Leipzig, 1918).

George of Pisidia, *Expeditio Persica*, ed. A. Pertusi, *Giorgio di Pisidia poemi* 1 (Ettal, 1959).

———, *In restitutionem S. Crucis*, ed. A. Pertusi, *Giorgio di Pisidia poemi* 1 (Ettal, 1959).

Germanus I of Constantinople, *Homily on the deliverance of Constantinople*, ed. V. Grumel, "Homélie de Saint Germain sur la délivrance de Constantinople", *R.E.Byz.* 16 (1958): 183–205.

History of the Patriarchs of Alexandria, ed. and tr. B. Evetts, P.O. 1(2, 4), 5(1), 10(5).

Ibn al-Balkhi, *Fars-nama*, ed. G. Le Strange and R. A. Nicholson (London, 1921).

Ibn Ishaq, *Sirat an-Nabi*, ed. F. Wüstenfeld (Göttingen, 1858–60); tr. A. Guillaume, *The life of Muhammad: A translation of Ishāq's Sirat rasūl allāh* (Karachi, 1955).

al-Jarir, *Naqaid*, ed. A. A. Bevan, *The Naḳā'iḍ of Jarīr and al-Farazdaḳ* (Leiden, 1905–12); tr. A. Wormhoudt (Oskaloosa, Ia., 1974).

Jerome, *Adversus Jovinianum*, ed. *P.L.* 23.221–352.

———, *In Hiezechielem*, ed. F. Glorie, *C.C.S.L.* 75.

———, *In Matheum*, ed. E. Bonnard, *S.C.* 242, 259.

John Bar Penkaye (John of Phenek), *Ris Melle*, ed. A. Mingana, *Sources syriaques* 1 (Leipzig, 1908) 1*–171* (book XV, tr. pp. 172*–197*); Eng. tr. of end of book XIV and parts of book XV in S. P. Brock, "North Mesopotamia in the late seventh century. Book XV of John Bar Penkāyē's *Rīš Mellē*", *J.S.A.I.* 9 (1987): 51–75.

John Malalas, ed. L. Dindorf (Bonn, 1831).

John of Ephesus, *H.E., pars tertia*, ed. and tr. E. W. Brooks, *C.S.C.O.* 105–6, *Syr.* 54–55.

———, *Lives of the Eastern saints*, ed. and tr. E. W. Brooks, *P.O.* 17(1), 18(4), 19(2).

John of Nikiu, *Chronicle*, ed. and tr. H. Zotenberg (Paris, 1883); tr. R. H. Charles (London, 1916).

Joshua the Stylite, *Chronicle*, ed. and tr. (1) W. Wright (Cambridge, 1882); (2) J. B. Chabot, *C.S.C.O.* 91, *Syr.* 43.235–317 (text), *C.S.C.O.* 121, *Syr.* 66.174–233 (translation).

Julian, *Contra Galilaeos*, ed. E. Masaracchia (Rome, 1990).

Kebra Nagast, ed. and tr. C. Bezold (Munich, 1905); tr. E.A.W. Budge, *The Queen of Sheba and her only son Menyelek (I)* (Oxford, 1932²).

Kephalaia, ed. and tr. H. J. Polotsky and A. Böhlig, *Manichäische Handschriften der Staatlichen Museen Berlin* 1: *Kephalaia*, 1. *Hälfte* (Stuttgart, 1940) (pp. 1–244); A. Böhlig, *Kephalaia*, 2. *Hälfte* (Stuttgart, 1966) (pp. 244–91); A. Böhlig, "Ja und Amen in manichäischer Deutung", *Z.P.E.* 58 (1985): 59–70 (p. 292).

Kirdir, Inscription of, ed. and tr. D. N. MacKenzie in G. Herrmann, *The Sasanian rock reliefs at Naqsh-i Rustam (Iranische Denkmäler* Reihe 2: *Iranische Felsreliefs* Lieferung 13 = I) (Berlin, 1989), 35–72.

Leges Constantini Theodosii Leonis, various versions in Syriac, Armenian, and Arabic, ed. and tr. K. G. Bruns and E. Sachau, *Syrisch-römisches Rechtsbuch aus dem fünften Jahrhundert* (Leipzig, 1880); E. Sachau, *Syrische Rechtsbücher* 1 (Berlin, 1907); further bibliography in H. Kaufhold, "Die Überlieferung der Sententiae syriacae und ihr historischer und literarischer Kontext", in D. Simon, ed., *Akten des 26. Deutschen Rechtshistorikertages, Frankfurt am Main, 22. bis 26. September 1986* (Frankfurt am Main, 1987), 505 n. 1.

Leges Homeritarum, ed. *P.G.* 86.567–620.

Letter of Pisentius, ed. and tr. A. Périer, "Lettre de Pisuntius, évêque de Qeft, à ses fidèles", *Revue de l'Orient chrétien* 19 (1914): 79–92, 302–23, 445–46.

Letter of Tansar, ed. M. Minovi (Teheran, 1932); tr. M. Boyce (Rome, 1968).

Malchus, ed. R. C. Blockley, *The fragmentary classicising historians of the later Roman Empire* 2 (Liverpool, 1983), 401–62.

Marinus, *Vita Procli*, ed. R. Masullo (Naples, 1985).

al-Masudi, *Kitab al-tanbih wa'l-ishraf*, ed. M. J. de Goeje (Leiden, 1894); tr. B. Carra de Vaux, *Maçoudi: Le livre de l'avertissement et de la revision* (Paris, 1897).

———, *Kitab muruj al-dhahab*, ed. and tr. (1) C. Barbier de Meynard and J.-B. Pavet de Courteille, *Maçoudi: Les prairies d'or* (Paris, 1861–77); (2) C. Pellat (text, Beirut, 1965–79; tr. (revision of Barbier de Meynard and Pavet de Courteille, Paris, 1962–74) (but see M. G. Morony's comments, *Iraq after the Muslim conquest* [Princeton, 1984], 566–67).

Menander Rhetor, ed. D. A. Russell and N. G. Wilson (Oxford, 1981).

Michael the Syrian, *Chronicle*, ed. and tr. J.-B. Chabot (Paris, 1899–1910).

Minucius Felix, *Octavius*, ed. J. Beaujeu (Paris, 1964).

Mishnah, ed. and tr. P. Blackman (London, 1951–56); tr. J. Neusner (ed.), *The Mishnah: A new translation* (New Haven, 1988).

Moses Khorenatsi, *History of the Armenians*, ed. M. Abelean and S. Yarutiwnean (Tiflis, 1913); tr. R. W. Thomson (Cambridge, Mass., 1978).

al-Nadim, *Kitab al-fihrist*, ed. (1) G. Flügel (Leipzig, 1871–72); (2) R. Tajaddod (Tehran, 1973²); tr. B. Dodge, *The Fihrist of al-Nadīm* (New York, 1970).

Nicephorus, *Breviarium*, ed. C. Mango, *Nikephoros Patriarch of Constantinople: Short history* (Washington, D.C., 1990).

Oraculum Sibyllinum XIII, ed. D. S. Potter, *Prophecy and history in the crisis of the Roman Empire: A historical commentary on the Thirteenth Sibylline Oracle* (Oxford, 1990).

Orbelian, Stephen, *History of Siounia*, ed. (1) G. Schahnazarian (Paris, 1859), (2) M. Emin (Moscow, 1861); tr. M. Brosset (St Petersburg, 1864–66).

Origen, *Epistola ad Africanum*, ed. N.R.M. de Lange, *S.C.* 302.469–578.

Passio Sanctorum Scilitanorum, ed. F. Ruggiero, "Atti dei martiri Scilitani", *M.A.L.* (1991): 39–139.

"Pawstos Buzand", *Epic histories*, ed. *Patmutiwn Hayoc i cors dprutiwns* (Venice, 1933⁴); tr. N. G. Garsoian, *The Epic histories attributed to P'awstos Buzand (Buzandaran Patmut 'iwnk')* (Cambridge, Mass., 1989).

Petrus Patricius, ed. C. Müller, *Fragmenta historicorum graecorum* 4 (Paris, 1851), 181–91.

Philippus (Bardaisan), *The book of the laws of countries*, ed. and tr. H.J.W. Drijvers (Assen, 1965).

Philostorgius, *H.E.*, ed. J. Bidez and F. Winkelmann (Berlin, 1981³).

Porphyry, *De imaginibus*, ed. J. Bidez, *Vie de Porphyre, le philosophe néoplatonicien* (Gent, 1913), 1*–23*.

———, *Vita Plotini*, ed. P. Henry and H.-R. Schwyzer, *Plotini opera* 1 (Paris, 1951), 1–41; 1² (Oxford, 1964), 1–38.

Priscus, ed. R. C. Blockley, *The fragmentary classicising historians of the later Roman Empire* 2 (Liverpool, 1983), 221–400.

Publilius Optatianus Porfyrius, *carmina*, ed. I. Polara (Turin, 1973).

Res gestae divi Saporis, ed. and tr. M. Back, *Die sassanidischen Staatsinschriften* (Leiden, 1978), 284–371; tr. R. Frye, *The history of ancient Iran* (Munich, 1984), 371–73.

Rufinus, *H.E.*, ed. T. Mommsen in E. Schwartz, ed., *Eusebius Werke* 2(2) (Leipzig, 1908), 957–1040.

"Sebeos, *History of Heraclius*", ed. V. G. Abgarian (Erevan, 1979); tr. F. Macler, *Histoire d'Héraclius par l'évêque Sebêos* (Paris, 1904).

Sententiae syriacae, ed. and tr. W. Selb (Vienna, 1990).

Severus of Antioch, *epistolae*, ed. and tr. E. W. Brooks, *P.O.* 12(2), 14(1).

———, *hymni*, ed. and tr. E. W. Brooks, *P.O.* 6(1), 7(5).

Simeon of Beth-Arsham, *Letter G*, ed. and tr. I. Shahîd, *The martyrs of Najrân: New documents* (Brussels, 1971) I–XXXII, 43–64.

Socrates Scholasticus, *H.E.*, ed. (1) R. Hussey (Oxford, 1853); (2) *P.G.* 67.29–842.

Sophronius of Jerusalem, *Epistola synodica ad Sergium Patriarcham Constantinopolitanum*, ed. *P.G.* 87.3147–3200.

Sozomen, *H.E.*, ed. J. Bidez (Berlin, 1960).

al-Tabari, *Tarikh al-rusul wa'l-muluk*, ed. M. J. de Goeje and others (Leiden, 1879–1901); partial tr. T. Nöldeke, *Geschichte der Perser und Araber zur Zeit der Sasaniden: Aus der arabischen Chronik des Tabari übersetzt* (Leiden, 1879); tr. ed. E. Yar-Shater (Albany, 1985–).

Tabula Peutingeriana, facsimile ed. with commentary, E. Weber (Graz, 1976).

Talmud, Babylonian, ed. I. Epstein, with tr. by various hands (London, 1935–48).

Tatian, *Oratio ad Graecos*, ed. M. Whittacker (Oxford, 1982).

Tertullian, *Adversus Judaeos*, ed. E. Kroymann, *C.C.S.L.* 2.1339–96.

Theodoret of Cyrrhus, *H.E.*, ed. L. Parmentier and F. Scheidweiler (Berlin, 1954²).

———, *Historia religiosa*, ed. P. Canivet and A. Leroy-Molinghen, *S.C.* 234, 257.

Theophanes, *Chronographia*, ed. C. de Boor (Leipzig, 1883–85).

Theophylact Simocatta, *Historia universalis*, ed. C. de Boor, re-ed. P. Wirth (Stuttgart, 1972).

Timothy I (Catholicos), *epistulae*, ed. and tr. O. Braun, *C.S.C.O.* 74–75, *Syr.* 67.

Vita S. Danielis Stylitae (*vita antiquior*), ed. H. Delehaye, *Les saints stylites* (Brussels, 1923), 1–94.

Vita S. Gregentii archiepiscopi Homeritarum, ed. A. Vasiliev, *Vizantijskij vremennik* 14 (1907): 23–67.

Yaqubi, *Kitab al-buldan*, ed. M. J. de Goeje, *Bibliotheca geographorum arabicorum* (Leiden, 1870–94), 7.231–373; tr. G. Wiet, *Ya'kubi: Les pays* (Cairo, 1937).

BIBLIOGRAPHY

SECONDARY LITERATURE

This bibliography is intended only as an explanation of the abbreviated references provided in the notes. Articles in encyclopedias and chapters in the *C.H.Ir.* have been excluded.

Abdel Sayed, G. G., *Untersuchungen zu den Texten über Pesyntheus, Bischof von Koptos (569–632)* (Bonn, 1984).

Abel, A., "L'Ethiopie et ses rapports avec l'Arabie préislamique jusqu'à l'émigration de ca. 615", *IV cong.int.st.etiop.* 405–20.

———, "La figure d'Alexandre en Iran", in *La Persia e il mondo greco-romano (Roma 11–14 aprile 1965)* (Rome, 1966), 119–36.

Abu-Lughod, J. L., *Before European hegemony: The world system A.D. 1250–1350* (New York, 1989).

Ahrweiler, H., *Byzance et la mer: La marine de guerre, la politique et les institutions maritimes de Byzance aux VIIᵉ–XVᵉ siècles* (Paris, 1966).

Akbar, M. J., "At the center of the world: Afghanistan, Iran and the rise of a new Islamic commonwealth", *New York Times* (10 January 1992): A13.

Alexander, P. J., ed. D. deF. Abrahamse, *The Byzantine apocalyptic tradition* (Berkeley, 1985).

———, *Religious and political history and thought in the Byzantine Empire* (London, 1978).

Allchin, F. R., and K. R. Norman, "Guide to the Aśokan inscriptions," *South Asian studies* 1 (1985): 43–50.

Almagro, M., and others, *Qusayr ʿAmra: Residencia y baños omeyas en el desierto de Jordania* (Madrid, 1975).

Anderson, R. D., P. J. Parsons, and R.G.M. Nisbet "Elegiacs by Gallus from Qasr Ibrîm", *J.R.S.* 69 (1979): 125–55.

Andreas, F. C., and W. Henning, "Mitteliranische Manichaica aus Chinesisch-Turkestan", *S.P.A.W.* (1932): 175–222, (1933): 294–363, (1934): 848–912.

Asche, U., *Roms Weltherrschaftsidee und Aussenpolitik in der Spätantike im Spiegel der Panegyrici Latini* (Bonn, 1983).

Atlas of Israel (Jerusalem, 1970²).

Avi-Yonah, M., *The Jews under Roman and Byzantine rule: A political history of Palestine from the Bar Kokhba war to the Arab conquest* (New York, 1984).

Barceló, P.A., *Roms auswärtige Beziehungen unter der Constantinischen Dynastie (306–363)* (Regensburg, 1981).

Barnes, T. D., "The consecration of Ulfila", *J.Th.S.* 41 (1990): 541–45.

———, *Constantine and Eusebius* (Cambridge, Mass., 1981).

———, "Constantine and the Christians of Persia", *J.R.S.* 75 (1985): 126–36.

———, "Religion and society in the age of Theodosius", in H. A. Meynell, ed., *Grace, politics and desire: Essays on Augustine* (Calgary, 1990), 157–75.

Bashear, S., "Apocalyptic and other materials on early Muslim-Byzantine wars: a review of Arabic sources", *J.R.A.S.* 1 (1991): 173–207.

Bates, M. L., "History, geography and numismatics in the first century of Islamic coinage", *S.N.R.* 65 (1986): 231–63.

Bazin, L., "Manichéisme et syncrétisme chez les Ouïgours", *Turcica* 21–23 (1991): 23–38.

Beck, H.-G., *Ideen und Realitaeten in Byzanz: Gesammelte Aufsaetze* (London, 1972).

Beck, R., 'Merkelbach's Mithras', *Phoenix* 41 (1987): 296–316.

————, "Mithraism since Franz Cumont", *A.N.R.W.* II.17.4 (1984): 2002–2115.

————, "Thus spake not Zarathuštra: Zoroastrian pseudepigrapha of the Greco-Roman world", in Boyce and Grenet, *History of Zoroastrianism* 3.491–565.

Becker, C. H., *Islamstudien* (Leipzig, 1924–32).

Beckingham, C. F., *Between Islam and Christendom: Travellers, facts and legends in the Middle Ages and the Renaissance* (London, 1983).

Beedham, B., "Turkey: Star of Islam", *Economist* (14 December 1991), 3–18 (Survey).

Bello, I. A., *The medieval Islamic controversy between philosophy and orthodoxy: Ijmāʿ and taʾwīl in the conflict between al-Ghazālī and Ibn Rushd* (Leiden, 1989).

Berchem, M. van, *Matériaux pour un Corpus inscriptionum arabicarum* 2(2) (*Mémoires de l'Institut Français d'Archéologie Orientale* 44) (Cairo, 1927).

Bianchi, U., "Sviluppi della teologia zoroastriana in età tardo-antica", in L. Lanciotti, ed., *Incontro di religioni in Asia tra il III e il X secolo d.C.* (Florence, 1984), 55–78.

Bleckmann, B., "Die Chronik des Johannes Zonaras und eine pagane Quelle zur Geschichte Konstantins", *Historia* 40 (1991): 343–65.

Bloch, H., "A new document of the last pagan revival in the West, 393–394 A.D.", *H.Th.R.* 38 (1945): 199–244.

Blockley, R. C., "The division of Armenia between the Romans and the Persians at the end of the fourth century A.D.", *Historia* 36 (1987): 222–34.

Blois, F. de., "The date of the 'martyrs of Nagrān' ", *Arabian archaeology and epigraphy* 1 (1990): 110–28.

Boccaccini, G., *Middle Judaism: Jewish thought, 300 B.C.E. to 200 C.E.* (Minneapolis, 1991).

Bodoff, L., "Was Yehudah Halevi racist?", *Judaism* 38 (1989): 174–84.

Bonneau, D., *La crue du Nil, divinité égyptienne, à travers mille ans d'histoire (332 av.–641 ap. J.-C.)* (Paris, 1964).

Bosworth, A. B., *Conquest and empire: The reign of Alexander the Great* (Cambridge, 1988).

Bowersock, G. W., *Hellenism in late antiquity* (Cambridge, 1990).

————, "The imperial cult: perceptions and persistence", in B. F. Meyer and E. P. Sanders, eds., *Jewish and Christian self-definition 3: Self-definition in the Graeco-Roman world* (London, 1982), 171–82.

————, *Roman Arabia* (Cambridge, Mass. 1983).

———, Review of Shahîd, *B.A.FO.C.*, *C.R.* 36 (1986): 111–17.

Boyce, M. (vol. 3 with F. Grenet), *A history of Zoroastrianism* (Leiden 1975–; vol. 1, corrected reprint, 1989).

———, *Textual sources for the study of Zoroastrianism* (Manchester, 1984).

———, *Zoroastrians: Their religious beliefs and practices* (London, 1979).

Braudel, F., *La Méditerranée et le monde méditerranéen à l'époque de Philippe II* (Paris, 1982⁵).

Braund, D., "The Caucasian frontier: myth, exploration and the dynamics of imperialism", in P. Freeman and D. Kennedy, eds., *The defence of the Roman and Byzantine East: Proceedings of a colloquium held at the University of Sheffield in April 1986* (Oxford, 1986) 31–49.

Briant, P., "Conquête territoriale et stratégie idéologique: Alexandre le Grand et l'idéologie monarchique achéménide', in *Actes du colloque international sur l'idéologie monarchique dans l'antiquité, Cracovie-Mogilany du 23 au 26 octobre 1977* (Warsaw, 1980), 37–83.

———, "Polythéismes et empire unitaire. (Remarques sur la politique religieuse des Achéménides)", in *Les grandes figures religieuses: Fonctionnement pratique et symbolique dans l'antiquité. Besançon 25–26 avril 1984* (Paris, 1986), 425–43.

Brice, W. C., ed., *An historical atlas of Islam* (Leiden, 1981).

Brock, S., *Syriac perspectives on late antiquity* (London, 1984).

Brown, P., *Society and the holy in late antiquity* (London, 1982).

———, *The world of late antiquity AD 150–750* (London 1971; reprint with revised bibliography, 1989).

Budge, E.A.W., *A history of Ethiopia* (London, 1928).

Bulliet, R. W., *Conversion to Islam in the medieval period: An essay in quantitative history* (Cambridge, Mass., 1979).

Buraselis, K., Θεία δωρεά. Μελέτες πάνω στὴν πολιτικὴ τῆς δυναστείας τῶν Σεβήρων καὶ τὴν *Constitutio Antoniniana* (Athens, 1989).

Busse, H., "Tempel, Grabeskirche und Haram aš-šarif. Drei Heiligtumer und ihre gegenseitigen Beziehungen in Legende und Wirklichkeit", in H. Busse and G. Kretschmar, eds., *Jerusalemer Heiligtums-traditionen in altkirchlicher und frühislamischer Zeit* (Wiesbaden, 1987), 1–27.

Calder, N., review of Crone and Hinds, *God's Caliph, J.S.S.* 32 (1987): 375–78.

Cameron, Averil, "Agathias on the Sassanians", *D.O.P.* 23–24 (1969–70): 67–183.

———, *Christianity and the rhetoric of empire: The development of Christian discourse* (Berkeley, 1991).

———, *Continuity and change in sixth-century Byzantium* (London, 1981).

———, "Eusebius of Caesarea and the rethinking of history", in E. Gabba, ed., *Tria corda: Scritti in onore di Arnaldo Momigliano* (Como, 1983), 71–88.

Canard, M., *Byzance et les musulmans du Proche Orient* (London, 1973).

Chabot, J. B., ed., *Documenta ad origines monophysitarum illustrandas* (*C.S.C.O., Syr.* 37, 52) (Paris, 1907; Louvain, 1933).

———, *Synodicon orientale ou recueil de synodes nestoriens* (Paris, 1902).

Chadwick, H., *Heresy and orthodoxy in the early Church* (London, 1991).

———, *History and thought of the early Church* (London, 1982).

———, *Origen : Contra Celsum* (Cambridge, 1953; corrected reprint, 1980).

Chastagnol, A., *L'évolution politique, sociale et économique du monde romain de Dioclétien à Julien* (Paris, 1982).

Chaudhuri, K. N., *Asia before Europe: Economy and civilisation of the Indian Ocean from the rise of Islam to 1750* (Cambridge, 1990).

Chaumont, M.-L., "L'Arménie entre Rome et l'Iran I. De l'avènement d'Auguste à l'avènement de Dioclétien", *A.N.R.W.* II.9.1(1976): 71–194.

———, *La christianisation de l'empire iranien des origines aux grandes persécutions du IVe siècle* (Louvain, 1988).

———, "Conquêtes sassanides et propagande mazdéenne (IIIème siècle)", *Historia* 22 (1973): 664–710.

———, *Recherches sur l'histoire d'Arménie de l'avènement des Sassanides à la conversion du royaume* (Paris, 1969).

Chelhod, J., *Introduction à la sociologie de l'Islam: De l'animisme à l'universalisme* (Paris, 1958).

Choksy, J. K., "Sacral kingship in Sasanian Iran", *B.A.I.* 2 (1988): 35–52.

Christensen, A., *L'Iran sous les Sassanides* (Copenhagen, 1944²).

Christol, A., "Les édits grecs d'Aśoka: étude linguistique 2. Sramenai. Morphologie d'un emprunt" *J.A.* 278 (1990): 45–70.

Chrysos, E., "Some aspects of Romano-Persian legal relations", *Κληρονομία* 8 (1976): 1–60.

Chwolsohn D., *Die Ssabier und der Ssabismus* (St Petersburg, 1856).

Clauss, M., *Mithras: Kult und Mysterien* (Munich, 1990).

Clover, F. M., "Le culte des empereurs dans l'Afrique vandale", *B.C.T.H.* 15–16B (1984): 121–28.

Clover, F. M., and R. S. Humphreys, "Toward a definition of late antiquity", in F. M. Clover and R. S. Humphreys, eds., *Tradition and innovation in late antiquity* (Madison, 1989), 3–19.

Cohen, S.J.D., "Crossing the boundary and becoming a Jew", *H.Th.R.* 82 (1989): 13–33.

———, "The rabbinic conversion ceremony", *J.J.S.* 41 (1990): 177–203.

Collins, R., *The Arab conquest of Spain 710–797* (Oxford, 1989).

Colpe, C., "Heidnischer und christlicher Hellenismus in ihren Beziehungen zum Buddhismus", in *Vivarium: Festschrift Theodor Klauser zum 90. Geburtstag* (Münster, 1984), 57–81.

Cook, M., *Muhammad* (Oxford, 1983; corrected reprint, 1985).

Cowley, R. W., *Ethiopian Biblical interpretation: A study in exegetical tradition and hermeneutics* (Cambridge, 1988).

Cracco Ruggini, L., " 'Felix temporum reparatio': realtà socio-economiche in movimento durante un ventennio di regno (Costanzo II Augusto, 337–361 D.C.)", *E.A.C.* 34 (1989): 179–249.

———, "Universalità e campanilismo, centro e periferia, città e deserto nelle Storie ecclesiastiche", in *La storiografia ecclesiastica nella tarda antichità:*

Atti del convegno tenuto in Erice (3–8 XII 1978) (Messina, 1980), 159–94.

Creswell, K.A.C., *Early Muslim architecture* (Oxford 1969² [vol. 1], 1940 [vol. 2]).

Cribb, J., "Numismatic evidence for Kushano-Sasanian chronology", *Stud.Ir.* 19 (1990): 151–93.

Croke, B., and J. Harries, *Religious conflict in fourth-century Rome: A documentary study* (Sydney, 1982).

Crone, P., *Meccan trade and the rise of Islam* (Princeton, 1987).

———, *Roman, provincial and Islamic law: The origins of the Islamic patronate* (Cambridge, 1987).

———, *Slaves on horses: The evolution of the Islamic polity* (Cambridge, 1980).

Crone, P., and M. Cook, *Hagarism: The making of the Islamic world* (Cambridge, 1977).

Crone, P., and M. Hinds, *God's Caliph: Religious authority in the first centuries of Islam* (Cambridge, 1986).

Crum, W. E., and H. G. Evelyn White, *The Monastery of Epiphanius at Thebes* (New York, 1926).

Dagorn, R., *La geste d'Ismaël d'après l'onomastique et la tradition arabes* (Geneva, 1981).

Dagron, G., "L'empire romain d'orient au IVᵉ siècle et les traditions politiques de l'hellénisme: le témoignage de Thémistios", *T.&M.Byz.* 3 (1968): 1–242.

———, *Naissance d'une capitale: Constantinople et ses institutions de 330 à 451* (Paris, 1974).

Dagron, G., and V. Déroche, "Juifs et chrétiens dans l'Orient du VIIᵉ siècle", *T.&M.Byz.* 11 (1991): 17–273.

dal Covolo, E., *I Severi e il cristianesimo: Ricerche sull'ambiente storico-istituzionale delle origini cristiane tra il secondo e il terzo secolo* (Rome, 1989).

Dandamaev, M. A., *A political history of the Achaemenid Empire* (Leiden, 1989).

Dandamaev, M. A., and V. G. Lukonin, *The culture and social institutions of ancient Iran* (Cambridge, 1989).

Dauvillier, J., *Histoire et institutions des Eglises orientales au Moyen Age* (London, 1983).

Decker, D. de, and G. Dupuis-Masay, "L' 'épiscopat' de l'empereur Constantin", *Byzantion* 50 (1980): 118–57.

Décobert, C., "La mémoire monothéiste du Prophète", *Studia Islamica* 72 (1990): 19–46.

———, *Le mendiant et le combattant: L'institution de l'Islam* (Paris, 1991).

Decret, F., "Les conséquences sur le christianisme en Perse de l'affrontement des empires romain et sassanide de Shâpûr Iᵉʳ à Yazdgard Iᵉʳ", *Rec.Aug.* 14 (1979): 91–152.

Den Heijer, J., *Mawhūb ibn Manṣūr ibn Mufarriǧ et l'historiographie copto-*

arabe: Etude sur la composition de l'Histoire des Patriarches d'Alexandrie (Louvain, 1989).

Derenk, D., *Leben und Dichtung des Omaiyadenkalifen al-Walīd ibn Yazīd: Ein quellenkritischer Beitrag* (Freiburg im Breisgau, 1974).

Dihle, A., "L'ambassade de Théophile l'Indien ré-examinée", in *Arabie préislamique* 461–68.

———, *Antike und Orient: Gesammelte Aufsätze* (Heidelberg, 1984).

Dörner, F. K., and T. Goell, *Arsameia am Nymphaios: Die Ausgrabungen im Hierothesion des Mithradates Kallinikos von 1953–1956* (Berlin, 1963).

Dombrowski, B.W.W., and F. A. Dombrowski, "Frumentius/Abbā Salāmā: Zu den Nachrichten über die Anfänge des Christentums in Äthiopien", *O.C.* 68 (1984): 114–69.

Donadoni, S., "Trois nouvelles stèles de Ghazali", in M. Krause, ed., *Nubische Studien: Tagungsakten der 5. internazionalen Konferenz der International Society for Nubian Studies, Heidelberg, 22.–25. September 1982* (Mainz am Rhein, 1986), 223–29.

Donceel-Voûte, P., *Les pavements des églises byzantines de Syrie et du Liban: Décor, archéologie et liturgie* (Louvain-la-Neuve, 1988).

Donner, F. M., *The early Islamic conquests* (Princeton, 1981).

———, "The formation of the Islamic state", *J.A.O.S.* 106 (1986): 283–96.

Drijvers, H.J.W., *Bardaisan of Edessa* (Assen, 1966).

———, *Cults and beliefs at Edessa* (Leiden, 1980).

Drinkwater, J. F., "The 'catastrophe' of 260: towards a more favourable assessment of the Emperor Valerian I', *R.S.A.* 19 (1989) [1991]: 123–35.

Dvornik, F., *Early Christian and Byzantine political philosophy: Origins and background* (Washington, D.C., 1966).

Engelhardt, I., *Mission und Politik in Byzanz: Ein Beitrag zur Strukturanalyse byzantinischer Mission zur Zeit Justins und Justinians* (Munich, 1974).

Enoki, K., "The Nestorian Christianism in China in mediaeval time according to recent historical and archaeological researches", in *Atti del convegno internazionale sul tema: L'Oriente cristiano nella storia della civiltà* (Rome, 1964), 45–83.

Ettinghausen, R., *From Byzantium to Sasanian Iran and the Islamic world: Three modes of artistic influence* (Leiden, 1972).

Ettinghausen, R., and O. Grabar, *The art and architecture of Islam: 650–1250* (London, 1987).

Faris, N. A., and H. W. Glidden, "The development of the meaning of Koranic ḥanīf", *Journal of the Palestine Oriental Society* 19 (1939–41): 1–13.

Felix, W., *Antike literarische Quellen zur Aussenpolitik des Sāsānidenstaates* 1 (Vienna, 1985).

Fiaccadori, G., "Teofilo Indiano", *S.C.O.* 33 (1983): 295–331; 34 (1984): 271–308.

Fiey, J. M., *Assyrie chrétienne* (Beirut, 1965–68).

———, "Iconographie syriaque: Hulagu, Doquz Khatun . . . et six ambons?", *Muséon* 88 (1975): 59–68.

———, *Jalons pour une histoire de l'Eglise en Iraq* (Louvain, 1970).

187

Firestone, R., *Journeys in holy lands: The evolution of the Abraham-Ishmael legends in Islamic exegesis* (Albany, 1990).

Foss, C., *History and archaeology of Byzantine Asia Minor* (London, 1990).

Fowden G., *The Egyptian Hermes: A historical approach to the late pagan mind* (Cambridge, 1986; corrected reprint Princeton, 1993).

——, "Nicagoras of Athens and the Lateran obelisk", *J.H.S.* 107 (1987): 51–57.

Frei, P., and K. Koch, *Reichsidee und Reichsorganisation im Perserreich* (Freiburg, 1984).

Frend, W.H.C., *Archaeology and history in the study of early Christianity* (London, 1988).

——, "Fragments of a version of the Acta S. Georgii from Q'asr Ibrim", *Jb.A.C.* 32 (1989): 89–104.

——, *The rise of Christianity* (London, 1984).

——, *The rise of the Monophysite movement. Chapters in the history of the Church in the fifth and sixth centuries* (Cambridge, 1972; corrected reprint, 1979).

Frend, W.H.C., and G. Dragas, "A eucharistic sequence from Q'asr Ibrim", *Jb.A.C.* 30 (1987): 90–98.

Frézouls, E., "Les fluctuations de la frontière orientale de l'empire romain", in *La géographie administrative et politique d'Alexandre à Mahomet: Actes du colloque de Strasbourg 14–16 juin 1979* (Leiden, 1981), 177–225.

Frye, R. N., *The history of ancient Iran* (Munich, 1984).

Fussman, G., "Chronique des études kouchanes (1978–1987)", *J.A.* 275 (1987): 333–400.

Gagé, J., "Le 'Templum Urbis' et les origines de l'idée de 'Renovatio' ", *A.I.Ph.O.* 4 (1936) (= *Mélanges Franz Cumont*), 151–87.

Gager, J. G., *The origins of anti-Semitism: Attitudes toward Judaism in pagan and Christian antiquity* (New York, 1983).

Garsoian, N., *Armenia between Byzantium and the Sasanians* (London, 1985).

——, *The Epic histories attributed to P'awstos Buzand (Buzandaran Patmuk 'iwnk')* (Cambridge, Mass., 1989).

Gautier-van Berchem, M., "The mosaics of the Dome of the Rock in Jerusalem and of the Great Mosque in Damascus", in Creswell, *Early Muslim architecture* 1.211–372.

Gebhardt, O. von, *The miniatures of the Ashburnham Pentateuch* (London, 1883).

Gero, S., *Barṣauma of Nisibis and Persian Christianity in the fifth century* (Louvain, 1981).

Ghedini, F., *Giulia Domna tra Oriente e Occidente: Le fonti archeologiche* (Rome, 1984).

Gignoux, P., "Le mage Kirdīr et ses quatre inscriptions", *C.R.A.I.* (1989): 689–99.

Gnoli, G., *De Zoroastre à Mani* (Paris, 1985).

——, *The idea of Iran: An essay on its origin* (Rome, 1989).

Gonda, J., *The Vedic god Mitra* (Leiden, 1972).

Goodenough, E. R., *Jewish symbols in the Greco-Roman period* (New York, 1953–68).

Goodman, M., "Nerva, the *Fiscus Judaicus* and Jewish identity", *J.R.S.* 79 (1989): 40–44.

———, "Proselytising in rabbinic Judaism", *J.J.S.* 40 (1989): 175–85.

———, *State and society in Roman Galilee, A.D. 132–212* (Totowa, N.J., 1983).

Grabar, O., *The formation of Islamic art* (New Haven, 1987²).

———, "The meaning of the Dome of the Rock", in M. J. Chiat and K. L. Reyerson, eds., *The medieval Mediterranean: Cross-cultural contacts* (St. Cloud, Minn., 1988), 1–10.

———, "Note sur une inscription grecque à Qusayr ʿAmrah", *Revue des études islamiques* 54 (1986): 127–32.

———, "The painting of the six kings at Qusayr ʿAmrah", *Ars orientalis* 1 (1954): 185–87.

———, *Studies in medieval Islamic art* (London, 1976).

Graf, D. F., "Zenobia and the Arabs", in D. H. French and C. S. Lightfoot, eds., *The eastern frontier of the Roman Empire: Proceedings of a colloquium held at Ankara in September 1988* (Oxford, 1989), 143–67.

Grandjean, Y., *Une nouvelle arétalogie d'Isis à Maronée* (Leiden, 1975).

Green, H. B., "Matthew 28:19, Eusebius, and the *lex orandi*", in R. Williams, ed., *The making of orthodoxy: Essays in honour of Henry Chadwick* (Cambridge, 1989), 124–41.

Guillou, A., *Régionalisme et indépendance dans l'empire byzantin au VIIᵉ siècle: L'exemple de l'Exarchat et de la Pentapole d'Italie* (Rome, 1969).

Günther, W., "Didyma. Bericht über die Arbeiten 1969/70. C. Inschriften", *M.D.A.I.(I.)* 21 (1971): 97–108.

Habicht, C., *Altertümer von Pergamon VIII.3: Die Inschriften des Asklepieions* (Berlin, 1969).

Hahn, W., *Moneta Imperii Byzantini: Rekonstruktion des Prägeaufbaues auf synoptisch-tabellarischer Grundlage* (Vienna, 1973–).

Haldon, J. F., *Byzantium in the seventh century: The transformation of a culture* (Cambridge, 1990).

Halsberghe, G. H., *The cult of Sol invictus* (Leiden, 1972).

Hannestad, K., "Les relations de Byzance avec la Transcaucasie et l'Asie Centrale aux 5ᵉ et 6ᵉ siècles", *Byzantion* 25–27 (1955–57): 421–56.

Harris, W. V., *Ancient literacy* (Cambridge, Mass., 1989).

Hayman, P., "Monotheism—a misused word in Jewish studies?", *J.J.S.* 42 (1991): 1–15.

Heather, P., and J. Matthews, *The Goths in the fourth century* (Liverpool, 1991).

Hermann, A., "Der Nil und die Christen", *Jb.A.C.* 2 (1959): 30–69.

Herrin, J., *The formation of Christendom* (Princeton, 1987; corrected reprint, 1989).

Hewsen, R. H., "In search of Tiridates the Great," *J.S.A.S.* 2 (1985–86): 11–49.

Hillenbrand, R., "*La dolce vita* in early Islamic Syria: the evidence of later Umayyad palaces", *Art history* 5 (1982): 1–35.

Humphrey, J., *Roman circuses: Arenas for chariot racing* (London, 1986).

Huyse, P., "Noch einmal zu Parallelen zwischen Achaimeniden- und Sāsānideninschriften", *A.M.Iran* 23 (1990): 177–83.

Illawi, I. A., *Les cités musulmanes abbasides, la pensée d'Abu 'l-Ala al-Ma 'ari et ses prolongements contemporains* (diss., Paris, 1981).

Innemée, K. C., "Parallels between Nubian and Byzantine liturgical vestments", *Jb.A.C.* 32 (1989): 181–85.

Irmscher, J., "Die hellenistische Weltreichsidee", *Klio* 60 (1978): 177–82.

——, "Sulle origini del concetto *Romania*", in *Popoli e spazio romano* 421–29.

Isaac, B., *The limits of empire: The Roman army in the East* (Oxford, 1990); corrected reprint, 1992.

Itō, G., "Aśokan inscriptions, Laghmān I and II", *Stud.Ir.* 8 (1979): 175–83.

Jameson, S., "Chronology of the campaigns of Aelius Gallus and C. Petronius", *J.R.S.* 58 (1968): 71–84.

Jerphanion, G. de, *Une nouvelle province de l'art byzantin: Les églises rupestres de Cappadoce* (Paris, 1925–42).

Juynboll, G.H.A., *Muslim tradition: Studies in chronology, provenance and authorship of early ḥadīth* (Cambridge, 1983).

Kaegi, W. E., *Army, society and religion in Byzantium* (London, 1982).

——, *Byzantium and the decline of Rome* (Princeton, 1968).

——, *Byzantium and the early Islamic conquests* (Cambridge, 1992).

——, "Challenges to late Roman and Byzantine military operations in Iraq (4th–9th centuries)", *Klio* 73 (1991): 586–94.

Kaplan, S., *The monastic holy man and the Christianization of early Solomonic Ethiopia* (Wiesbaden, 1984).

Kaufhold, H., "Die Überlieferung der Sententiae syriacae und ihr historischer und literarischer Kontext", in D. Simon, ed., *Akten des 26. Deutschen Rechtshistorikertages, Frankfurt am Main, 22. bis 26. September 1986* (Frankfurt am Main, 1987), 505–18.

Kedourie, E., *The Chatham House Version and other Middle-Eastern Studies* (Hanover, N.H., 1984[2]).

Kennedy, H., *The Prophet and the Age of the Caliphates: The Islamic Near East from the sixth to the eleventh century* (London, 1986).

Kenney, J. P., "Monotheistic and polytheistic elements in classical Mediterranean spirituality", in A. H. Armstrong, ed., *Classical Mediterranean spirituality: Egyptian, Greek, Roman* (London, 1986), 269–92.

Kessler, C., " 'Abd al-Malik's inscription in the Dome of the Rock: a reconsideration", *J.R.A.S.* (1970): 2–14.

Kettenhoffen E., "Die Einforderung des Achämenidenerbes durch Ardašīr: eine interpretatio romana", *O.L.P.* 15 (1984): 177–90.

——, Review of Winter, *Friedensverträge*, *B.O.* 47 (1990): 163–78.

Kinzig, W., "'Non-separation': closeness and co-operation between Jews and Christians in the fourth century", *V.Chr.* 45 (1991): 27–53.

Kister, M. J., *Studies in Jāhilliya and early Islam* (London, 1980).

Klein R., *Constantius II. und die christliche Kirche* (Darmstadt, 1977).

Klimkeit, H.-J., *Die Begegnung von Christentum, Gnosis und Buddhismus an der Seidenstrasse* (Opladen, 1986).

——, "Buddhistische Übernahmen im iranischen und türkischen Manichäismus", in W. Heissig and H.-J. Klimkeit, eds, *Synkretismus in den Religionen Zentralasiens* (Wiesbaden, 1987), 58–75.

——, "Das manichäische Königtum in Zentralasien", in K. Sagaster and M. Weiers, eds, *Documenta barbarorum: Festschrift für Walther Heissig zum 70. Geburtstag* (Wiesbaden, 1983), 225–44.

Knoche, U., "Über die Dea Roma. Ein Sinnbild römischer Selbstauffassung", in R. Klein, ed., *Prinzipat und Freiheit* (Darmstadt, 1969), 488–516.

Kolb, F., *Diocletian und die Erste Tetrarchie. Improvisation oder Experiment in der Organisation monarchischer Herrschaft?* (Berlin, 1987).

——, 'L'ideologia tetrarchica e la politica religiosa di Diocleziano', in G. Bonamente and A. Nestori, eds, *I cristiani e l'impero nel IV secolo. Colloquio sul Cristianesimo nel mondo antico* (Macerata, 1988), 17–44.

——, "Zu chronologischen Problemen der ersten Tetrarchie", *Eos* 76 (1988): 105–25.

Konow, S., ed., *Kharoshṭhī inscriptions (Corpus inscriptionum indicarum 2[1])*, (Calcutta, 1929).

Krause, M., "Zur Kirchengeschichte Nubiens", in T. Hägg, ed., *Nubian culture past and present: Main papers presented at the sixth international conference for Nubian studies in Uppsala, 11–16 August, 1986* (Stockholm, 1987), 293–308.

Kunst, K., *Rhetorische Papyri* (Berlin, 1923).

Lane Fox, R., *Pagans and Christians* (Harmondsworth, 1986).

Lassner, J., *The shaping of ʿAbbāsid rule* (Princeton, 1980).

Lee, A. D., "The role of hostages in Roman diplomacy with Sasanian Persia", *Historia* 40 (1991): 366–74.

Lepage, C., "Contribution de l'ancien art d'Ethiopie à la connaissance des autres arts chrétiens", *C.R.A.I.* (1990): 799–822.

Lepelley, C., *Les cités de l'Afrique romaine au Bas-Empire* (Paris, 1979–81).

Letsios, D. G., "The case of Amorkesos and the question of the Roman foederati in Arabia in the Vth century", in *Arabie préislamique* 525–38.

Lewis, B., *Race and slavery in the Middle East: An historical enquiry* (New York, 1990).

Lieberman, S., *Greek in Jewish Palestine: Studies in the life and manners of Jewish Palestine in the II–IV centuries C.E.* (New York, 1942).

——, *Hellenism in Jewish Palestine* (New York, 1950).

Lieu, S.N.C., *Manichaeism in the later Roman Empire and medieval China* (Tübingen, 1992²).

Lim, R., "Unity and diversity among Western Manichaeans: a reconsideration of Mani's *sancta ecclesia*", *R.E.Aug.* 35 (1989): 231–50.

Linder, A., *The Jews in Roman imperial legislation* (Detroit, 1987).

Lingat, R., ed. G. Fussman and E. Meyer, *Royautés bouddhiques: Aśoka et La fonction royale à Ceylan* (Paris, 1989).

Little, D. P., *History and historiography of the Mamlūks* (London, 1986).

Litvinsky, B.A., "Outline history of Buddhism in Central Asia", in *Kushan studies in U.S.S.R.: Papers presented by the Soviet scholars at the UNESCO conference on history, archaeology and culture of Central Asia in the Kushan period, Dushanbe 1968* (Calcutta, 1970), 53–132.

MacCoull, L.S.B., "The paschal letter of Alexander II, Patriarch of Alexandria: a Greek defense of Coptic theology under Arab rule", *D.O.P.* 44 (1990): 27–40.

Mackerras, C., "The Uighurs", in D. Sinor, ed., *The Cambridge history of early inner Asia* (Cambridge, 1990), 317–42.

Makris, D., and G. Myrtsidou, "Στην Ορμύλια σήμανε η ώρα της Ορθοδοξίας', *Καθημερινή* (1 March 1992): 3.

Manandian, H. A., *The trade and cities of Armenia in relation to ancient world trade* (Lisbon, 1965).

Mango, C., "Deux études sur Byzance et la Perse Sassanide", *T.&M.Byz.* 9 (1985): 91–118.

Markus, R., "Chronicle and theology: Prosper of Aquitaine", in C. Holdsworth and T. P. Wiseman, eds, *The inheritance of historiography 350–900* (Exeter, 1986), 31–43.

Martinez, F. J., "The apocalyptic genre in Syriac: the world of Pseudo-Methodius", in H.J.W. Drijvers, R. Lavenant, C. Molenberg, and G. J. Reinink, eds, *IV symposium syriacum 1984: Literary genres in Syriac literature (Groningen—Oosterhesselen 10–12 September)* (Rome, 1987), 337–52.

Mary (Mother), and K. Ware, *The festal Menaion* (London, 1969).

Mastino, A., "*Orbis*, κόσμος, οἰκουμένη: aspetti spaziali dell'idea di impero universale da Augusto a Teodosio", in *Popoli e spazio romano* 63–162.

Matthews, J., *The Roman Empire of Ammianus* (London, 1989).

Mazza, M., *Le maschere del potere: Cultura e politica nella tarda antichità* (Naples, 1986).

Merkelbach, R., *Mithras* (Königstein, 1984).

Meslin, M., "Nationalisme, état et religions à la fin du IVᵉ siècle", *Archives de sociologie des religions* 18 (1964): 3–20.

Metzler, D., "Über das Konzept der 'Vier grossen Königreiche' in Manis Kephalaia (cap. 77)", *Klio* 71 (1989): 446–59.

Meyendorff, J., *Imperial unity and Christian divisions: The Church 450–680 A.D.* (Crestwood, N.Y., 1989).

——, *Introduction à l'étude de Grégoire Palamas* (Paris, 1959).

Meyer, M., "Die Felsbilder Shapurs I.", *J.D.A.I.* 105 (1990): 237–302.

Mielich, A. L., "Die Aufnahme der Malereien", in Musil and others, *Ḳuṣejr ʿAmra* 1.190–99.

Miles, G. C., "The earliest Arab gold coinage", *Museum notes (American Numismatic Society)* 13 (1967): 205–29.

Millar, F., "Emperors, frontiers and foreign relations, 31 B.C. to A.D. 378", *Britannia* 13 (1982): 1–23.

————, "Empire, community and culture in the Roman Near East: Greeks, Syrians, Jews and Arabs", *J.J.S.* 38 (1987): 143–64.

————, *The Roman Empire and its neighbours* (New York, 1981²).

Miquel, A., *La géographie humaine du monde musulman jusqu'au milieu du 11ᵉ siècle* (Paris, 1967–88; I², 1973).

Molè, C., "La terminologia dello spazio romano nelle fonti geografiche tardoantiche", in *Popoli e spazio romano* 321–50.

Momigliano, A., *Ottavo contributo alla storia degli studi classici e del mondo antico* (Rome, 1987).

Monneret de Villard, U., "'Aksūm e i quattro re del mondo", *Annali Lateranensi* 12 (1948): 125–80.

Moorhead, J., "The Monophysite response to the Arab invasions", *Byzantion* 51 (1981): 579–91.

Morony, M. G., "The Age of Conversions: a reassessment", in M. Gervers and R. J. Bikhazi, eds, *Conversion and continuity: Indigenous Christian communities in Islamic lands, eighth to eighteenth centuries* (Toronto, 1990), 135–50.

————, *Iraq after the Muslim conquest* (Princeton, 1984).

Mottahedeh, R. P., *Loyalty and leadership in an early Islamic society* (Princeton, 1980).

Müller, C.D.G., "Damian, Papst und Patriarch von Alexandrien," *O.C.* 70 (1986): 118–42.

Mukherjee, B. N., *Studies in Aramaic edicts of Aśoka* (Calcutta, 1984).

Munro-Hay, S. C., *Aksum: An African civilisation of late antiquity* (Edinburgh, 1991).

————, "The dating of Ezana and Frumentius," *Rassegna di studi etiopici* 32 (1988): 111–27.

Musil, A., and others, *Ḳuṣejr ʿAmra* (Vienna, 1907).

Nasrallah, J., "L'Eglise melchite en Iraq, en Perse et dans l'Asie centrale," *Proche-Orient Chrétien* 25 (1975): 135–73, 26 (1976): 16–33, 319–53.

Nassar, N., "Saljuq or Byzantine: Two related styles of Jazīran miniature painting," in J. Raby, ed., *The art of Syria and the Jazīra 1100–1250* (Oxford, 1985), 85–98.

Newby, G. D., *The making of the last prophet: A reconstruction of the earliest biography of Muhammad* (Columbia, S.C., 1989).

Nicolet, C., *L'inventaire du monde: Géographie et politique aux origines de l'empire romain* (Paris, 1988).

Nikolaos, Metropolitan of Aksum, Διάσκεψις Ἀνατολικῶν Ὀρθοδόξων Ἐκκλησιῶν ἐν Ἀδὶς Ἀβέβα, 15–21 Ἰανουαρίου 1965 (Athens, 1965).

Nilsson, M. P., *Geschichte der griechischen Religion* (Munich, 1967–74³).

Nock, A. D., ed. Z. Stewart, *Essays on religion and the ancient world* (Oxford, 1972).

Nylander, C., "Achaemenid imperial art", in *Power and propaganda* 345–59.

Oates, D., *Studies in the ancient history of northern Iraq* (London, 1968).

Obolensky, D., *The Byzantine Commonwealth: Eastern Europe, 500–1453* (London, 1971).

Olderogge, D. A., "L'Arménie et l'Ethiopie au IV siècle (à propos des sources de l'alphabet arménien)", *IV cong.int.st.etiop.* 195–203.

O'Meara, D., *Pythagoras revived. Mathematics and philosophy in late antiquity* (Oxford, 1989).

Ostrogorsky, G., *Zur byzantinischen Geschichte: Ausgewählte kleine Schriften* (Darmstadt, 1973).

Pagden, A., *Spanish imperialism and the political imagination: Studies in European and Spanish-American social and political theory 1513–1830* (New Haven, 1990).

Palmer, A., "King Abgar of Edessa, Eusebius and Constantine", in H. Bakker, ed., *The sacred centre as the focus of political interest: Proceedings of the symposium held on the occasion of the 375th anniversary of the University of Groningen, 5–8 March 1989* (Groningen, 1992), 3–29.

Panitschek, P., "Zur Darstellung der Alexander- und Achaemenidennachfolge als politische Programme in kaiserzeitlichen Quellen", *Klio* 72 (1990): 457–72.

Papastathis, C. K., "Περί των 'Νόμων' των Ομηριτών του Αγίου Γρηγεντίου", *Graeco-Arabica* 4 (1991): 115–26.

Parke, H. W., *Oracles of Apollo in Asia Minor* (London, 1985).

Patlagean, E., *Structure sociale, famille, chrétienté à Byzance. IVe–XIe siècle* (London, 1981).

Patoura, S., "Τὸ Βυζάντιο καὶ ὁ ἐκχριστιανισμὸς τῶν λαῶν τοῦ Καυκάσου καὶ τῆς Κριμαίας (6ος αἰ.)", *Σύμμεικτα* (Κέντρον Βυζαντινῶν Ἐρευνῶν, Ἐθνικὸν Ἴδρυμα Ἐρευνῶν, Athens) 8 (1989): 405–35.

Peters, F. E., "Byzantium and the Arabs of Syria", *Annales archéologiques arabes syriennes* 27–28 (1977–78): 97–113.

Peterson, E., *Der Monotheismus als politisches Problem: Ein Beitrag zur Geschichte der politischen Theologie im Imperium Romanum* (Leipzig, 1935).

Pietri, C., "La politique de Constance II: Un premier 'césaropapisme' ou l' *imitatio Constantini?*", *E.A.C.* 34 (1989): 113–78.

Pigulewskaja, N., *Byzanz auf den Wegen nach Indien: Aus der Geschichte des byzantinischen Handels mit dem Orient vom 4. bis 6. Jahrhundert* (Berlin, 1969).

Pipes, D., *Slave soldiers and Islam: The genesis of a military system* (New Haven, 1981).

Potter, D., *Prophecy and history in the crisis of the Roman Empire: A historical commentary on the thirteenth Sibylline Oracle* (Oxford, 1990).

Price, S.R.F., *Rituals and power: The Roman imperial cult in Asia Minor* (Cambridge, 1984).

Rabbat, N., "The meaning of the Umayyad Dome of the Rock", *Muqarnas* 6 (1989): 12–21.

Raven, W., "Some early Islamic texts on the Negus of Abyssinia", *J.S.S.* 33 (1988): 197–218.

Rehm, A., *Didyma 2: Die Inschriften* (Berlin, 1958).

Reinink, G. J., "Der edessenische 'Pseudo-Methodius'", *B.Z.* 83 (1990): 31–45.

———, "Ps.-Methodius: a concept of history in response to the rise of Islam", in Averil Cameron and L. I. Conrad, eds, *The Byzantine and early Islamic Near East I: Problems in the literary source material* (Princeton, 1992), 149–87.

———, "Pseudo-Methodius und die Legende vom römischen Endkaiser", in W. Verbeke, D. Verhelst, and A. Welkenhuysen, eds, *The use and abuse of eschatology in the Middle Ages* (Leuven, 1988), 82–111.

Remnick, D., "Defending the faith," *New York Review of Books* (14 May 1992): 44–51.

Reynolds, J. M., and R. Tannenbaum, *Jews and God-fearers at Aphrodisias* (Cambridge, 1987).

Reynolds, J. M., and J. B. Ward-Perkins, *The inscriptions of Roman Tripolitania* (Rome, 1952).

Rickert, F., "Zu den Stadt- und Architekturdarstellungen des Ashburnham Pentateuch (Paris, Bibl.nat. NAL 2334)", in *Actes du XIe congrès international d'archéologie chrétienne: Lyon, Vienne, Grenoble, Genève et Aoste (21–28 septembre 1986)* (Rome, 1989), 1341–54.

Ries, J., "Le culte de Mithra en Iran", *A.N.R.W.* II.18.4 (1990): 2728–75.

Robin, C., "Aux origines de l'état Ḥimjarite: Ḥimyar et Dhû-Raydân", in M. M. Ibrahim, ed., *Arabian studies in honour of Mahmoud Ghul: Symposium at Yarmouk University, December 8–11, 1984* (Wiesbaden, 1989), 104–12.

Rösger, A., "Princeps mundi. Zum römischen Weltherrshaftsgedanken in der Historia Augusta", in *Bonner Historia-Augusta-Colloquium 1979/1981* (Bonn, 1983), 255–73.

Romanis, F. de, "Romanukharaṭṭa e Taprobane: sui rapporti Roma-Ceylon nel I sec.d.C.", *Helikon* 28 (1988): 5–58.

Rosen-Ayalon, M., *The early Islamic monuments of Al-Ḥaram al-Sharīf : An iconographic study* (Jerusalem, 1989).

Rosenfield, J. M., *The dynastic arts of the Kushans* (Berkeley, 1967).

Rotter, G., *Die Umayyaden und der zweite Bürgerkrieg (680–692)* (Wiesbaden, 1982).

Roueché, C., *Aphrodisias in late antiquity* (London, 1989).

Rubin, Z., "Byzantium and southern Arabia—the policy of Anastasius", in D. H. French and C. S. Lightfoot, eds, *The eastern frontier of the Roman Empire: Proceedings of a colloquium held at Ankara in September 1988* (Oxford, 1989), 383–420.

———, "The Mediterranean and the dilemma of the Roman Empire in late antiquity", *M.H.R.* 1 (1986): 13–62.

Ruether, R. R., *Faith and fratricide: The theological roots of anti-Semitism* (New York, 1974).

Runciman, S., *A history of the Crusades* (Cambridge, 1951–54).

Russell, J. R., "Kartīr and Mānī: a shamanistic model of their conflict", in *Iranica varia: Papers in honor of Professor Ehsan Yarshater* (Leiden, 1990), 180–93.

———, *Zoroastrianism in Armenia* (Cambridge, Mass., 1987).

Rutgers, L. V., "Archaeological evidence for the interaction of Jews and non-Jews in late antiquity", *A.J.A.* 96 (1992): 101–18.

Sahlins, M., "Cosmologies of capitalism: the trans-Pacific sector of 'the world system'", *P.B.A.* 74 (1988): 1–51.

Sarre, F., and E. Herzfeld, *Archäologische Reise im Euphrat- und Tigris-Gebiet* (Berlin, 1911–20).

Sartre, M., *Trois études sur l'Arabie romaine et byzantine* (Brussels, 1982).

Sauvaget, J., "Les Ghassanides et Sergiopolis", *Byzantion* 14 (1939): 115–30.

———, "Remarques sur les monuments omeyyades', *J.A.* 231 (1939): 1–59.

Schick, R., *The fate of the Christians in Palestine during the Byzantine-Umayyad transition, A.D. 600–750* (diss., Chicago, 1987).

Schindler, A., ed., *Monotheismus als politisches Problem? Erik Peterson und die Kritik der politischen Theologie* (Gütersloh, 1978).

Schmidt, C., and H. J. Polotsky, "Ein Mani-Fund in Ägypten. Originalschriften des Mani und seiner Schüler", *S.P.A.W.* (1933): 4–90.

Scholz, P., "Kusch—Meroë—Nubien", *A.W.* Sondernummer (1986, 1987).

Schürer, E., ed. G. Vermes and others, *The history of the Jewish people in the age of Jesus Christ (175 B.C.–A.D. 135)* (Edinburgh, 1973–87).

Seidl, E., *Rechtsgeschichte Agyptens als römischer Provinz (Die Behauptung des ägyptischen Rechts neben dem römischen)* (Sankt Augustin, 1973).

Selb, W., *Orientalisches Kirchenrecht* (Vienna, 1981–89).

———, *Zur Bedeutung des syrisch-römischen Rechtsbuches* (Munich, 1964).

Serjeant, R. B., and R. Lewcock, eds, *Ṣanʿāʾ: An Arabian Islamic city* (London, 1983).

Shahîd, I., *Byzantium and the Arabs in the fifth century* (Washington, D.C., 1989). [*B.A.FI.C.*]

———, *Byzantium and the Arabs in the fourth century* (Washington, D.C., 1984). [*B.A.FO.C.*]

———, *Byzantium and the Semitic Orient before the rise of Islam* (London, 1988).

———, "The Iranian factor in Byzantium during the reign of Heraclius", *D.O.P.* 26 (1972): 293–320.

———, *The martyrs of Najrân: New documents* (Brussels, 1971).

Shaki, M., "The Dēnkard account of the history of the Zoroastrian scriptures", *Arch.orient.* 49 (1981): 114–25.

Sherwin-White, S., "Seleucid Babylonia: a case-study for the installation and development of Greek rule", in A. Kuhrt and S. Sherwin-White, eds, *Hellenism in the East: The interaction of Greek and non-Greek civilizations from Syria to Central Asia after Alexander* (London, 1987), 1–31.

Shinnie, P. L., "Christian Nubia", in J. D. Fage, ed., *The Cambridge history of Africa* 2 (Cambridge, 1978), 556–88.

Shitomi, Y., "De la chronologie de la persécution de Nagran", *Orient* (Tokyo) 26 (1990): 27–42.

Sidebotham, S. E., "Ports of the Red Sea and the Arabia-India trade", in *Arabie préislamique* 195–223.

Simon, M., 'Mithra, rival du Christ?', in *Etudes Mithriaques. Actes du 2ᵉ Congrès international, Téhéran, du 1ᵉʳ au 8 septembre 1975* (Leiden, 1978), 457–78.

Sinclair, T. A., *Eastern Turkey: An architectural and archaeological survey* (London, 1987–90).

Smith, R.R.R., "The imperial reliefs from the Sebasteion at Aphrodisias", *J.R.S.* 77 (1987): 88–138.

———, "*Simulacra gentium:* the *ethne* from the Sebasteion at Aphrodisias", *J.R.S.* 78 (1988): 50–77.

Sophrony (Archimandrite), tr. R. Edmonds, *The monk of Mount Athos: Staretz Silouan 1866–1938* (London, 1973).

Soucek, P., "The temple of Solomon in Islamic legend and art", in J. Gutmann, ed., *The Temple of Solomon: Archaeological fact and medieval tradition in Christian, Islamic and Jewish art* (Missoula, Mont., 1976), 73–123.

Spain, S., " 'The promised blessing': the iconography of the mosaics of S. Maria Maggiore", *Art Bulletin* 61 (1979): 518–40.

Spuler, B., "Die Nestorianische Kirche", in *Handbuch der Orientalistik* I.8.2 (Leiden, 1961), 120–69.

Štaerman, E. M., "Le culte impérial, le culte du Soleil et celui du Temps", in M.-M. Mactoux and E. Geny, eds, *Mélanges Pierre Lévêque* 4 (Paris, 1990), 361–79.

Stavisk(ij)(y), B. J., *La Bactriane sous les Kushans: Problèmes d'histoire et de culture* (Paris, 1986).

———, "Buddhist monuments of Central Asia and the Sasanians", *B.A.I.* 4 (1990): 167–70.

St. Clair, A., "The Torah shrine at Dura-Europus: a re-evaluation", *Jb.A.C.* 29 (1986): 109–17.

Steiner, G., "Altorientalische 'Reichs'-Vorstellungen im 3. Jahrtausend", in *Power and propaganda* 125–43.

Stern H., "Notes sur les mosaïques du Dôme du Rocher et de la mosquée de Damas, à propos d'un livre de Mᵐᵉ Marguerite Gautier van Berchem", *C.Arch.* 22 (1972): 201–32.

Stevenson, J., *Creeds, councils and controversies: Documents illustrative of the history of the Church A.D. 337–461* (London, 1966).

———, rev. W.H.C. Frend, *A new Eusebius: Documents illustrating the history of the Church to AD 337* (London, 1987²).

Strobel, K., "Aspekte des politischen und sozialen Scheinbildes der rabbinischen Tradition: Das spätere 2. und das 3. Jh.n.Chr.", *Klio* 72 (1990): 478–97.

Suermann, H., *Die geschichtstheologische Reaktion auf die einfallenden Muslime in der edessenischen Apokalyptik des 7. Jahrhunderts* (Frankfurt am Main, 1985).

Sundermann, W., *Mitteliranische manichäische Texte kirchengeschichtlichen Inhalts* (Berlin, 1981).

Tambiah, S. J., *World conqueror and world renouncer: A study of Buddhism and polity in Thailand against a historical background* (Cambridge, 1976).

Tardieu, M., "Les calendriers en usage à Ḥarrān d'après les sources arabes et le commentaire de Simplicius à la Physique d'Aristote", in I. Hadot, ed., *Simplicius: Sa vie, son oeuvre, sa survie. Actes du colloque international de Paris (28 sept.-1er oct. 1985)* (Berlin, 1987), 40–57.

——, "La diffusion du bouddhisme dans l'empire kouchan, l'Iran et la Chine, d'après un kephalaion manichéen inédit", *Stud.Ir.* 17 (1988): 153–82.

——, *Les paysages reliques: Routes et haltes syriennes d'Isidore à Simplicius* (Louvain, 1990).

——, "Ṣābiens coraniques et 'Ṣābiens' de Ḥarrān", *J.A.* 274 (1986): 1–44.

Tcherikover, V. A., A. Fuks, and M. Stern, eds., *Corpus papyrorum Judaicarum* (Cambridge, Mass., 1957–64).

Teixidor, J., "Deux documents syriaques du IIIe siècle après J.-C., provenant du Moyen Euphrate", *C.R.A.I.* (1990): 144–63.

Thelamon, F., *Païens et chrétiens au IVe siècle: L'apport de l'"Histoire ecclésiastique" de Rufin d'Aquilée* (Paris, 1981).

Times atlas of the world (London, 1990[8]).

Török, L., "The historical background: Meroe, North and South", in T. Hägg, ed., *Nubian culture past and present: Main papers presented at the sixth international conference for Nubian studies in Uppsala, 11–16 August, 1986* (Stockholm, 1987), 139–229.

——, "Kush and the external world", in S. Donadoni and S. Wenig, eds, *Studia Meroitica 1984: Proceedings of the fifth international conference for Meroitic studies, Rome 1984* (Berlin, 1989), 49–215.

——, *Late antique Nubia: History and archaeology of the southern neighbour of Egypt in the 4th–6th c.A.D.* (Budapest, 1988).

Trebilco, P. R., *Jewish communities in Asia Minor* (Cambridge, 1991).

Trimingham, J. S., *Christianity among the Arabs in pre-Islamic times* (London, 1979).

Tubach, J., *Im Schatten des Sonnengottes: Der Sonnenkult in Edessa, Ḥarrān und Ḥaṭrā am Vorabend der christlichen Mission* (Wiesbaden, 1986).

Turcan, R., "Le culte impérial au IIIᵒ siècle", *A.N.R.W.* II.16.2 (1978): 996–1084.

——, *Les cultes orientaux dans le monde romain* (Paris, 1989).

——, "Les dieux et le divin dans les mystères de Mithra", in R. van den Broek, T. Baarda, and J. Mansfeld, eds, *Knowledge of God in the Graeco-Roman world* (Leiden, 1988), 243–61.

——, *Les sarcophages romains à représentations dionysiaques: Essai de chronologie et d'histoire religieuse* (Paris, 1966).

———, "Terminus et l'universalité hétérogène: idées romaines et chrétiennes", in *Popoli e spazio romano* 49–62.

Ullendorff, E., *Ethiopia and the Bible* (London, 1968).

Unruh, F., *Das Bild des Imperium Romanum im Spiegel der Literatur an der Wende vom 2. zum 3. Jh. n. Chr.* (Bonn, 1991).

Vanderspoel, J., "The background to Augustine's denial of religious plurality", in H. A. Meynell, ed., *Grace, politics and desire: Essays on Augustine* (Calgary, 1990), 179–93.

Vantini, G., *Christianity in the Sudan* (Bologna, 1981).

———, "Le roi Kirki de Nubie à Baghdad: un ou deux voyages?" in E. Dinkler, ed., *Kunst und Geschichte Nubiens in christlicher Zeit: Ergebnisse und Probleme auf Grund der jüngsten Ausgrabungen* (Recklinghausen, 1970), 41–48.

Vermaseren, M. J., *Corpus inscriptionum et monumentorum religionis Mithriacae* (The Hague, 1956–60).

Versnel, H. S., *Inconsistencies in Greek and Roman religion 1: Ter unus. Isis, Dionysos, Hermes. Three studies in henotheism* (Leiden, 1990).

Veyne, P., "Une évolution du paganisme gréco-romain: injustice et piété des dieux, leurs ordres ou 'oracles' ", *Latomus* 45 (1986): 259–83.

Vööbus, A., *History of the School of Nisibis* (Louvain, 1965).

Waldmann, H., *Der kommagenische Mazdaismus* (Tübingen, 1991).

Wallerstein, I., *Geopolitics and geoculture: Essays on the changing world-system* (Cambridge, 1991).

———, *The modern world-system* (New York, 1974–80).

Wallinga, H. T., "The ancient Persian navy and its predecessors", in H. Sancisi-Weerdenburg, ed., *Achaemenid history 1: Sources, structures and synthesis. Proceedings of the Groningen 1983 Achaemenid history workshop* (Leiden, 1987), 47–77.

Watson, A. M., *Agricultural innovation in the early Islamic world: The diffusion of crops and farming techniques, 700–1100* (Cambridge, 1983).

Weitzmann, K., and H. L. Kessler, *The frescoes of the Dura synagogue and Christian art* (Washington, D.C., 1990).

Wendell, C., "Baghdād: *Imago mundi*, and other foundation-lore", *International Journal of Middle East Studies* 2 (1971): 99–128.

Westenholz, A., "The Old Akkadian Empire in contemporary opinion", in *Power and propaganda* 107–24.

Whitby, M., *The Emperor Maurice and his historian: Theophylact Simocatta on Persian and Balkan warfare* (Oxford, 1988).

Wiesehöfer, J., "Iranische Ansprüche an Rom auf ehemals achaimenidische Territorien", *A. M. Iran* 19 (1986): 177–85.

Wilken, R. L., "Pagan criticism of Christianity: Greek religion and Christian faith", in W. R. Schoedel and R. L. Wilken, eds, *Early Christian literature and the classical intellectual tradition in honorem Robert M. Grant* (Paris, 1979), 117–34.

Will, E., "Philon et les prosélytes," in P. Goukowsky and C. Brixhe, eds,

Hellènika symmikta: Histoire, archéologie, épigraphie (Nancy, 1991), 151–68.

———, "Pline l'Ancien et Palmyre: un problème d'histoire ou d'histoire littéraire?", *Syria* 62 (1985): 263–69.

Williams, M. H., "Θεοσεβὴς γὰρ ἦν—The Jewish tendencies of Poppaea Sabina", *J.Th.S.* 39 (1988): 97–111.

Williams, R., *Arius: Heresy and tradition* (London, 1987).

Williams, R. A., *The American Indian in Western legal thought: The discourses of conquest* (New York, 1990).

Wink, A., *al-Hind: The making of the Indo-Islamic world* (Leiden, 1991–).

Winkelmann, F., "Zur Geschichte des Authentizitätsproblems der Vita Constantini", *Klio* 40 (1962): 187–243.

Winkler, G., "An obscure chapter in Armenian Church history (428–39)", *R.E.Arm.* 19 (1985): 85–179.

Winter, E., "Legitimität als Herrschaftsprinzip: Kaiser und 'König der Könige' im wechselseitigen Verkehr", in H.-J. Drexhage and J. Sünskes, eds, *Migratio et commutatio. Studien zur alten Geschichte und deren Nachleben Thomas Pekáry zum 60. Geburtstag am 13. September 1989 dargebracht von Freunden, Kollegen und Schülern* (St Katharinen, 1989), 72–92.

———, *Die sāsānidisch-römischen Friedensverträge des 3. Jahrhunderts n.Chr.—ein Beitrag zum Verständnis der aussenpolitischen Beziehungen zwischen den beiden Grossmächten* (Frankfurt am Main, 1988).

Wolfram, H., *History of the Goths* (Berkeley, 1988).

Wolski, J., "Sur l'impérialisme des Parthes Arsacides", in L. de Meyer and E. Haerinck, eds., *Archaeologia iranica et orientalis: Miscellanea in honorem Louis vanden Berghe* (Gent, 1989), 637–50.

Zaborski, A., "Marginal notes on medieval Nubia", in M. Krause, ed., *Nubische Studien: Tagungsakten der 5. internationalen Konferenz der International Society for Nubian Studies, Heidelberg, 22.–25.September 1982* (Mainz am Rhein, 1986), 403–12.

Zekiyan, B.L., "La rupture entre les églises géorgienne et arménienne au début du VIIe siècle. Essai d'une vue d'ensemble de l'arrière-plan historique", *R.E.Arm.* 16 (1982): 155–74.

Index

ITALY

B Y Z A

SICILY
Messina

C
Epi

M E D I T E R

Taxila

E M

L I B Y

S A H A R

INDIA

0

0

na